ACCELERATING PRIVATE SECTOR AND GREEN TRANSFORMATION IN UZBEKISTAN

Edited by Kiyoshi Taniguchi and Begzod M. Djalilov

JANUARY 2025

ASIAN DEVELOPMENT BANK

6 ADB Avenue, Mandaluyong City, 1550 Metro Manila, Philippines
Tel +63 2 8632 4444; Fax +63 2 8636 2444
www.adb.org

ISBN 978-92-9277-071-6 (print); 978-92-9277-072-3 (PDF); 978-92-9277-073-0 (ebook)
Publication Stock No. TCS240578-2
DOI: http://dx.doi.org/10.22617/TCS240578-2

Notes:
In this publication, "$" refers to United States dollars.
ADB recognizes "China" as the People's Republic of China and "Kyrgyzstan" as the Kyrgyz Republic.
ADB placed its regular assistance to Afghanistan on hold effective 15 August 2021.

Cover design by Joe Mark Ganaban. All photos by ADB.

Contents

Tables, Figures, Boxes, and Map

Tables

Figures

Boxes

Map

Preface

Since 2017, Uzbekistan has accelerated its pace of reform to open its markets. The public sector used to dominate the domestic market. Since it was opened to the private sector and outside the country, Uzbekistan's growth has been robust. Expansionary fiscal policy, buoyant private consumption, and increased fixed investment propelled gross domestic product growth to reach 6% in 2023.

Uzbekistan adopted a new Constitution in 2023. In addition, Uzbekistan embarked on its medium-term development framework, "Uzbekistan 2030" (the Strategy). The Strategy sets an overarching objective of building a free, prosperous, and strong New Uzbekistan. The Strategy's aspiration is that Uzbekistan will achieve upper-middle-income status through sustainable development. The Strategy addresses critical reform areas, including human capital development, natural resource management, water scarcity, and governance. Furthermore, the Government of Uzbekistan considers climate change and environmental degradation to be critical challenges for long-term sustainable growth. Hence, the government adopted the Program on the Transition to a "green" economy and ensuring "green" growth in the Republic of Uzbekistan until 2030. The Government of Uzbekistan focuses on two broad areas of needed reforms: market orientation with private sector development and climate change.

This country diagnostic study, *Accelerating Private Sector and Green Transformation in Uzbekistan*, presents an in-depth analysis of ways in which the country can best consolidate achievements from its recent policy reforms and continue reform efforts to achieve goals set in the Strategy. This study identifies key elements critical for sustaining inclusive growth, private sector development, and green transformation of the economy.

The study concludes that the government should focus on three priority areas to achieve the development aspirations stipulated in the Strategy. First, the government must reduce the heavy public footsteps in the market. Private sector development is critical at this juncture. Second, with support from development aid agencies, the government should support green transition. Green transition entails not only investment in renewable energy but also examining the entire value chain to maximize knowledge and technology transfer. Third, human capital development to accommodate these changes cannot be neglected. An educated and well-trained workforce can better accommodate new ideas and technology to make economic transformation successful.

We sincerely hope that the findings in this study will support the Government of Uzbekistan in its endeavor to accelerate reforms for inclusive growth, market orientation, and green transformation. We look forward to continuing dialogue and engagement with the government and are fully committed to supporting Uzbekistan in achieving its development aspirations.

Eugene Zhukov
Director General
Central and West Asia Department
Asian Development Bank

Albert F. Park
Director General/Chief Economist
Economic Research and Development Impact Department
Asian Development Bank

Acknowledgments

This country diagnostic study, *Accelerating Private Sector and Green Transformation in Uzbekistan*, was prepared by the Asian Development Bank (ADB) under the regional technical assistance project (TA 6811-REG) Economic Diagnostic Studies in Asia and the Pacific Subproject 1: Economic Diagnostic Studies in Asia and the Pacific. The study aims to contribute to the analysis of ongoing economic reforms taken by the Government of Uzbekistan. The study focuses on three critical aspects of ongoing reforms, including inclusive growth, market orientation through private sector development, and human capital development.

The study was undertaken by the "One ADB" team from the Central and West Asia Department (CWRD) and the Economic Research and Development Impact Department (ERDI), under the overall guidance and supervision of Kanokpan Lao-Araya, the country director for the Uzbekistan Resident Mission (URM), CWRD, ADB and Kiyoshi Taniguchi, regional lead economist for CWRD, ERDI, ADB. The study was led by Begzod M. Djalilov, regional cooperation specialist, Regional Cooperation and Integration Unit, CWRD.

Each chapter was prepared by a team of ADB staff and consultants: Chapter 1 (macroeconomic overview) by Kiyoshi Taniguchi (ERDI, ADB), Begzod M. Djalilov (CWRD, ADB), and Roman Mogilevskii (CWRD, ADB); Chapter 2 (green growth) by Jin Murakami (Singapore University of Technology and Design); Chapter 3 (agriculture development and food security) by Nodir Djanibekov (Leibniz Institute of Agricultural Development in Transition Economies [IAMO]); Chapter 4 (private sector development) by Begzod M. Djalilov (CWRD, ADB), Adham Kuchkarov (senior private sector development officer, ADB), Ajay Bhandoola (TA consultant), and Elbek Rikhsiyev (staff consultant, ADB); Chapter 5 (human capital development) by Daryll Naval (TA consultant) and Kiyoshi Taniguchi (ERDI, ADB); and Chapter 6 (regional cooperation and integration) by Turdakun Tashbolotov (TA consultant, ADB).

Overall, Kiyoshi Taniguchi and Begzod M. Djalilov provided technical review and economic editing to ensure the coherence and quality of the chapter studies. Maria Rowena Cham, Sayyora Pulatova, and Bhabhani Dewan provided overall research and technical support. Cherry Lynn Zafaralla and Alastair Mcindoe copy edited the volume, with the assistance of Daryll Naval as proofreader. Joe Mark Ganaban performed graphic design, layout, and typesetting.

The study is a product of extensive consultations with key government ministries in Uzbekistan, its think-tank agencies, and research institutions supporting development and strategy planning. The study team expresses special gratitude to the Institute of Macroeconomic and Regional Studies; Ministry of Economy and Finance; Central Bank of Uzbekistan; Ministry of Investment, Industry, and Trade, Ministry of Labor and Poverty Reduction; and Ministry of Higher Education, Science and Innovations.

Other stakeholders who contributed to this study through consultation include the Central Asian Green University, the European Bank for Reconstruction and Development, the Global Green Growth Institute, and the World Bank.

Abbreviations

ADB	Asian Development Bank
CAREC	Central Asia Regional Economic Cooperation
CBU	Central Bank of Uzbekistan
PRC	China, People's Republic of
CIS	Commonwealth of Independent States
CO_2	carbon dioxide
COVID-19	coronavirus disease
CWRD	Central and West Asia Department
EAEU	Eurasian Economic Union
ERDI	Economic Research and Development Impact Department
FAO	Food and Agriculture Organization of the United Nations
FDI	foreign direct investment
GDP	gross domestic product
GHG	greenhouse gas
HCI	Human Capital Index
ICT	information and communication technology
IEA	International Energy Agency
IFC	International Finance Corporation
IPO	intial public offering
JSC	joint-stock company
LMIC	lower-middle-income country
MSMEs	micro, small, and medium-sized enterprises
NDS	National Development Strategy
NFIS	National Financial Inclusion Strategy
NO_2	nitrogen dioxide
NPL	nonperforming loans
OECD	Organisation for Economic Co-operation and Development
PISA	Programme for International Student Assessment
PPP	public–private partnership
SEZ	special economic zone
SMEs	small and medium-sized enterprises
SOBs	state-owned banks
SOEs	state-owned enterprises
TRACECA	Transport Corridor Europe-Caucasus-Asia
UNDP	United Nations Development Programme

UNESCO	United Nations Educational, Scientific and Cultural Organization
UNFCC	United Nations Framework Convention on Climate Change
UNICEF	United Nations Children's Fund
USAID	United States Agency for International Development
WHO	World Health Organization
WTO	World Trade Organization

Executive Summary

In 2017, Uzbekistan initiated an ambitious reform program to liberalize its economy after years of state control. From 2017 to 2022, gross domestic product (GDP) grew at an average rate of 5.2%, while GDP per capita increased by 3.3% annually. Although the economic boom following the 2017 reforms is commendable, it has heavily relied on energy-intensive, resource-dependent, and low-value-added sectors, with insufficient emphasis on green growth. Additionally, this growth has also disproportionately excluded women, small and medium-sized enterprises (SMEs), and small-scale farmers.

This country diagnostic study aims to explore how Uzbekistan can build on its recent economic gains and achieve sustainable and green growth. The first chapter presents a detailed analysis of the country's macroeconomic indicators; the second chapter explores opportunities for green growth within the sectors of energy, transport, and urban development; the third reviews Uzbekistan's agricultural reforms, strategic policies for sector development, and efforts toward ensuring food security; the fourth chapter emphasizes the need to enhance the role of the private sector in improving the investment climate; the fifth underscores the critical importance of investing in human capital to maintain economic momentum; and the last chapter examines recent advancements in regional cooperation and integration, focusing on the impacts of foreign trade and the development of connectivity.

Macroeconomic Conditions

Uzbekistan's structural transformation has been marked by a shift from agriculture to services and manufacturing as part of its industrialization policy. From 2017 to 2022, economic expansion was primarily driven by gross value-added growth in services (40%) and industry (26%). Despite this shift, agricultural reforms remain focused on boosting production and enhancing agri-food exports. In 2024 and 2025, growth is projected to weaken in the services and agriculture sectors while remaining robust in the industrial sector.

From 2017 to 2022, exports nearly doubled due to tariff reductions and new trade agreements. Meanwhile, imports more than doubled as demand for cars, equipment, and petroleum products rose. The widening trade deficit was financed by increased foreign direct investment and remittances, primarily from the Russian Federation. However, declining remittance inflows in 2024 and 2025 are expected to reduce household income, thereby slowing consumption growth.

The fiscal deficit grew from 3.9% of GDP in 2022 to an estimated 5.5% in 2023 due to increased social spending, higher subsidies for state-owned enterprises (SOEs), and recurrent expenditures. Despite this, the government plans to sustain high capital spending in social sectors while limiting unexpected public expenditures and subsidies for SOEs as part of structural reforms.

Strategic Investment for Green Growth

In 2022, Uzbekistan outlined its green growth strategy and action plan for transitioning to a green economy by 2030. This strategy aims to boost resilience to climate change and external shocks. Green growth will be pursued through three main paths: (i) improving resource efficiency and productivity, (ii) reducing environmental costs and climate risks, and (iii) creating inclusive jobs in value-added sectors. Green growth will be necessary for Uzbekistan to meet its second nationally determined contribution target of reducing the country's greenhouse gas (GHG) emissions per unit of GDP by 35% below 2010 levels by 2030.

Uzbekistan's heavy reliance on natural gas, oil, and other fossil fuels has led to high GHG emissions—the second-highest in Central Asia—and an energy intensity twice the global average as of 2019. While hydropower accounted for about 10% of the country's total electricity production capacity in 2018, solar and wind power contributions remain negligible despite Uzbekistan's geographical advantages for solar energy. Additionally, fossil fuel subsidies for end-users continue to hamper efforts to scale up renewable energy systems.

The rapid growth in passenger and freight transportation and fragmented supply chains are increasing GHG emissions and worsening air pollution. Uzbekistan ranks among the world's most polluted countries, particularly in terms of particulate matter (PM2.5), and its nitrogen oxide concentrations are continuously increasing. The country's roads are generally in poor condition, and only about 50% of the railway network has been modernized. While electric vehicles are gaining popularity, greater investment is needed in both domestic electric vehicle production and public charging infrastructure.

The country's land, water, and air pollution problems, as well as GHG emissions, are being worsened by inadequate solid waste disposal, especially in rapidly growing cities. The country generates an estimated 4 million tons of municipal solid waste annually, projected to rise to 7 million tons by 2030, with only about 10% being recycled in urban areas.

Green growth will require substantial investments, and Uzbekistan has already emerged as the region's largest recipient of multilateral development bank climate finance. However, better leveraging of these investments is essential, particularly in critical areas such as energy, transport, information and communication technology, water and waste management, agriculture, forestry, and land use. Modernizing outdated infrastructure and advancing digital technologies will be key components of these efforts.

Decarbonization of electricity and widespread electrification of end uses, including of transport services, will be central to Uzbekistan's strategy for transformative climate action. Efforts should capitalize on the country's significant potential for large-scale solar photovoltaic projects. Additionally, urbanization patterns must be aligned with green growth principles to ensure sustainable development.

Agriculture Development and Food Security Policy

Agriculture constitutes about 25% of Uzbekistan's economy and employment. Since 2017, the government has implemented groundbreaking reforms under the Agriculture Development Strategy, 2020–2030. The liberalization of the cotton market has raised both farmgate gate prices and cotton output. The creation of cotton-textile clusters has provided farmers greater access to inputs, thereby boosting processing efficiency. Similarly, wheat liberalization has positively impacted productivity, and state policies leveraging comparative advantages in horticulture, including export subsidies, have lifted production and exports from 2018 to 2021. As a result of these reforms, agriculture has become a pillar of resilience during the pandemic. In 2020, the sector grew by 2.9%—surpassing the 2.0% GDP growth in 2020—and continued to expand by 4.0% in 2021.

Despite sweeping reforms, significant issues threaten the sector's sustainable and inclusive growth. Firstly, *dekhqan* farms or smallholders—the primary producers of fruits, vegetables, and livestock—receive insufficient support from state policies, which predominantly favor large commercial farms. Smallholders face limited access to financial services and advanced technologies, as well as processors, storage, and packaging facilities. Addressing the needs of smallholders is crucial for fostering more sustainable and inclusive development.

Secondly, the government's alternating policies of consolidating and fragmenting farms to optimize sizes in response to productivity issues have created widespread insecurity over land tenure among farmers. This top-down approach has discouraged farmers from investing in soil fertility, irrigation, and sustainable technologies, leading to lower land productivity and increased vulnerability to climate change. Establishing an independent farmers' association to represent and defend the interests of farmers is essential for empowering them and ensuring their needs are addressed.

Lastly, despite the high share of public spending on agriculture in the government's total public expenditure, this has not translated into a pattern of agricultural growth that is both climate-resilient and inclusive. More public subsidies should be directed toward smallholders and initiatives that increase climate-resilient production, including education, research, and advisory services. The distribution of subsidies must be transparent, well-coordinated, and coherent to positively impact productivity, incomes, and growth.

Private Sector Development, Privatization, and Access to Finance

The 2017 reforms have created an enabling environment for private investments and an influx of development finance into the country. Between 2017 and 2022, these reforms led to tangible outcomes such as the reduction of various taxes and the partial or complete abolishment of import customs duties and excise taxes on numerous goods.

Under the Development Strategy from 2022 to 2026, the government is focusing on three main objectives to boost private sector participation: (i) expanding public–private partnership (PPP) agreements, (ii) increasing trade volume in the stock market, and (iii) divesting state assets. Given Uzbekistan's substantial share of PPPs relative to its GDP, expanding PPP agreements is feasible, though enhancing project finance capacity is essential for achieving this goal.

The country's stock market remains nascent, with a 2022 market capitalization of $200 million, significantly below the ambitious $7 billion target for 2026. Companies must foster confidence through stringent regulatory compliance and solid performance to attract more investors. Developing robust information technology infrastructure is crucial to ensure quick and reliable settlements.

State-owned enterprises still dominate key sectors in Uzbekistan, enjoying advantages such as preferential market access, government guarantees, tax breaks, and concessional loans. This presents considerable challenges for private firms facing hefty tax and regulatory hurdles. In response, a 2021 reform strategy was implemented to decrease the number of SOEs by 75% and improve their corporate governance and transparency. The state-owned banking sector is a crucial area for advancing private sector development and financial inclusion. The government has set a goal to increase the proportion of private sector borrowers in the banking system's loan portfolio from 28% in 2020 to 70% by 2025.

Supporting small and medium-sized enterprises (SMEs) is also vital for private sector growth, as SMEs contributed to over half of the nation's GDP and employed nearly 80% of the workforce in 2023. However, SMEs face challenges in accessing finance due to limited financing options that meet their needs. Additionally, the financial technology startup ecosystem is underdeveloped due to a lack of funding. Nonetheless, several initiatives, including the creation of a Fintech Association, have been implemented to expedite its development. The lending volume of nonbank credit organizations remains low, but new regulations aim to increase this from 0.3% in 2020 to 4.0% by 2025.

Progress in gender equality in the business sphere is evident, with the share of women-owned businesses rising from 20% in 2017 to 30% in 2022, a trend expected to continue following the adoption of gender equality policies.

Unlocking the Productivity Potential Through Enhanced Education

Investments in education and human capital not only drive long-term economic growth and reduce income inequality but are also essential for improving climate adaptation. For Uzbekistan, continuous investment in human capital is key to maintaining sustained economic progress, particularly during its current demographic dividend stage. However, this window of opportunity is expected to close by 2040, underscoring the urgency of capitalizing on these advantages now.

The government places significant emphasis on education, allocating an average of 5.9% of GDP to this sector from 2013 to 2022, which is higher than in other similar-income countries. However, despite substantial government investment, a financing gap of SUM44.3 billion was forecasted for 2019 to 2023.

The financing gap manifests itself in various ways, evident in inadequate teacher pay, which is among the country's most underpaid professionals. As a result, many teachers move to private education or leave the country for better economic opportunities. The shortage of teachers and school facilities, coupled with rising enrollment, has led to the widespread implementation of double shifts in schools. Additionally, the quality of school infrastructure, as well as access to water, sanitation, and hygiene, needs to be improved to provide students with safe and conducive learning environments.

Learning outcomes are currently not adequately assessed due to the lack of effective assessment methods. In 2022, Uzbekistan participated for the first time in the Programme for International Student Assessment, which measures student performance in reading, math, and science. However, at the time of writing (July 2024), the results were not yet available. A study conducted in 2018 among grade 4 students showed that students could answer only half of the test questions correctly. They performed better in science and environmental studies compared to reading comprehension and math.

Access to basic education is generally good, but early childhood education and higher education face challenges despite significant investments in these levels. Preschool gross enrollment rates (GER) increased from 28% in 2018 to 44% in 2021, driven by initiatives such as the establishment of the Ministry of Preschool Education in 2017. The GER at the primary and secondary levels has consistently been above or close to 100% from 2003 to 2021. In contrast, GERs in tertiary education have been relatively low, ranging from 8% to 14% from 2003 to 2019 and rising to 21% in 2021, still among the lowest in Central Asia. The low participation in higher education is not due to a lack of demand but rather limited spaces, leading to high selectivity.

Additionally, there is a notable gender disparity at the tertiary education level, particularly in high-paying fields such as sciences, engineering, manufacturing, and construction, which male students predominantly choose. Women are also significantly underrepresented in research roles. Improving women's access to higher education is vital for stabilizing the labor market. In response to this issue, the government has implemented the Women's Education Support Program for 2022–2026.

Lastly, the workforce is grappling with a skills mismatch, given the significant discrepancy between the number of graduates in various fields of study and the demand for jobs in those fields. This is especially true in the industry, services, construction, transport, and communication sectors. A 2021 survey indicates that the primary challenge firms face when hiring young workers is their lack of relevant skills or work experience. To address this, there needs to be enhanced collaboration between employers and educational institutions to better align graduate skills with the demands of the labor market.

Regional Cooperation and Integration

Since its 2017 reforms, the Government of Uzbekistan has enhanced its regional and global economic ties, signing trade agreements with 47 countries by 2022.

Trade liberalization significantly increased Uzbekistan's foreign trade from $24 billion in 2016 to $50 billion in 2022, with the Russian Federation and the People's Republic of China (PRC) as top export destinations and Kazakhstan, the Republic of Korea, and Türkiye as major import sources. Concurrently, an improved business climate and the establishment of special economic zones has led to foreign direct investment (FDI) inflows rising from $1.8 billion in 2017 to $2.0 billion in 2021, with a quarter directed toward manufacturing. In the short to medium term, renewable energy is identified as an attractive sector for FDI, which would be essential for driving green growth.

Regional integration is being bolstered through enhanced transport connectivity. Uzbekistan's strategic location in Central Asia positions it as a vital transit hub, linking to the PRC, the European Union (EU), the Middle East, and the Russian Federation. Efforts are underway to develop transport corridors with neighboring countries.

Uzbekistan is actively engaging with international and regional organizations and initiatives, including the Eurasian Economic Union (EAEU), Shanghai Cooperation Organisation, Central Asia Regional Economic Cooperation Program, and World Trade Organization (WTO).

Uzbekistan became an observer in the EAEU in 2022, a strategic move given the country's increasing trade with the union's member countries, which reached 31% of total foreign trade in 2022. Full membership in the EAEU would not only boost trade but also greatly benefit the millions of Uzbek migrants in the Russian Federation by easing employment restrictions. Additionally, Uzbekistan's educational and professional qualifications would be recognized across the EAEU.

Negotiations for Uzbekistan to join the WTO resumed in 2017. The government has not yet disclosed the status of these negotiations. Joining the WTO has benefits and challenges, but it undeniably promotes market liberalization. The country's accession to WTO will intensify competition, leading to the decline of nonviable SOEs and the rise of genuinely competitive businesses in the country, further attracting foreign direct investment.

Uzbekistan actively cooperates with countries both within and outside Central Asia to enhance trade and regional connectivity. Within the region, Kazakhstan is Uzbekistan's biggest partner and its third-largest import market in 2021. Together, Kazakhstan and Uzbekistan account for 70% of regional trade and have started constructing the Central Asia International Centre for Trade and Economic Cooperation, set to become a significant industrial, trade, and logistics hub. Meanwhile, the Kyrgyz Republic was its fifth-largest export partner in 2021. In 2021, the two countries signed a 3-year agreement to regulate water consumption and energy exchange.

Outside the region, the PRC is Uzbekistan's largest trading partner, major investor, and key lender. Uzbekistan plays a significant role in the Central Asia–PRC gas pipeline. Uzbekistan is also enhancing transport connectivity with Afghanistan and Pakistan to access South Asian markets and seaports. Key initiatives like the Trans-Afghan railway and a rail link with the PRC are set to further boost Uzbekistan's regional cooperation and development in the coming years.

The European Union and the United Kingdom (UK) are also important economic partners. The EU countries accounted for 9.2% of Uzbekistan's total trade, 3.3% of exports, and 13.0% of imports. In 2021, the EU accepted Uzbekistan as a beneficiary of its generalized scheme of preferences, allowing Uzbekistan to export 6,200 tariff-free products to the EU. A similar agreement was made with the UK to export 7,800 types of locally produced goods with zero tariffs.

To achieve sustainable and green growth, Uzbekistan must build on the positive outcomes of its 2017 reforms. Continuing structural reforms, including efforts for regional integration, are essential to enhance the business climate, strengthen the private sector, and attract investments, particularly in the energy and transport sectors. The agriculture sector, a crucial component of the economy, is vital for ensuring food security and a significant source of exports. Prioritizing support for smallholders is key to promoting a more sustainable and inclusive development of this sector. Furthermore, ongoing investments in human capital are necessary to ensure education is accessible and of high quality. Aligning the education system with labor market needs will maximize its effectiveness and relevance.

CHAPTER 1

Macroeconomic Performance, Opportunities, and Challenges of Uzbekistan

Kiyoshi Taniguchi, Begzod M. Djalilov, and Roman Mogilevskii

Uzbekistan is the most populous country in Central Asia, with a population of 36.8 million as of 2023. Uzbekistan is classified as a lower-middle-income country (LMIC) as per World Bank's classification.[1] Uzbekistan has been implementing multifaceted structural reforms since it embarked on an ambitious reform program in 2017. The main goals of the reforms are to sustain economic growth, liberalize markets, and reduce the involvement of the public sector.

This chapter reviews Uzbekistan's recent macroeconomic performance, including economic growth; discusses the various structural reforms the government has enacted since 2017; and analyzes future macroeconomic developments. It offers some policy options that the government could explore.

Macroeconomic Conditions

Uzbekistan began liberalizing its economy in 2017 following years of state management after gaining independence on 31 August 1991. As a result, Uzbekistan's economy expanded with an average annual gross domestic product (GDP) growth of 5.2% and gross national income per capita in the local currency at 20.2% between 2017 and 2023 (Figure 1.1). These growth rates are higher than those of emerging economies in the European Union (EU), Central Asia, and other LMICs around the world. As of 2022, per capita gross national income stood at $2,280.

The official nominal exchange rate of the Uzbek sum (SUM) against the United States (US) dollar depreciated in 2018, resulting from the foreign exchange liberalization in 2017, from an average of SUM2,966 per dollar in 2016 to SUM8,072 per dollar by 2018. Owing to the Central Bank of Uzbekistan (CBU) commitment to exchange rate flexibility, the sum further depreciated in 2022, but only by a modest 3.9%. The nominal exchange rate reached SUM11,736 per dollar in 2023 (Figure 1.2).

1 See World Bank. World Bank Country and Lending Groups (accessed 20 August 2024).

Figure 1.1: Gross Domestic Product Growth and Gross National Income per Capita

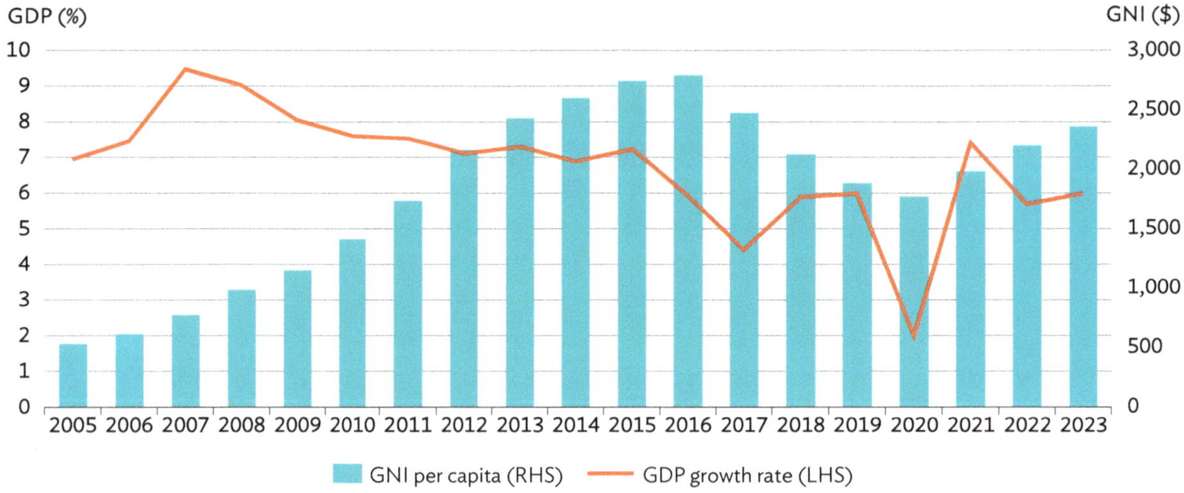

GDP = gross domestic product, GNI = gross national income, LHS = left-hand side, RHS = right-hand side.
Source: World Development Indicators (accessed 1 June 2024).

Figure 1.2: Nominal Exchange Rates
(Sum per $)

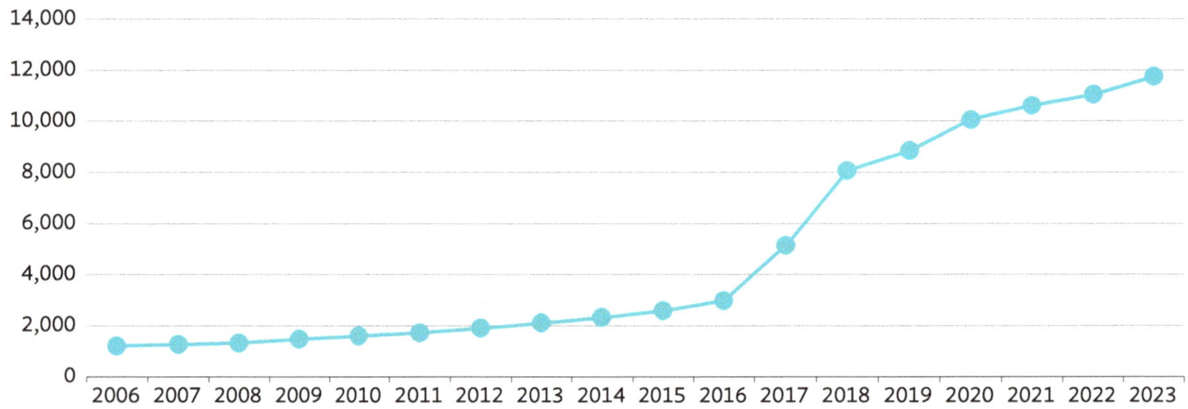

Sources: World Bank Development Indicators; Havar Analytics (accessed 1 June 2024).

Uzbekistan's economy has successfully recovered from the coronavirus disease (COVID-19) pandemic, posting a strong GDP growth rebound in 2021. Likewise, contrary to initial sentiments, a positive economic spillover occurred after the start of Russia's war in Ukraine. Anecdotal evidence shows that there was an inflow of highly skilled labor and capital into Uzbekistan at the onset.

Uzbekistan's structural transformation is characterized by a shift from agriculture to manufacturing and services as the government pursues an industrialization policy to emphasize manufacturing. From 2017 to 2022, the country's rapid economic expansion was driven by gross value-added growth in services (40.0%) and industry (25.5%). Agriculture grew at an average of 2.5% annually from 2017 to 2022, slower than overall GDP. Agriculture's share in gross value-added also shrank from 32.2% in

2017 to 25.2% in 2022 with the ongoing structural transformation. Nonetheless, agriculture reform has focused on establishing a market-driven crop structure, discontinuing mandatory cotton and wheat production, increasing domestic processing of raw materials, and changing farm structure.

On the demand side, the key drivers of GDP growth from 2017 to 2022 have been private consumption and gross capital investments. The share of private consumption in GDP averaged 61.0%, while gross capital investments accounted for 38.1%. Net exports remained negative, and their share expanded from 6.3% of GDP in 2017 to 14.5% in 2022. Coupled with elevated demand for imported capital goods for industrial and infrastructure upgrading, the average 6.7% annual growth in private consumption expanded the share of import of goods and services in GDP from 27.0% in 2017 to 39.0% in 2022.

The simultaneous increase in exports and imports has contributed to further opening of the economy, with trade rising from 47.8% of GDP in 2017 to 71.6% in 2022. The accelerated growth of imports was driven by the increasing demand for imported machinery and equipment financed by foreign direct investment (FDI) inflows and the general liberalization of foreign trade.

Growth is forecast to weaken in 2024 and 2025 especially in services and agriculture. Administered price increases are expected to limit a rise in real domestic demand. On the supply side, growth in services is anticipated to decelerate in 2024 and 2025 due to subdued demand for food and accommodation, storage, and transportation services. The agriculture sector's growth is expected to decline due to expected water shortages. Industry growth will be sustained due to rising external demand for food and textiles and domestic demand for mining and quarrying.

Inflation

High inflation expectations have lowered the demand for money.[2] In response to high inflation and to manage inflation expectations, the CBU adopted an inflation target of 5% to be achieved by the second half of 2024.[3] From 2017 to 2023, inflation reached 12.4% on average primarily due to food price increases (Figure 1.3). The periodic increases in electricity and natural gas tariffs and import inflation penetration further aggravated inflation.[4]

2 CBU. 2023. Inflationary Expectations of Population and Firms (accessed 19 July 2023). Key elements of inflationary expectations among the population are (i) cost escalation in imported goods, including foodstuff; (ii) exchange rate changes; (iii) artificial price increases; (iv) increase in fuel and energy resource prices; (v) rise in wages and social benefits; (vi) price hikes in housing and rent; and (vii) high level of price differences between supermarkets and food markets. Key factors in building inflationary expectations among firms are (i) exchange rate changes, (ii) cost escalation in fuel and transport, (iii) increase in wages and social benefits, (iv) price increase in imported inputs for production, (v) worsening competition environment in the economy, (vi) existence of tariff and nontariff barriers for import of selected goods, and (vii) increase in rent payment for commercial estate.

3 CBU. 2022. *Monetary Policy Guidelines for 2023 and the Period of 2024–2025*.

4 Structural reforms launched in 2017 entailed adjustments of power and natural gas prices to reach their cost-recovery level in generation, transmission, and distribution. The government had raised tariffs up until the outbreak of the COVID-19 pandemic in 2020. In 2021, the government postponed implementation of this structural reform. This was to avoid passing costs of reforms on to the population during the pandemic, and to accelerate economic recovery without high inflation. As of 2023, the government has not resumed the tariff increases.

Figure 1.3: Inflation Primarily Led by Food Inflation (2017 = 100)

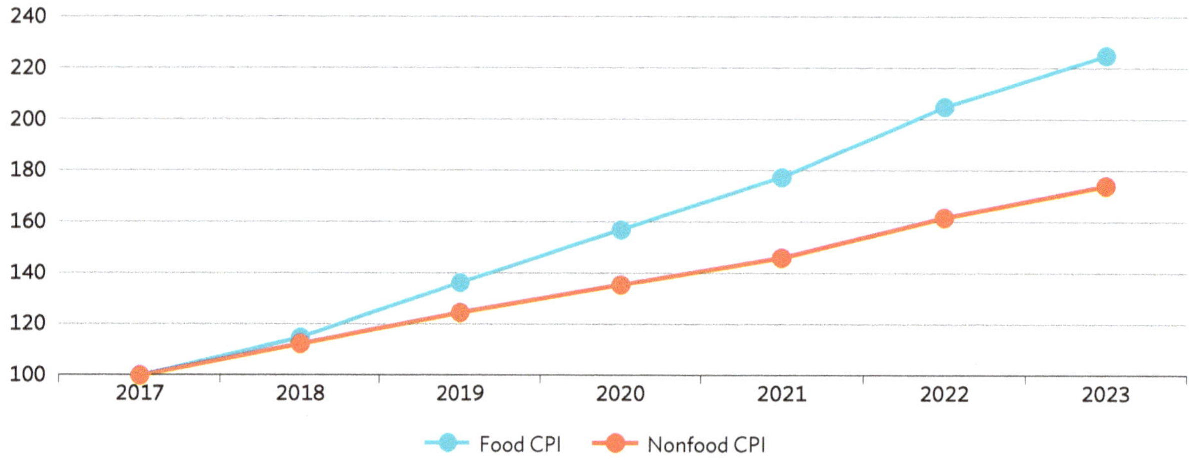

CPI = consumer price index.
Source: Havar Analytics (accessed 1 June 2024).

Monetary policy effectiveness is constrained by low financial inclusion,[5] high dollarization,[6] and subsidized government lending. Monetary tightening contributes to the financial system's health and brings down inflation, which was successfully lowered to 8.8% in 2023. However, high interest rates have been retained: as of the end of 2022, the weighted average interest rate was equal to 22.4% for commercial loans in national currency and 7.0% for loans in US dollars.[7]

Inflation is projected to have minimal change in 2024 and 2025 as continuing tight monetary policy under the structural reforms is expected to manage inflation. Under the tight monetary policy environment, commercial banks are also expected to continue limiting micro- and consumer lending, including auto loans. The government will likewise tighten fiscal expenditures, reduce energy subsidies and policy lending, and improve the targeting of social protection payments to narrow the fiscal deficit.

Trade and Current Account Balance

Uzbekistan's key trade partners are the Russian Federation, the PRC, and the European Union. From 2017 to 2022, Uzbekistan's trade geography changed, with the share of Central Asian neighbors in total merchandise trade rising from 11.0% in 2017 to 16.0% in 2022. From 2017 to 2022, exports of goods and services almost doubled, and imports increased more than twice over. Increasing FDI and remittances—mostly from the Russian Federation—financed the widening trade deficit. The increase

5 In 2021 in Uzbekistan, account ownership at a financial institution or with a mobile money service provider was 44.1% for the population aged 15+; for comparison, in the same year this share was 81.1% in Kazakhstan and 62.4% in average for LMICs. See World Bank. World Development Indicators Database (accessed 1 June 2024).

6 At the end of 2022, the share of loans denominated in foreign currency was 47.0% of total commercial bank credits. Source: CBU. Currency Rates (accessed 1 June 2024r).

7 International Monetary Fund. 2022. Republic of Uzbekistan. 2022 Article IV Consultation—Press Release; Staff Report; and Statement by the Executive Director for the Republic of Uzbekistan. *IMF Country Report*. No. 22/189.

in exports was mostly from textiles, vegetables, fruits, fertilizers, and tourism. Imports grew for a broad range of products, notably machinery and equipment associated with industrialization and food products, reflecting the shift from a self-sufficiency policy to agriculture commercialization.

In 2020, Uzbekistan became an observer in the Eurasian Economic Union, facilitating dialogue with its member states without legal and policy implications for Uzbekistan. The following year, in 2021, Uzbekistan fully acceded to the Commonwealth of Independent States' free trade agreement (CIS FTA), liberalizing Uzbekistan's trade with its neighbors. Since July 2023, Uzbekistan has been in bilateral market access negotiations on goods and services.[8] The government prioritized access to the World Trade Organization and halved the average most-favorable-nation tariff from 14.9% in 2015 to 7.4% by 2021.

The current account deficit widened in 2023 mainly due to the surge in imports of cars, equipment, and petroleum products arising from robust aggregate demand. The depreciation of the Uzbek sum further pushed the value of imports higher. Higher gold exports backed by high gold prices accelerated exports, but the exports were insufficient to counter the surge in imports. The large current account deficit in 2023 according to the Central Bank of Uzbekistan was covered by the inflow of foreign direct investments and private-sector borrowing.

Figure 1.4: Current Account Balance and Balances on Goods, Services, and Income
($ million)

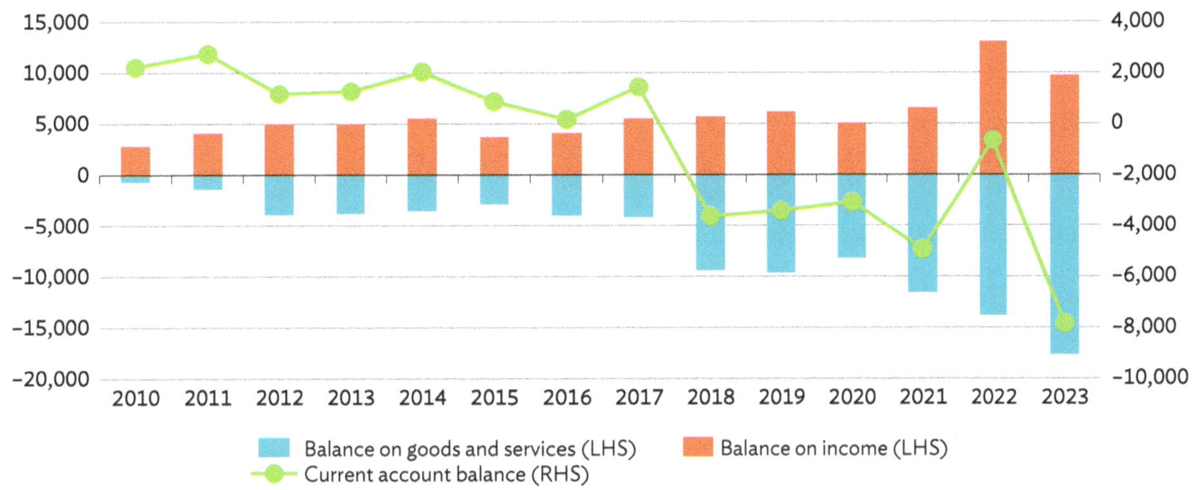

LHS = left-hand side, RHS = right-hand side.
Source: Havar Analytics (accessed 1 June 2024).

As the number of migrant Uzbek workers in the Russian Federation decreased, remittance growth returned to its medium-term trend, registering 12.9% of GDP in 2023. The depreciation of the Russian ruble further accelerated the out-migration of Uzbek overseas workers from Russia. As a result, foreign reserves edged down to $35.6 billion, or 9 months of import cover, in 2023. Remittance inflows from the Russian Federation are expected to continue declining in 2024 and 2025, curbing household income that will slow consumption growth.

8 World Trade Organization (WTO). 2023. Accessions: Uzbekistan—Current Status of Accession (accessed 24 July 2023)

Fiscal Balance and Fiscal Issues

The fiscal deficit expanded from 4.0% of GDP in 2022 to an estimated 5.5% in 2023. High commodity prices of gold, copper, and petrochemicals are mainly produced by state-owned enterprises (SOEs) and improved tax collection, but fiscal revenues decreased from 32.0% of GDP in 2022 to 30.1% in 2023. At the same time, fiscal outlays slightly decreased from 36.0% in 2022 to 35.6% in 2023. Most of the fiscal deficit was financed by public debt.

Structural reforms will limit unanticipated public expenditures and subsidies for SOEs. The government plans to maintain high spending for capital projects for social sectors, including education, health care, and social protection. Structural reform will reduce the fiscal deficit to 4.0% of GDP in 2024 and 3.0% in 2025. Furthermore, the government set a limit for public external borrowing with an overall rule that public and publicly guaranteed debt should not exceed the equivalent of 60% of GDP. The government will further tighten policies if debt reaches 50% of GDP.[9] In 2023, the new public borrowing limit was $4.5 billion, of which $2 billion was allocated to budget support and $2.5 billion to investment projects.[10] To reduce fiscal risks associated with borrowings by SOEs, the government limits their borrowing based on the risk classification of each SOE seeking to borrow.

Government Development Strategy

Uzbekistan's development has accelerated since 2017. Currently, the government's efforts are framed within the development strategy called "Uzbekistan–2030" and the national development strategy for 2022–2026, providing a comprehensive program of reforms. The country faces challenges requiring swift and coordinated action from all interested parties, including Uzbekistan's development partners, to implement this strategy.

The government needs to accelerate the pace of structural reforms, especially on the fiscal front, to support sustainable growth, contain inflation, and protect vulnerable households. One of the most challenging reforms is fiscal consolidation, including reducing the subsidy to SOEs. SOE reform is critical for sustainable growth, and the government must maintain minimum interference in the economy for the private sector to grow.

With a rapidly growing labor force, the economy should generate adequate new jobs to avoid a possible brain drain. New jobs will mainly come from small and medium-sized enterprises; hence, the government should create a level playing field for the private sector to enhance productivity. The government should improve governance and strengthen the rule of law.

Uzbekistan has set a target of reducing greenhouse gas (GHG) emissions per unit of GDP by 35% below 2010 levels by 2030. Furthermore, Uzbekistan aims to generate at least 30% of its electricity from renewable sources. Along with these targets, Uzbekistan is progressing in diversifying its electricity generation using renewable sources. A green development policy will accelerate the country's transition to a green economy.

---

9 Republic of Uzbekistan. 2023. Law of the Republic of Uzbekistan No. 836 "On Public Debt".

10 H. Son and B. Djalilov. 2023. How Central Asia and the Caucasus Can Cut Debt and Foster Inclusive Growth. *Asian Development Blog*. 24 November.

CHAPTER 2

Strategic Investment for Green Growth

Jin Murakami

Uzbekistan, in partnership with the Asian Development Bank (ADB) and other development partners, is expected to take a range of transformative actions to advance economic development and poverty reduction based on the concept of green growth.[1] The Organisation for Economic Co-operation and Development (OECD) defines green growth as economic progress that fosters environmentally sustainable, low-carbon, and socially inclusive development.[2] Green growth makes economies more resilient by enhancing the adaptive capacity of industries and societies to climate change, natural hazards, and other external shocks.[3] The scope of green growth is closely related to the nationwide or even regionwide transition toward a green economy, characterized by substantially increased investment in renewable energy, low-carbon transport, energy- and water-efficient production, and sustainable agriculture and forest management systems.

The greening of critical infrastructure, focused on climate change mitigation and adaptation, is as an essential element of Uzbekistan's long-term economic development vision and its roadmap for economic transition. In other words, climate change is not the single issue for Uzbekistan as a low-middle-income country with a gross domestic product (GDP) per capita of about $2,500 and a poverty rate of around 14% as of 2022. One of the key principles of the Strategy for the Transition to a Green Economy, 2019–2030 is "the priority of applying green tools and approaches to achieve the goals of socio-economic development."[4]

Uzbekistan is one of the Central Asia's fastest-growing economies due in large part to a series of market reforms taken since 2017. Gross domestic product at constant prices was 780.3 trillion sum (SUM), or $71.3 billion in 2022, against SUM266.6 trillion in 2017 by recording real GDP growth of 192.7% in nominal terms over 2017–2022.[5] Uzbekistan, being rich in natural gas, oil, coal, copper, gold, silver, and uranium, is largely meeting the growing needs of domestic and regional production systems by consuming its own natural resources.[6] The main consumers of the country's energy sources are the energy sector (33.6%), followed by industry and construction (22.3%), households (20.6%), and transport (16.3%). Agriculture (cotton and grain primarily, as well as fruit and vegetables)

1 K. Anderson, E. Ginting, and K. Taniguchi. 2020. *Uzbekistan Quality Job Creation as a Cornerstone for Sustainable Economic Growth*; World Bank. 2022b. *Towards a Greener Economy in Uzbekistan*; United Nations Development Programme (UNDP). 2022b. *Green Growth Strategic Framework Uzbekistan*.

2 OECD. 2015. *OECD Work on Green Growth*.

3 ADB. 2012. *Green Growth, Resources and Resilience: Environmental Sustainability in Asia and the Pacific*.

4 Government of Uzbekistan. 2022.

5 International Monetary Fund. National Summary Data Page—Uzbekistan (accessed 20 August 2023).

6 United Nations Framework Convention on Climate Change (UNFCC). 2016. *Third National Communication of the Republic of Uzbekistan under the UN Framework Convention on Climate Change*; International Energy Agency (IEA). 2020. *Uzbekistan Energy Profile*.

uses 90% of water resources. The water resources of Uzbekistan and upstream Central Asian countries are being sharply depleted by climate change, and a shortage of fresh water is likely to threaten the region's food production and ecosystems. Uzbekistan's recent economic growth has been driven by the energy-intensive and natural resource–dependent industry sector, such as manufacturing, mining and quarrying, construction, and electricity, gas, steam, and air conditioning, while agriculture, forestry, and fishing, and food services have continued to be low value-added industries against the concept of green growth (Table 2.1).

Table 2.1: Industrial Gross Value Added in Uzbekistan, 2017–2022

Sector	2017	2018	2019	2020	2021	2022	2017–2022 (% change)
Gross value added of industries	100.0	100.0	100.0	100.0	100.0	100.0	
Agriculture, forestry, and fishing	31.1	30.4	28.9	26.9	25.9	25.8	(5.3)
Mining and quarrying	2.9	4.3	4.8	4.8	4.1	4.0	1.1
Manufacturing	15.0	15.5	17.9	20.3	20.8	20.9	5.9
Electricity, gas, steam, and air conditioning	1.7	1.6	1.5	1.9	2.0	1.9	0.3
Water supply, sewerage, and waste management	0.2	0.2	0.2	0.2	0.2	0.2	0.0
Construction	5.7	5.8	6.7	6.7	6.6	6.7	0.9
Wholesale and retail trade	7.1	6.8	6.4	6.1	6.3	6.4	(0.7)
Accommodation and food services	0.8	0.7	0.7	0.5	0.6	0.6	(0.1)
Transport and storage	7.5	6.8	6.1	5.4	5.6	5.5	(1.9)
Information and communication	2.2	2.1	1.8	1.8	1.9	2.0	(0.2)
Other services	25.9	25.8	25.0	25.4	26.1	25.9	0.0

() = negative.
Source: International Monetary Fund. National Summary Data Page—Uzbekistan (accessed 20 August 2023).

Uzbekistan's economic growth model faces serious constraints and transformative forces in a rapidly changing global market and environmental policy landscape that includes environmental, social, and governance factors; investing criteria; net zero emissions targets and scenarios, carbon tax and pricing schemes; and uncertainties in global demand for fossil fuels and natural gas trading.[7] Close policy attention is being paid to the impacts of recent external shocks on Uzbekistan's trade, energy, and industry sectors, such as the coronavirus disease (COVID-19) pandemic, Russian's war in Ukraine, global supply chain crisis, and rising inflation globally. These shocks have not only slowed the country's growth but also heightened a regionwide awareness of environmental costs and climate change risks to the production systems of Central Asia, Europe, and other regions. The recoveries from the economic impact of the pandemic in several countries in Asia and the Pacific, including Uzbekistan, are using "green recovery" measures to satisfy immediate monetary needs and to help achieve long-term green growth.[8]

7 The technical assistance (TA) project conducted a small-scale survey among state-owned enterprises and developed a methodology for these firms to adopting environmental, social, and governance principles. See ADB. Technical Assistance (TA) 6545-UZB: Assessment of Socio-Economic Impacts of COVID-19 and Institutional Strengthening for Policy Responses.

8 ADB. 2022a. *Implementing a Green Recovery in Southeast Asia*; World Bank. Green Recovery Initiative (GRI).

Although several international organizations use the concept of green growth to describe a range of strategies for a country's economic transition and recovery from the pandemic, this chapter views green growth for Uzbekistan as an overall economic gain that can be achieved through three main paths: (i) resource-use efficiency and productivity improvements, (ii) environmental cost and climate change risk–expected economic loss-reduction; and (iii) job creation through inclusive growth in less energy-intensive and natural resource-dependent but more higher value-added sectors by diversifying sources of energy generation, such as renewable energy.[9] The economic gains from taking these paths justifies increasing investments in low-carbon, climate-resilient infrastructure to implement the country's Strategy for the Transition to a Green Economy, and to achieve the targets of its nationally determined contributions (NDC) in the Paris climate change agreement by 2030.[10]

Low-Carbon, Climate-Resilient Infrastructure Investment Needs

Uzbekistan signed the Paris agreement in 2017 and submitted its second NDC in October 2021 with a target of reducing the country's greenhouse gas (GHG) emissions per unit of GDP by 35% below 2010 levels by 2030. According to Climate Watch,[11] in 2019, Uzbekistan emitted 185.4 million tons of carbon dioxide (CO_2) equivalent (tCO_2e), accounting for 0.4% of global GHG emission. It ranked 41st out of 197 countries in terms of share of global emissions. Uzbekistan's GHG emissions per GDP are high. Figure 2.1 shows that the country ranks 24th and second-highest among Central Asia's region's five countries.

Figure 2.1: Greenhouse Gas Emissions per Gross Domestic Product in Central Asia, 2019
(tCO_2e/$ million)

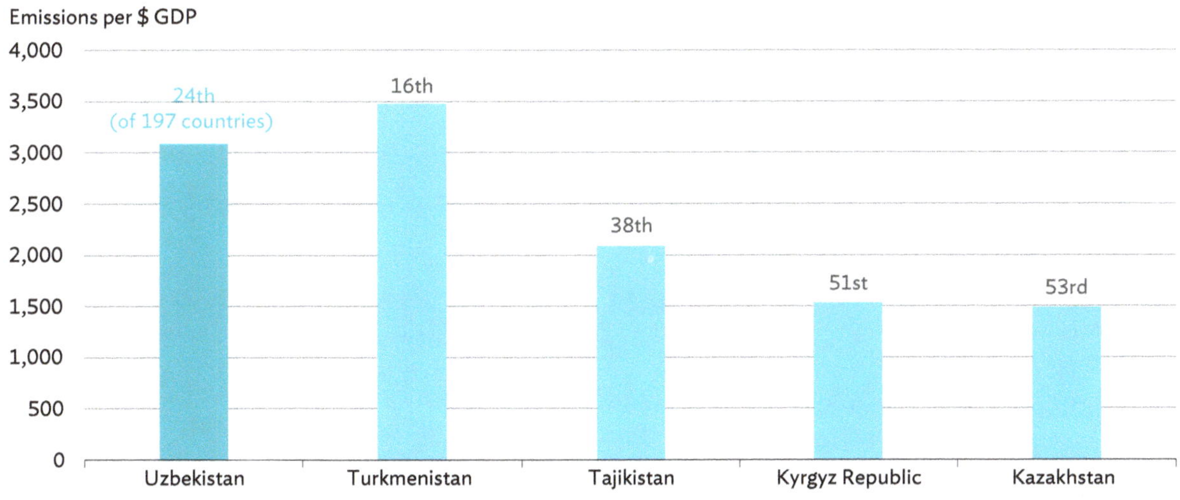

GHG = greenhouse gas, tCO_2e = ton of carbon dioxide equivalent.
Source: Climate Watch (accessed 20 August 2023).

9 Health care, education, finance, information and communication technology, and new agriculture production technology and services, and natural resource management services are examples for higher value-added sectors.
10 UNDP. 2022b. *Green Growth Strategic Framework Uzbekistan*.
11 Climate Watch (accessed 20 August 2023).

Table 2.2 shows the distribution of Uzbekistan's GHG emissions across inventory sectors over 1990–2019. Here, the largest contribution consistently comes from energy (82.8%–85.1% of total emissions over the period), followed by agriculture (10.0%–13.3%), waste (2.9%–3.5%), and industrial processes (1.0%–2.6%). The increased energy usage for electricity, heating, manufacturing, construction, and transport, along with considerable fugitive emissions, were mainly responsible for the recent resurgence of GHG emissions from the energy sector. Forestry and land use sequestered 11.6 tCO_2e for major forest plantation projects in the Aral Sea basin during 2005–2010; however, the degree of sequestration decreased in 2016–2019 (3.4 tCO_2e), possibly from further desertification.

Table 2.2: Greenhouse Gas Emissions Inventory in Uzbekistan, 1990–2019
(tCO_2e)

Year	Energy	Industrial Processes	Agriculture	Waste	Total Emissions	Forestry and Land Use	Net Emission
1990	136.9	1.7	21.9	4.8	165.2	(0.8)	164.5
1995	118.3	3.2	16.7	5.0	143.2	(0.8)	142.4
2000	147.3	3.1	17.3	5.3	173.0	(0.7)	172.3
2005	143.3	4.4	19.4	5.5	172.6	(11.6)	161.0
2010	149.6	5.9	25.6	6.1	187.1	(11.6)	175.5
2015	116.3	6.4	31.7	6.7	161.0	(3.1)	157.9
2016	122.9	6.5	34.7	6.8	170.9	(3.4)	167.5
2017	127.3	6.7	35.4	6.9	176.3	(3.4)	172.9
2018	133.9	6.8	36.1	7.0	183.8	(3.4)	180.4
2019	138.1	6.9	36.6	7.2	188.8	(3.4)	185.4
Contribution, %							
1990	82.8	1.0	13.3	2.9	100.0		
2000	82.6	2.2	11.7	3.5	100.0		
2010	85.1	1.8	10.0	3.0	100.0		
2019	83.0	2.6	11.2	3.2	100.0		

( ) = negative, tCO_2e = ton of carbon dioxide equivalent.
Source: Climate Watch (accessed 20 August 2023).

To meet the target of reducing GHG emissions per GDP by 2030, Uzbekistan's climate policy calls for a variety of mitigation measures, which can be summarized into three strategic approaches: modernization of production systems, diversification of energy sources, and pilot projects and international cooperation.[12] Uzbekistan's second NDC highlights the strategic importance of adaptation for the country's climate resilience in water management, agriculture, ecosystems, infrastructure and production facilities, as well as in the social sphere and Aral Sea disaster. Being a landlocked country, Uzbekistan is highly vulnerable to natural hazards, including high temperature, heat waves, droughts, heavy precipitation, floods, earthquakes, and landslides—and all these hazards are being worsened by the climate change around Central Asia.[13] A 2022 country risk profile by

12 UNDP. 2022b. *Green Growth Strategic Framework Uzbekistan*; UNFCC. 2016. *Third National Communication of the Republic of Uzbekistan under the UN Framework Convention on Climate Change*.

13 Asian Development Bank (ADB). 2021a. Climate Risk Country Profile: Uzbekistan.

the Central Asia Regional Economic Cooperation (CAREC) estimates Uzbekistan's average annual economic losses from floods at $396 million, affecting 220,000 people a year; and $214 million from earthquakes, affecting 160,000 people a year.[14] The 2021 Notre Dame Global Adaption Initiative Index ranks Uzbekistan 97th out of 192 countries in readiness to leverage private and public sector investments for adaptation projects. This is lower than Kazakhstan (51) but higher than the Kyrgyz Republic (100), Tajikistan (140), and Turkmenistan (183).

A group of nine multilateral development banks[15] are committed to ensuring consistent financial flows to low-carbon, climate-resilient capital investment programs beyond traditional infrastructure projects. The nine's climate finance commitments in low- and middle-income countries in 2021 totaled $50.7 billion, with 66% for climate change mitigation and the rest for adaptation.[16] Central Asia received $1.9 billion (3.8%), with 75% for mitigation and the rest for adaptation. Nearly $1.1 billion of this was invested in low-carbon, climate-resilient infrastructure for energy, transport, and building (55.0%); $443 million for cross-sectors (23.0%); $176 million for agriculture, forestry, and land use (9.1%); and $175 million for water and waste management (9.1%), as shown in Figure 2.2. Uzbekistan was the largest recipient country of the climate finance for Central Asia over 2015–2021 ($4.4 billion), followed by Kazakhstan ($2.6 billion) and Tajikistan ($1.1 billion). That Uzbekistan was the largest recipient reflected the sharply increased capital flows and infrastructure investment following 2017's market reforms (Figure 2.3).

Figure 2.2: Multilateral Development Bank Climate Mitigation and Adaptation Finance to Central Asia by Sector in 2021

($ million)

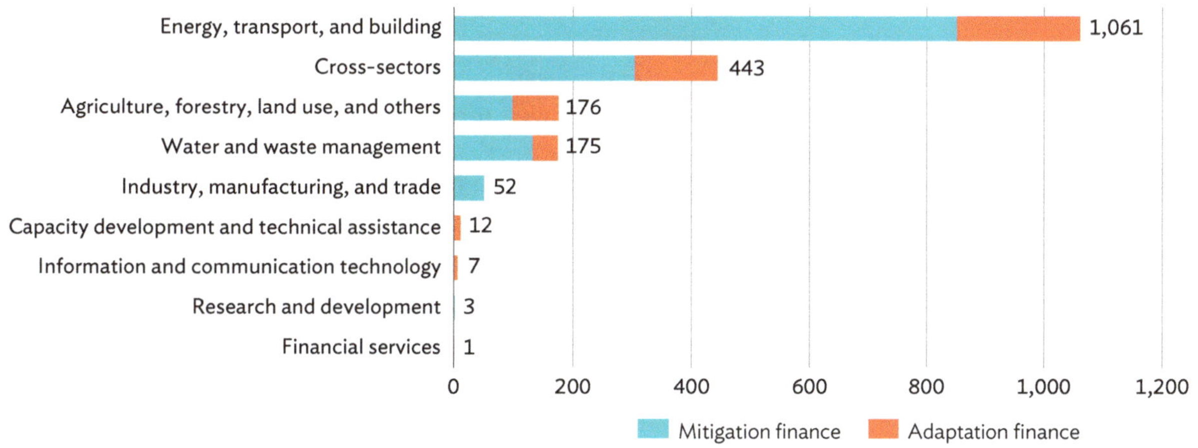

Source: European Investment Bank. 2022. *Joint Report on Multilateral Development Banks' Climate Finance*.

14 CAREC. 2022. *Country Risk Profile Uzbekistan*. Asian Development Bank.

15 African Development Bank, ADB, Asian Infrastructure Investment Bank, Council of Europe Development Bank, European Bank for Reconstruction and Development, European Investment Bank, Inter-American Development Bank Group, Islamic Development Bank, New Development Bank, and World Bank Group.

16 European Investment Bank. 2022. *Joint Report on Multilateral Development Banks' Climate Finance*.

Figure 2.3: Multilateral Development Bank Climate Finance in Central Asia, 2015–2021
($ million)

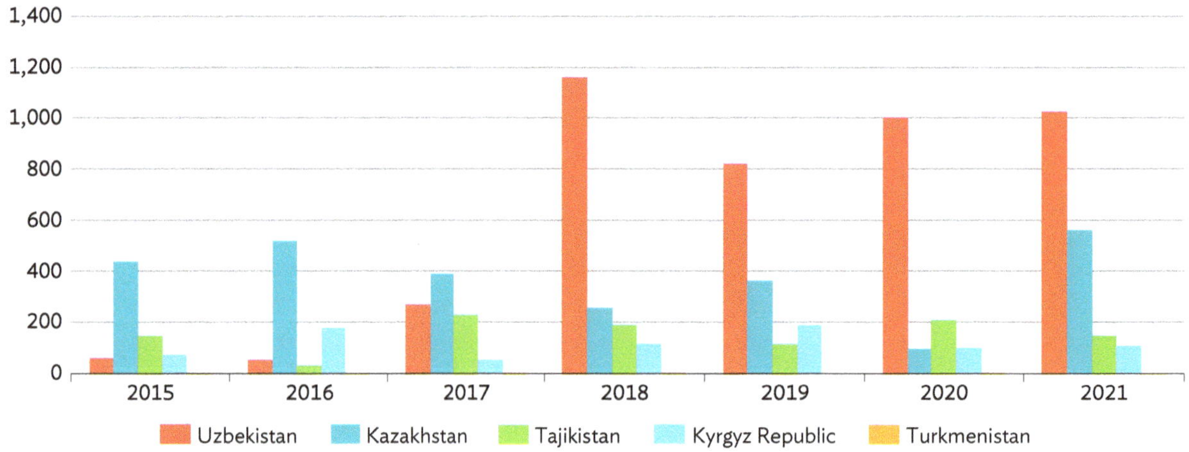

Source: European Investment Bank. 2022. *Joint Report on Multilateral Development Banks' Climate Finance*.

Strategic Investments in Critical Infrastructure

This section identifies critical infrastructure options for strategic investment in Uzbekistan's key sectors as part of a green growth strategy. Critical infrastructure can be broadly defined as systems or assets that are essential for the nation's economic and societal functions.[17] Based on this definition, critical infrastructure sectors can vary depending on a country's stage of development, industrial structure, socioeconomic characteristics, and climate risks and vulnerabilities. Even so, energy, transport, information and communication technology (ICT), water and waste management, and agriculture and food production systems are commonly critical infrastructure sectors in many countries, including Uzbekistan. Recent studies and intergovernmental policy reports on climate change use a systems approach to assess and strategize multiscale (region, country, city) climate mitigation and adaptation actions for synergies and trade-offs across interlinked critical infrastructure sectors.[18]

Energy

Uzbekistan produced 50 billion–60 billion cubic meters (bcm) of natural gas a year before the pandemic, of which 10–15 bcm (15%–25% of total production) was exported, mainly to the People's Republic of China (PRC), the Russian Federation, Kazakhstan, and other countries in Central Asia. Natural gas exports fell sharply to 3.6 bcm in 2020 and to 2.4 bcm in 2021.[19] In early 2020, the government decided to halt natural gas exports by 2025 because of domestic energy shortages. According to the International Energy Agency (IEA), domestic gas consumption is typically about

17 National Institute of Standards and Technology. Glossary: Critical Infrastructure (accessed 20 August 2023); OECD. 2019. *Good Governance for Critical Infrastructure Resilience*.

18 IPCC. 2022. *Climate Change 2022: Impacts, Adaptation, and Vulnerability. Contribution of Working Group II to the Sixth Assessment Report of the Intergovernmental Panel on Climate Change*. https://doi:10.1017/9781009325844; S. Lwasa et al. 2022: Urban Systems and Other Settlements. In P.R. Shukla et al. eds. *Climate Change 2022: Mitigation of Climate Change. Contribution of Working Group III to the Sixth Assessment Report of the Intergovernmental Panel on Climate Change*; World Economic Forum. 2022. *Delivering Climate-Resilient Cities Using a Systems Approach: Insight Report*.

19 CEIC. 2022. Uzbekistan Natural Gas: Exports.

39 bcm per year, and some 85% of electricity generation came from natural gas until 2019.[20] To meet growing energy consumption, in 2021, Uzbekistan imported additional crude petroleum, mainly from Turkmenistan, Kazakhstan, the Russian Federation, and the Kyrgyz Republic. Uzbekistan has become a net importer of electricity and other energy products since it signed an agreement to connect domestic electrical grids with the Central Asian Power System in July 2019 with Afghanistan, Kazakhstan, the Kyrgyz Republic, Tajikistan, and Turkmenistan.[21] Although interdependency between these connected countries has increased, the stability of the region's electricity supply has decreased. In Uzbekistan, this is manifested in more frequent blackouts in more territories because of an aged, poorly maintained, and inadequately operated cross-border network of systems put in operation during the former Soviet Union era.

Figure 2.4: Uzbekistan's Energy and Oil Products Trade, 2010–2022
($ million)

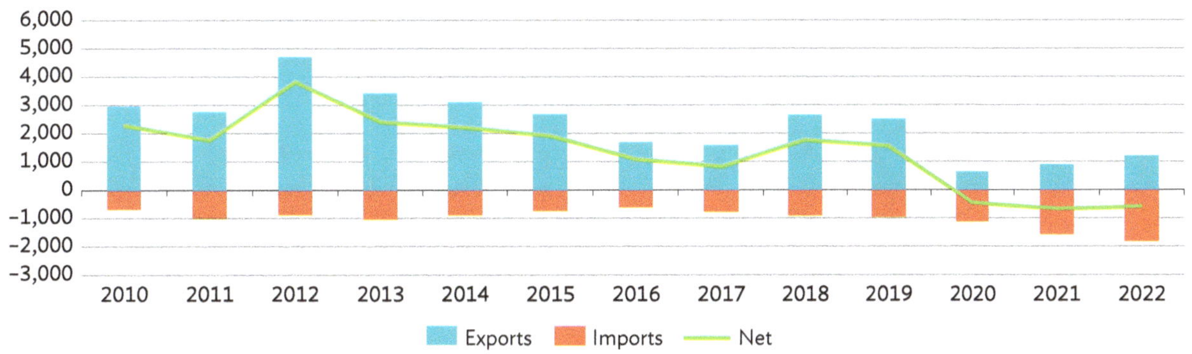

Source: International Monetary Fund. National Summary Data Page—Uzbekistan: Merchandise Trade (accessed 20 August 2023).

The economy's heavy dependence on natural gas, oil, and other fossil fuels continues to be a critical consideration for Uzbekistan in terms of energy security and energy intensity. The energy intensity of GDP has steadily decreased since 2000. Even so, the country's energy systems in 2019 had a higher level of intensity in primary energy, at 8.0 megajoules per 2017 dollar purchasing power parity than the global average of 4.7 megajoules due mainly to outdated infrastructure and equipment.[22] The single largest source of Uzbekistan's GHG emissions in energy is methane leaks from outdated natural gas transport systems, with fugitive emissions of 25.5 tCO_2e in 2019.[23] The modernization of energy supply facilities, especially gas pipeline networks, compressor stations, thermal power plants, electrical grids, and monitoring technologies would significantly advance Uzbekistan 's energy efficiency and mitigate climate change. The capital investment needed to upgrade Uzbekistan's energy systems is estimated at $3.7 billion a year over 2020–2030, according to one energy transition scenario.[24]

20 IEA. 2021. *Uzbekistan Energy Profile*.

21 IEA. 2022e. *Uzbekistan 2022: Energy Policy Review*.

22 World Bank. Energy Intensity Level of Primary Energy (MJ/$2017 PPP GDP)—Uzbekistan; World Bank. Sustainable Energy for All (SE4ALL) Database from the SE4ALL Global Tracking Framework led jointly by the World Bank, International Energy Agency, and the Energy Sector Management Assistance Program (accessed 20 August 2023).

23 IEA. 2022e. *Uzbekistan 2022: Energy Policy Review*; UNFCC. 2016. *Third National Communication of the Republic of Uzbekistan under the UN Framework Convention on Climate Change*.

24 European Bank for Reconstruction and Development. 2021. A Carbon-Neutral Electricity Sector in Uzbekistan: Summary for Policymakers.

Expanding renewable energy sources is projected to improve energy security and reduce GHG emissions. The government presently aims to increase Uzbekistan's share of renewable energy sources in total electricity generation to over 30% by 2030. In 2018, renewable energy from hydropower accounted for about 10% of total electricity production capacity, but the shares of solar and wind power were negligible. The country's geographical features are highly favorable for the expansion of solar power generation (Table 2.3). Since 2019, competitive bidding processes have attracted foreign direct investment in large solar photovoltaic (PV) projects, mainly in southern and southwestern regions where there is higher solar irradiation. The government also promoted small- and medium-scale solar power projects for households and enterprises to meet their energy consumption, such as by installing rooftop solar PVs in urban areas and developing off-grid solar PVs in remote areas. Renewable energy producers are legally allowed to develop local grids and trade electric and thermal energy units through these grids. This can create both substantial investment opportunities and market design challenges for integrating solar thermal heating and other renewable energy solutions for modernizing Uzbekistan's aging district heating networks, which have a total length of 4,965 kilometers (km) nationwide (footnote 20).[25]

Table 2.3: Renewable Energy Source Potential in Uzbekistan

Renewable Energy Source	Gross Potential	Technical Potential
Hydropower	9.2 Mtoe	2.0 Mtoe
Wind power	2.2 Mtoe	0.4 Mtoe
Solar power	50,973 Mtoe	177 Mtoe

Mtoe = million tons of oil equivalent.
Source: International Energy Agency. Uzbekistan Energy Profile: Sustainable Development (accessed 20 August 2023).

Fossil fuel subsidies for end-user consumption continue to hamper efforts to scale up Uzbekistan's relatively expensive renewable energy systems, which calls for tariff liberalization and market-based pricing mechanisms.[26] With the introduction of a green certification system in June 2023, the government plans to strategize a variety of financial incentive schemes for renewable energy producers, suppliers, and consumers, such as green tariffs, subsidies, and tax benefits. Nuclear power is a possible electricity generation option and also influences the scalability of private capital investments in newly emerging renewable energy sources. However, this must be cautiously discussed because Uzbekistan is prone to earthquakes and other natural hazards. Another important challenge for expanding the sources of renewable energy, especially hydropower and solar power, is developing sufficient storage systems, such as pumped storage hydropower and concentrating solar power plants, which can secure a flexible supply of energy through upgraded and extended grids nationwide.[27] Another challenge is managing end-of-life solar panels, as this is likely to generate substantial decommissioning costs and potentially harm the environment because the number of solar PV sites will rise sharply in the coming decades.

25 See also UNFCC. 2016. *Third National Communication of the Republic of Uzbekistan under the UN Framework Convention on Climate Change*.
26 See IEA. 2022b. Fossil Fuel Subsidies by Fuel in Uzbekistan, 2010-2020. See also International Monetary Fund. Fossil Fuel Subsidy Database 2022.
27 IEA. 2022d. *Solar Energy Policy in Uzbekistan: A Roadmap*.

Advances in digitalization and automation technologies in energy are expected to increase energy security, improve energy efficiency, and reduce GHG emissions. In Uzbekistan, this will be accompanied by the modernization of outdated energy infrastructure and equipment and the expansion of renewable energy sources at all levels. Projects with development partners to achieve this are already underway. In digital infrastructure, a new supervisory control and data acquisition system, an energy management system, and remote terminal units for the National Electric Grid have been implemented with support from ADB, the World Bank, and other international partners.[28] Digital infrastructure initiatives such as this aim to support Uzbekistan's "smart" energy transition along with several interrelated objectives. These are increasing the capacity of the transmission network capacity; integrating renewable energy produced by private entities into the national power grid; harnessing resource planning, system operation, and risk management functions with real-time data and computer-aided analysis; adjusting tariffs for full-cost recovery; mobilizing private capital investments in newly emerging renewable energy solutions; and ensuring stable energy supplies to millions of households and business consumers nationwide or even regionwide via grids connected to the Central Asian Power System.

According to the International Energy Agency (IEA),[29] the world's digital infrastructure investment in electrical grids steadily grew by 55.6% over 2015–2021 (Figure 2.5). About 78.5% of the $55.7 billion investment in 2021 went to the distribution sector's digital infrastructure, including the rollout of smart meters (38.4%), automation and management systems (24.6%), and networking and communications (15.4%). Electric vehicle (EV) public charging infrastructure accounted for less than 10% of the world's infrastructure investment in electrical grids in 2021, but has expanded by 587.5% since 2015, suggesting the increasing importance of an integrated systems approach to the planning and design of smart grids in coordination with other critical infrastructure sectors. This will be especially important for Uzbekistan's transport sector.

Figure 2.5: Global Digital Infrastructure Investment in Electrical Grids, 2015–2021

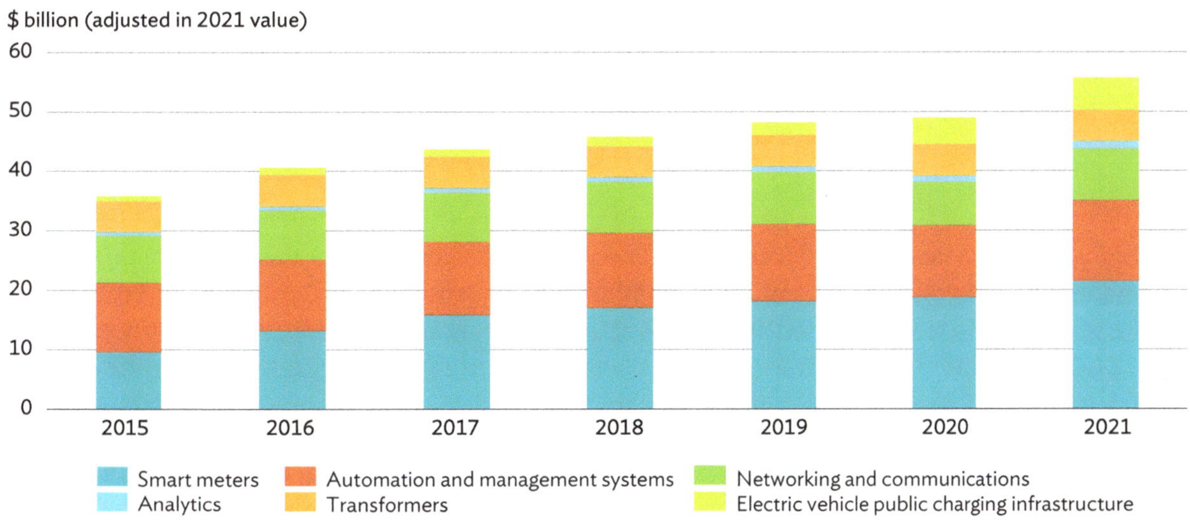

Source: International Energy Agency. 2022. Smart Grids: Analysis. Paris (accessed 23 August 2023).

28 World Bank. 2021. Uzbekistan to Reform and Green Its Electricity Sector, with World Bank Support. *Press release*. 25 June.
29 IEA. 2022d. *Smart Grids: Analysis*.

Transport

Passenger and freight transport play a vital role in Uzbekistan's economic development and poverty reduction. Traffic volume continues to grow steadily as the country industrializes and regional trade increases, as well as from the economic recovery from the pandemic. Uzbekistan's total passenger-kilometers grew by 66.0% over 2010–2019, predominately led by road transport, accounting for 98.4% of total passenger transport in 2019 (Figure 2.6).[30] Passenger-kilometers by rail transport fell by 56.0% in 2020 due to COVID-19 travel restrictions, and road transport declined 8.8%. The country's total tons-kilometers, an indicator of freight movements, increased by 27.1% over 2010–2020 (Figure 2.6). Rail transport is the primary mode of long-haul and cross-border freight movements, accounting for 59.3% of total transport services in 2020. Road transport is mainly for short-haul freight movements at 40.7%.[31] Total tons-kilometers by road grew faster than by rail over 2010–2020, by 75.0% and 5.2%, respectively.

Figure 2.6: Total Passenger and Freight Traffic Volume in Uzbekistan, 2010–2020

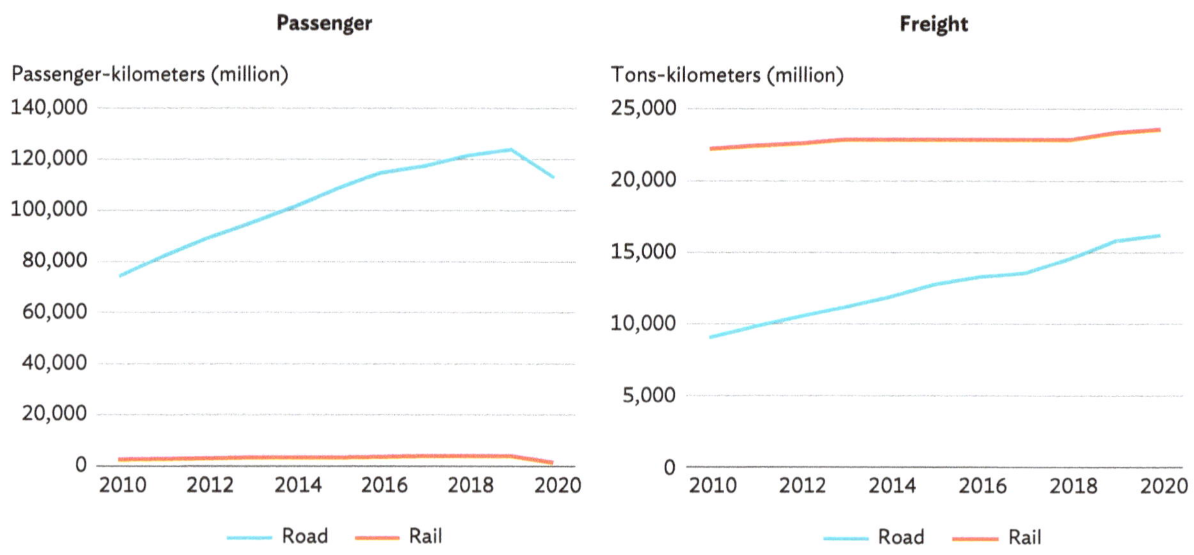

Source: OECD Statistics: Transport (accessed 23 August 2023).

The rapidly growing passenger and freight movements by road are not only an indicator of the country's strong economic progress but also of increased traffic congestion, air pollution, and GHG emissions. Traffic congestion is concentrated in Tashkent and Samarkand; urban centers with populations of 200,000 inhabitants; and around major transport corridors and border-crossing points. This congestion is holding back urban business, tourism, and logistics performance (Figure 2.7). IQAir ranks Uzbekistan 20th out of 131 countries and regions in annual average PM2.5 from vehicle emissions, dust storms, waste burning, and pollution from the mining and energy industries.[32] This is lower

30 OECD Statistics. Transport (accessed 23 August 2023).
31 K. Anderson, E. Ginting, and K. Taniguchi. 2020. Uzbekistan Quality Job Creation as a Cornerstone for Sustainable Economic Growth.
32 IQAir. 2023. Air Quality Historical Rankings 2022. Goldach. https://www.iqair.com.

than Tajikistan (10) but higher than the Kyrgyz Republic (24), Kazakhstan (40), and Turkmenistan (44). Tashkent, due largely to its increased and concentrated traffic congestion, ranked 383rd out of 7,323 polluted cities worldwide in 2022 and 6th out of 14 polluted cities regionwide in average PM2.5 concentration.[33] Over 2010–2017, Uzbekistan's PM2.5 air pollution exceeded the World Health Organization's guideline value, although the level declined over this period.[34] The country's nitrogen dioxide (NO_2) air pollution, however, grew by 69.7% over 2004–2017 (Figure 2.8) and is concentrated alongside main roadways (Map 2.1). Uzbekistan's GHG transport emissions are overwhelmingly from road transport (94%), followed by rail (5%) and in-country air transport (1%) (footnote 25). While the government continues to increase spending on road transport to increase economic growth and competitiveness, the Strategy for the Transition to a Green Economy aims to establish an integrated green transport system in accordance with the country's long-term urban development plans and environmental safety measures.

Figure 2.7: Uzbekistan's Logistic Performance Scores, 2007 and 2018

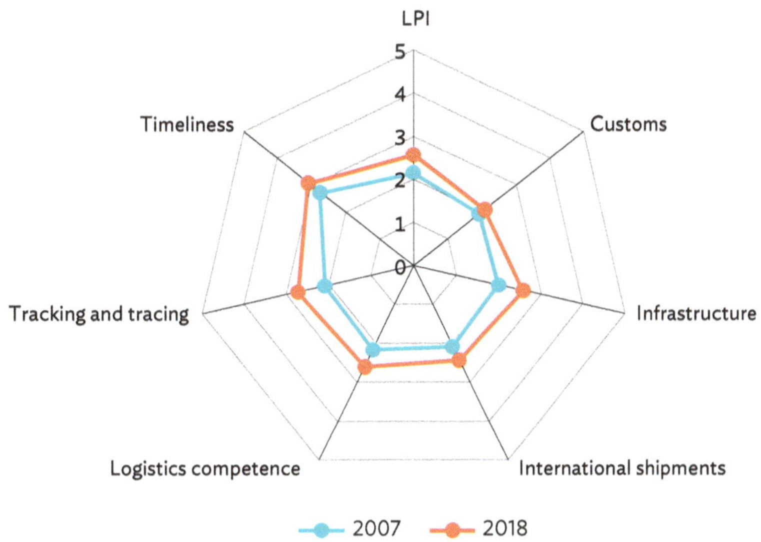

LPI = logistics performance index.
Note: The LPI is the weighted average of the scores on the six dimensions, ranging from 0 to 5.
Source: World Bank. Logistics Performance Index: International Scorecard Page (accessed 20 August 2023).

33 M. Tursumbayeva et al. 2023. Cities of Central Asia: New Hotspots of Air Pollution in the World. *Atmospheric Environment*. 309; IQAir. 2023. Air Quality Historical Rankings 2022. Goldach. https://www.iqair.com.

34 World Bank. PM2.5 Air Pollution, Mean Annual Exposure (micrograms per cubic meter)—Uzbekistan (accessed 20 August 2023).

Figure 2.8: Nitrogen Dioxide Emissions, 2000–2017 and Surface Concentration, 2017 in Uzbekistan
('000 tCO_2e)

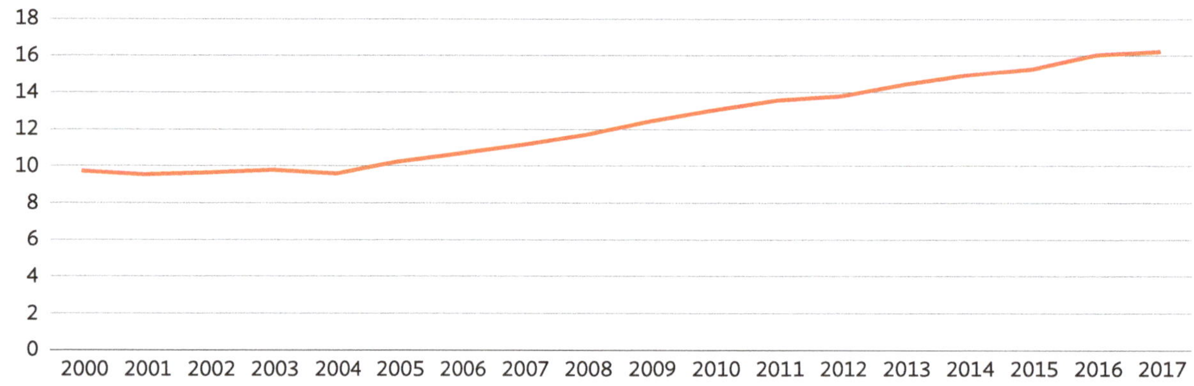

tCO_2e = tons of carbon dioxide equivalent.
Source: World Bank. Indicators (accessed 20 August 2023).

Map 2.1: Nitrogen Dioxide Emissions Surface Concentration in Uzbekistan, 2017

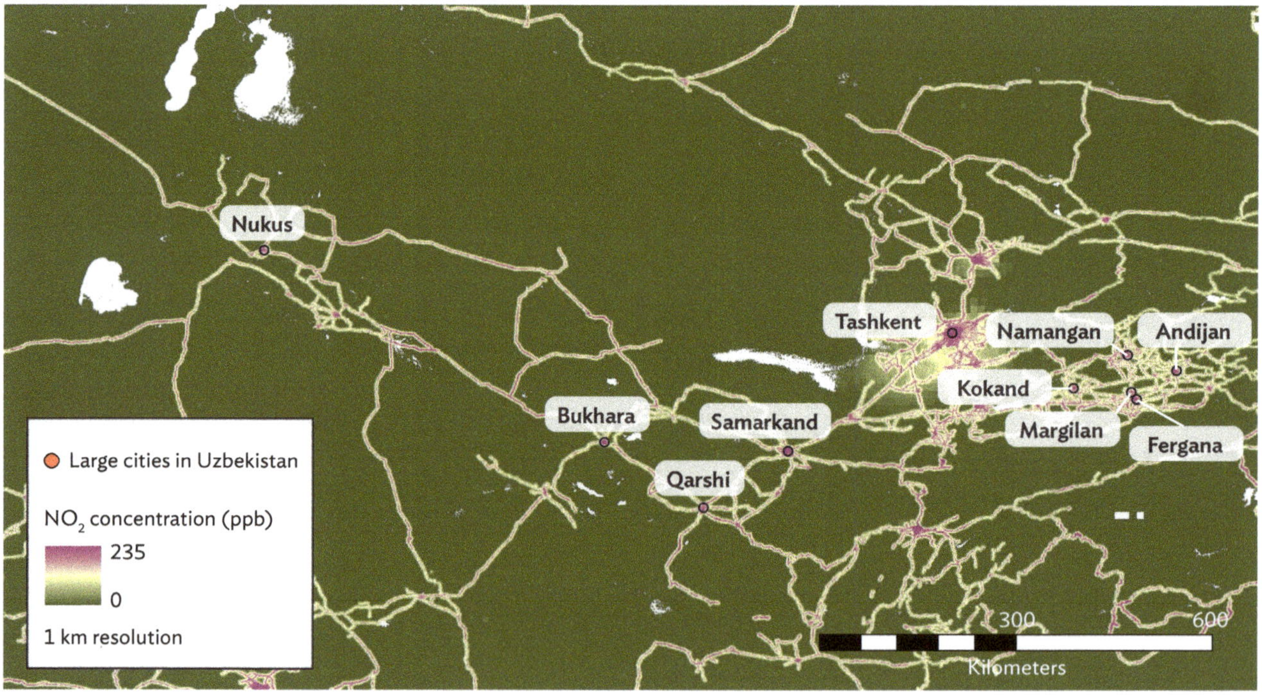

NO_2 = nitrogen dioxide; ppb = parts per billion.
Note: The boundaries, colors, denominations, and any other information shown on this map do not imply, on the part of the Asian Development Bank, any judgment on the legal status of any territory, or any other endorsement or acceptance of such boundaries, colors, denominations, or information.
Source: Author with data from Anenberg et al. 2022. Long-term Trends in Urban NO_2 Concentrations and Associated Paediatric Asthma Incidence: Estimates from Global Datasets. *The Lancet Planetary Health*. 6 (1). pp. 49–58.

Uzbekistan's 42,654 kms of main roads consist of international (3,979 km), national (14,069 km), and regional (24,606 km) roads. In addition, local governments manage 140,000 kms of urban and rural roads. The country's roads are generally poor because of outmoded design standards, inadequate maintenance and rehabilitation, and increased climatic anomalies and natural hazards (footnote 31). With technical assistance and financial support from ADB and other development partners, the modernization and reconstruction of selected sections of the road transport network are underway to improve road safety, mitigate air pollution and GHG emissions, and enhance climate resilience.[35] Road improvement projects are aligned with international transport corridors to enhance regional connectivity, cross-border trade, and foreign direct investment.[36] Filling gaps in the cross-border road transport network system, i.e., a "missing link" problem solution, is the most cost-effective option for investing in road infrastructure investment for Uzbekistan and its regionally connected countries that include Kazakhstan, the Kyrgyz Republic, Tajikistan, and Turkmenistan.[37]

Recent road modernization and reconstruction projects aim to reduce the country's physical barriers to cross-border freight traffic and improve its logistics performance (Figure 2.7). The economy, however, still suffers from the high cost of freight transport for several reasons, including the inefficiency of customs clearance processes. The country's major border-crossing points do not have the capacity to manage increased freight traffic due largely to the lack of investment in digital infrastructure and modern customs equipment (footnote 31).

Uzbekistan's logistics operations are also characterized by fragmented supply chains, as they are managed by different groups of transport companies and inefficient cargo handling procedures at transport and warehouse facilities. Cross-border freight transport relies on five main international logistics centers, including Navoi International Airport's cargo terminal developed and managed by Uzbekistan Airways and Korean Air and the Angren Logistics Center connected by the Angren–Pap Railway Line. To promote manufacturing, agriculture, and pharmaceutical production, Uzbekistan had designated some 20 free economic zones, 116 small industrial zones, 12 technology parks, and 440 clusters by 2023 through which regional and local logistics facilities and road transport infrastructure are separately invested and managed.[38] The experiences of other countries suggest the locational dispersion of modern logistics facilities through road transport networks is likely to result in "logistics sprawl" around large cities and thereby increasing frequent short-distance freight trips by small-size trucks along with the problem of first-mile and last-mile deliveries.[39] First-mile and last-mile deliveries account for a large percentage of the total cost of freight transport services and are increasingly recognized as a significant source of air pollution and GHG emissions.[40]

Uzbekistan's road transport system, including 140,00 kms of urban and rural segments, carries an estimated 90% of domestic short-distance freight traffic,[41] while the insufficiency of secondary and tertiary roads in the country's urban and rural areas was pointed out by ADB.[42] Very little has been done to tackle Uzbekistan's first-mile and last-mile delivery system development and management. Amid the expansion and advancement of e-commerce markets, various green logistics measures to

35 ADB. 2022b. Proposed Loan and Technical Assistance Grant Republic of Uzbekistan: National Road Development Project.
36 Ministry of Investments, Industry and Trade. Transport Corridors (accessed 20 August 2023).
37 World Bank. 2020a. *Uzbekistan Pap-Angren Railway (P146328)*.
38 Investment Promotion Agency. FEZ and SIZ (accessed 20 August 2023).
39 K. Aljohani and R. G. Thompson. 2016. Impacts of Logistics Sprawl on the Urban Environment and Logistics: Taxonomy and Review of Literature. *Journal of Transport Geography*. 57. pp. 255–263.
40 World Economic Forum. 2020. *The Future of the Last-Mile Ecosystem*.
41 Logistics Cluster. 2022. 3.2 Uzbekistan Transporters.
42 ADB. 2021b. *Harnessing Uzbekistan's Potential of Urbanization: National Urban Assessment*.

overcome the problem of first-mile and last-mile delivery services are progressively being adopted in many countries, cities, and districts. For example, the creation of "micro-hubs" is expected to consolidate delivery points and produce start-up delivery businesses with e-mobility and other low-carbon micromobility options suited for local street conditions.[43] The World Economic Forum notes that in less populated, remote areas, e-commerce giants in partnership with start-up companies might be able to offer drone delivery services as a cost-effective green logistics solution for relatively time-sensitive, high-value lightweight shipments—for example, medical supplies, perishable foods, and electronics—subject to given flight safety regulations, topographical and weather conditions, skyway network plans, air traffic control systems, building and port design standards, and charging infrastructure provisions (footnote 40).

Air transport plays a catalytic role in promoting Uzbekistan's economic growth, especially through international trade, high-tech manufacturing, and tourism by enhancing interregional connectivity and integrating the country's economic production systems into global value chains. Since the introduction of market-based reforms in 2017, air passenger movements grew by 20.6% over 2017–2019. Air cargo movements in the same period, however, declined by 44.9% amid increased international competition due to high costs and the inefficiency of the freight transport system.[44] The pandemic stalled growth in air transport markets worldwide. Nevertheless, the global aviation sector predicts that many cities will face airport capacity constraints after achieving full travel demand recovery and further growth across the global regions by around 2025, even in a pessimistic scenario.[45]

Uzbekistan has 11 airports, and until 2019 the growth of air transport demand was mainly at Tashkent International Airport, which handled 64% of the country's aircraft movements in that year.[46] Uzbekistan's airports are expected to see a significant increase in air passenger movements by 2040, driven by further market liberalization and economic progress as the country heads toward upper-middle-income status. Meeting this demand will require substantial brownfield investment in airport infrastructure and equipment; for example, increasing runway capacity and modernizing terminals to meet international airport design standards. On the other hand, during the past few years, international airport design standards and capital investment criteria progressively have given greater weight to decarbonization technology and policy, following green recovery plans.[47] The Intergovernmental Panel on Climate Change (IPCC) 6th assessment report in 2022 says that air transport is a "hard-to-decarbonize" sector not only for its heavy dependency on fossil fuels but also for its energy-intensive airport infrastructure and equipment that have long "lock-in" timescales. Green airport projects aiming to reduce aviation-related congestion, air pollution, and GHG emissions need to consider both "in-sector" solutions (e.g., green technologies, smart operations, alternative fuels) and "out-of-sector" solutions (e.g., intermodal transport connection, ground access transport development and management, high-speed rail modal substitution, and airport-linked special economic zone designation and land use coordination.[48]

---

43 European Environment Agency. 2019. *The First and Last Mile—the Key to Sustainable Urban Transport: Transport and Environment Report 2019*.

44 World Bank. Air Transport, Passengers Carried: International Civil Aviation Organization, Civil Aviation Statistics of the World and ICAO Staff Estimates (accessed 20 August 2023).

45 Airports Council International. 2021. *The Impact of COVID-19 on the Airport Business and the Path to Recovery*. Montreal.

46 International Civil Aviation Organization. 2020. Traffic Flow Global Data (Shape File). Montreal.

47 Airports Council International. 2022. *Green Airports Recognition 2022 Carbon Management*. Montreal.

48 P. Jaramillo et al. 2022: Transport. In P.R. Shukla et al. eds. *Climate Change 2022: Mitigation of Climate Change. Contribution of Working Group III to the Sixth Assessment Report of the Intergovernmental Panel on Climate Change*; H. Kato and J. Murakami. 2022. *Developing Airport Systems in Asian Cities: Spatial Characteristics, Economic Effects, and Policy Implications*. ADB; S. Lwasa et al. 2022: Urban Systems and Other Settlements. In P.R. Shukla et al. eds. *Climate Change 2022: Mitigation of Climate Change. Contribution of Working Group III to the Sixth Assessment Report of the Intergovernmental Panel on Climate Change.*

Uzbekistan's operational railway network totaled 4,732 km in 2021,[49] accompanied by the expansion of international transport corridors regionwide.[50] The main sections of regionwide railway networks were developed during the Russian Empire era and later extended by the former Soviet Union. In recent years, Uzbekistan Railways, with technical assistance and financial support from ADB and other development partners, worked on the reconstruction and modernization of the country's rail infrastructure and equipment, including the electrification of the railway system and the renewal of rolling stock.[51] Although some 50% of the railway network has been modernized, more investment is needed in rail infrastructure and rolling stock to increase the system's energy efficiency to improve international trade competitiveness and reduce air pollution and GHG emissions from aging diesel-powered locomotives for rail freight transport by 2030.

Increasing the share of passenger movements by better-performing public transport modes will be critical for achieving the scope of green growth. High-speed rail passenger services, branded as Afrosiyob, have been operating since 2011; these services have a design speed of 250 km/hour for a total network length of 831 km, connecting the capital and major tourist cities, such as Samarkand, Karshi, Navoi, and Bukhara. To develop a tourism-led economic corridor and reduce GHG emissions from increased intercity passenger movements, a further extension in the high-speed rail network and electrification projects are planned with technical assistance and financial support from ADB and the Asian Infrastructure Investment Bank.[52] In Samarkand, the country's most popular tourist city, two modern tram lines were inaugurated with a service length of 6.4 km in 2017 and 5.0 km in 2018 for managing intracity passenger movements by public transport across the Temir Yo'l Vokzali HSR station, ancient sites, and cultural places. Tashkent's metro system, initially built during the former Soviet Union era, has been extended to improve citywide access by public transport and reduce private cars in city-fringe areas with a planned new 55 km circle line. Tashkent is preparing to launch high-speed metrobus services with bus rapid transit corridors (dedicated bus lanes) to make public transport a faster option than going by car. The metrobus services will be accompanied by transit-oriented development principles (e.g., compact, mixed-use, and walkable built environments around public transport nodes); separate bike lanes; and electric bus fleets.[53] The transit-oriented development principles and separate bike lanes are expected to encourage short-distance travel by active transport modes, reduce traffic congestion and accidents, lower GHG and air pollution emissions, and improve public health, thus contributing to socioeconomic development.

Expanding the production and operation of green vehicles will be vital for advancing Uzbekistan's transition toa green economy by 2030. The United Nations Economic Commission for Europe (UNECE) Statistical Database shows the total number of passenger cars in Uzbekistan grew by 78.2% over 2013–2021, but passenger cars per 1,000 people remained at 91 vehicles in 2021 (Table 2.4). This is lower than the degree of motorization in other middle-income countries, such as Albania (211 vehicles in 2021) and Romania (398). Methane, a compressed natural gas, is the most widely used fuel in private passenger vehicles (65% of total passenger vehicles), followed by gasoline (24.4%), propane (8.4%), and diesel (2.2%).[54] The government is preparing to apply the minimum Euro-5 standard for the import and domestic production of passenger vehicles (footnote 17).[55] Of several

49 World Bank. Rail lines (total route-km)—Uzbekistan: Internation Union of Railways (UIC) (accessed 20 August 2023).
50 CAREC. 2021. Railway Sector Assessment for Uzbekistan. ADB.
51 ADB. 2019. Sector Assessment (Summary): Transport (Rail Transport [Non Urban]).
52 Asian Infrastructure Investment Bank. 2022. Republic of Uzbekistan: Bukhara–Miskin–Urgench–Khiva Railway Electrification Project.
53 UNDP. 2022c. Tashkent: Accelerating Investments in Low Emission Vehicles (TAILEV).
54 Statistics Agency. 2022b. *What Type of Fuel is Most Widely Used in Uzbekistan?*.
55 See also UNDP. 2022c. *Tashkent: Accelerating Investments in Low Emission Vehicles (TAILEV)*.

green vehicle fuel alternatives, EVs are gaining public attention and market popularity. Although the domestic production of EVs is still quite small, imports of EVs and plug-in hybrids mainly from the PRC are rising. Tashkent and Samarkand had several hundred PRC-made electric buses by early 2023.

Table 2.4: Motorization in Uzbekistan, 2013–2021

Year	Population ('000)	Passenger Vehicles ('000)	Vehicles (per '000 people)
2013	29,031	1,713	59
2014	29,334	1,819	62
2015	30,847	1,974	64
2016	31,651	2,057	65
2017	31,843	2,134	67
2018	32,460	2,272	70
2019	33,019	2,410	73
2020	33,339	2,767	83
2021	33,536	3,052	91

Source: United Nations Economic Commission for Europe Statistical Database. Transport Tables (accessed 20 August 2023).

Increasing Uzbekistan's EV sales calls for more investment not only in its domestic EV production systems but also in public charging infrastructure. To date, there are only about 70 EV charging stations. The government plans to increase this to 2,500 nationwide by 2025 through private sector initiatives—for example, public site auctions, which could be accompanied by the installation of solar PV systems and the development of microgrids.[56] The fast expansion of EV production and operations can, as seen in the PRC, generate considerable battery-waste materials at levels that are higher than the country's recycling capacity, which can cause additional environmental hazards. For Uzbekistan, the development of battery recycling systems needs to be carefully planned and incentivized for strategic investments to meet future demand for EV battery waste management in the automobile industry.

Advancing digital infrastructure enables Uzbekistan to adopt demand-responsive mobility services and other transformative solutions with dynamic information and data analytics. One of the most impactful transformations in transport has been the advent and growth of online platforms for ride-hailing and taxi services. In Uzbekistan, Yandex Go and MyTaxi.uz are the main mobility service apps. The government reports that taxi services accounted for 49.7% (SUM9.5 trillion) of the total volume of market services provided by road transport in the first half of 2022.[57] Despite the market significance of ride-hailing and taxi services, little information exists on their impact on traffic congestion, air pollution, and GHG emissions in the context of Uzbekistan's green transition. The adverse effects of ride-hailing services on behavioral adaptation—such as increasing vehicle kilometers traveled by road transport and decreasing the use of public transport services—have been observed in other countries' transport markets.[58] For Uzbekistan, more information, data, analytical

56 President of the Republic of Uzbekistan. 2022. Presidential Decree No. 443 on Measures of State Support to Establish Electric Vehicle Production.

57 Statistics Agency. 2022a. *What Is the Share of Taxis in the Volume of Road Transport Services?*

58 A. Tirachini. 2020. Ride-Hailing, Travel Behaviour and Sustainable Mobility: An International Review. *Transportation*. 47 (4). pp. 2011–2047.

research are needed to support evidence-based infrastructure investment decisions and demand-responsive mobility service solutions to establish an integrated green transport system with newly emerging disruptive technologies, such as ride-hailing, driverless cars, and the Internet of Things.

Information and Communication Technology

Uzbekistan's ICT sector contributed to only 1.8% of the gross value added of all industries in 2022 (Table 2.1). Even so, the development of digital technologies across transformative sectors is one of the national strategies for inclusive economic growth over the next decade of industrial and societal changes. The pace of digital adoption by citizens has accelerated since 2013. In 2019, only 10% of population (3.3 million people) subscribed to fixed telephone and broadband services, but the number of fixed broadband service subscribers rose from 3.1 million in 2019 to 6.8 million in 2021, up 120.9%, due in part to pandemic lockdowns and lifestyle changes (Figure 2.9, panel A). The country's mobile cellular services had 35 million subscriptions (103 subscriptions per 100 people) in 2021, up by 50.9% from 2018 (Figure 2.9, panel B).

Figure 2.9: Fixed Telephone, Broadband, and Mobile Subscriptions in Uzbekistan, 2005–2021
(million)

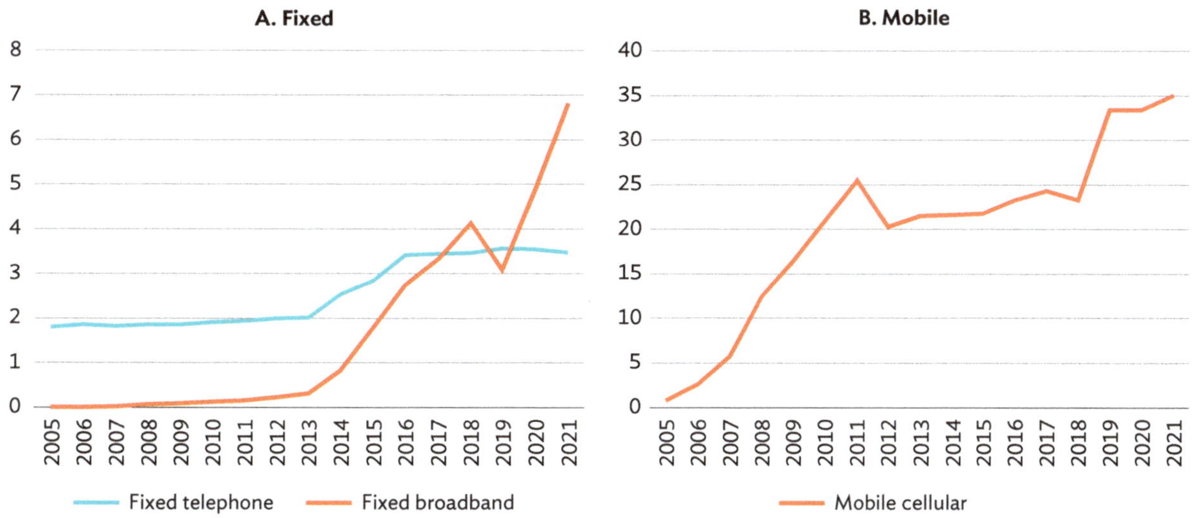

Source: World Bank. Indicators (accessed 20 August 2023).

Improving the internet's performance in capacity, reliability, and affordability is a critical challenge for Uzbekistan's market competitiveness and socioeconomic development. High-speed internet is unevenly concentrated in cities, which have a critical mass of affluent consumers. But demand for better online access to social services, such as in education and health care, is rising in rural towns and villages, and among the economically disadvantaged, especially women. According to the United States Agency for International Development (USAID), the country's digital divide between urban and rural populations and men and women calls for a digital transformation roadmap.[59]

[59] USAID. 2022. *Uzbekistan Digital Ecosystem Country Assessment (DECA)*.

A strategic pillar in the Digital Uzbekistan 2030 Strategy adopted in 2020 is the development of digital infrastructure; specifically, expanding the fiber-optic network to 250,000 km and attaining 100% high-speed internet coverage by 2030. With financial support from the Japan Bank for International Cooperation, the government extended the fiber-optic network from 36,600 km in 2019 to 81,700 km in 2021, a 123.1% increase. The country's major mobile operators have enlarged the coverage of middle-mile and last-mile connectivity infrastructure by increasing the number of mobile base stations from 26.1 million to 45.9 million in the same period, a 75.8% increase. In fulfillment of operator license requirements, this expansion has not only been in profitable cities but also in less profitable rural areas. The government has given special attention to enhancing digital connectivity infrastructure in social facilities, such as schools, hospitals, and local communities, which can be economized through cross-sector coordination with the construction and rehabilitation of other network infrastructure, such as energy grids, roads, and railways (footnote 59). As nationwide mobile and fixed broadband networks connect more people, goods, and services in larger areas, the data traffic generated and processed will grow exponentially in the coming years. The provision of hyperscale data centers is still limited in Uzbekistan, leaving substantial foreign direct investment opportunities to benefit from the growth of data usage and computing services.

Figure 2.10: Digital Infrastructure in Uzbekistan, 2013–2021

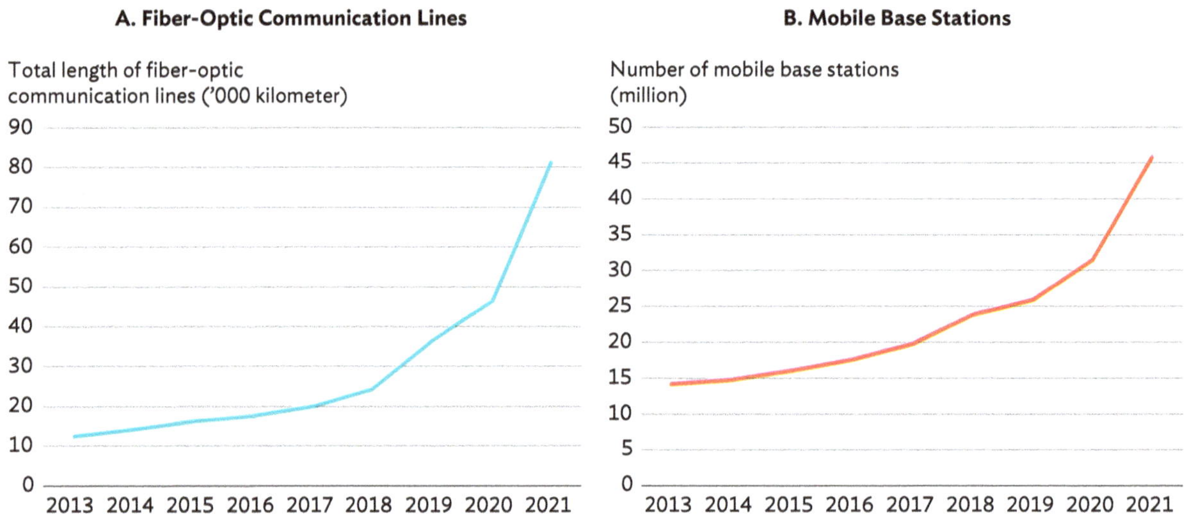

Source: Ministry of Digital Technologies (accessed 20 August 2023).

The proliferation of digital technologies will indirectly support industrial transitions toward green economies through the digitalization of energy, transport, and other critical infrastructure systems. However, the operation of digital infrastructure directly affects energy consumption and GHG emissions through the growth of data traffic. Data centers and transmission networks that underpin digitalization worldwide, excluding cryptocurrency mining, each accounted for 1.0%–1.5% of global electricity consumption, and generated 0.9% of the global energy-related GHG emissions in 2020.[60] The impact of emerging digital innovations, such as 6G and 7G, the Internet of Things, blockchain, artificial intelligence, and the metaverse on energy consumption and GHG emissions is still uncertain.

60 IEA. 2022c. *Smart Grids: Analysis*. Paris.

The world's four major ICT companies, Amazon, Microsoft, Meta, and Google, are proactively investing in renewable energy systems to safeguard the operation of digital infrastructure against potential energy crises and to mitigate climate change impacts under environmental, social, and governance investing criteria.[61] Hyperscale data centers are also driving the ICT sector's substantial renewable energy procurement through power purchase agreements (Figure 2.11). These global developments show that Uzbekistan's digital transformation roadmap by 2030 needs to be closely interlinked with green growth measures in other sectors.

Figure 2.11: Global Renewable Energy Power Purchase Agreements by Sector, 2010–2021
(gigawatt)

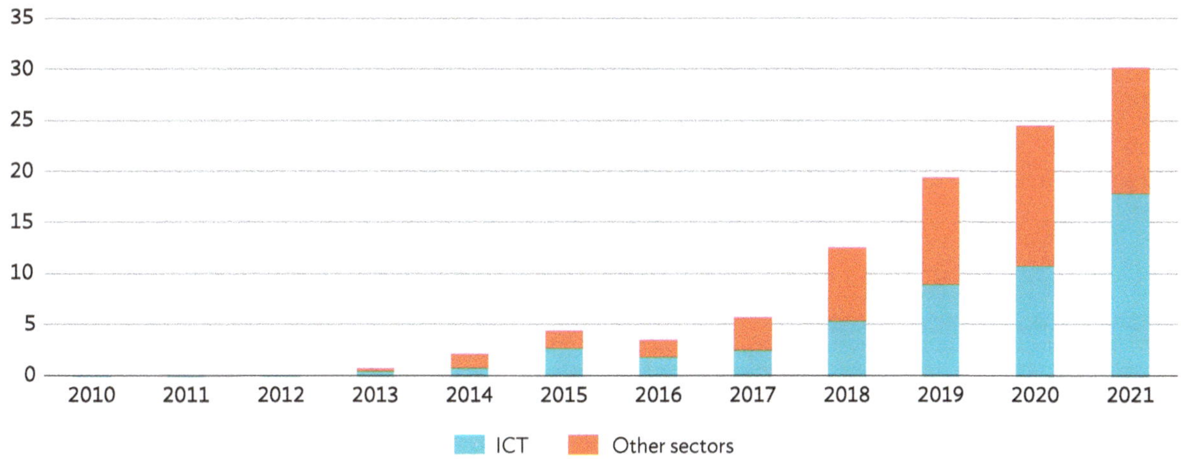

ICT = information and communication technology.
Source: International Energy Agency. 2022. Global Renewable Energy Power Purchase Agreements by Sector, 2010–2021 (accessed 20 August 2023).

The Digital Uzbekistan 2030 Strategy contains several measures to integrate digital technologies into key sectors for climate resilience, including agricultural production and water resource management. One of these measures is setting up a proposed unified national data platform to encourage knowledge sharing among farmers and stakeholders in agriculture to improve productivity through shared data and information, create new agribusiness opportunities, and contribute to the development of agri-food value chains. Smart agritechnology based on 5G, the Internet of Things, drones, and intelligent sensors are tested to monitor farming conditions, control water and other resource inputs, and make agricultural yields more predictable (footnote 59). Digital technologies can make a substantial contribution to Uzbekistan's climate change adaptation through a multi-hazard early warning system to enhance the capability of detecting, monitoring, analyzing, and forecasting climate-induced hazards, such as floods and landslides, for impact-based risk assessment and information dissemination in vulnerable areas.[62]

61 IEA. 2022a. *Data Centres and Data Transmission Networks*.
62 UNDP. 2022a. *Enhancing Multi-Hazard Early Warning System to Increase Resilience of Uzbekistan Communities to Climate Change-Induced Hazards*.

Water and Waste Management and Forestry and Other Land Use

Aqueduct 3.0 Country Rankings places Uzbekistan at 25th out of 165 countries in its 2019 survey in terms of baseline water stress—expressed as the ratio of total water withdrawal to available renewable water supply for agricultural, domestic, and industrial use.[63] Uzbekistan's water resources come from the surface runoff of the Amu Darya and Syr Darya Rivers (55%), runoff of small rivers (33%), underground water (10%), and collected water (2%). Most of these water resources are used to irrigate vast fields for cotton and grain production in the country's rural areas. It should be noted that cotton and grain is not only water-intensive but also energy-intensive due to water pumping requirements, and the country's cropping patterns are gradually shifting to more value-added crops, such as fruit and vegetables. Uzbekistan's water productivity—the economic output per unit of water consumption—was ranked 171st out of 178 countries in 2019 because of its inadequate irrigation and drainage practices.[64] About 70% of distributed irrigation water does not reach crops. Drainage water beyond irrigated fields also forms large disposal lakes, causing the salinization of croplands in vast areas, which is decreasing yields and degrading ecosystems.[65] The Aral Sea, once the world's fourth-largest lake with a surface area of 68,000 km^2, has shrunk by 90% since the 1960s due to the wasteful irrigation systems adopted during the former Soviet Union era. The desiccation of the Aral Sea has salinized water and soil, increased toxic dust and salt storms, jeopardized human health, and raised environmental risks.

The Strategy for the Transition to a Green Economy by 2030 contains several measures for climate resilience and socioeconomic development for the water sector. The modernization of irrigation and drainage systems continues to be the chief approach to improve the management of resources. The introduction of drip irrigation technologies on an agricultural area of up to 1 million hectares aims to increase its crop yields by 20%–40%, and the rehabilitation and reconstruction of on-farm and inter-farm water canals and gates around irrigated fields also increase the efficiency of water supplies to croplands by reducing 30%–50% of water losses.[66] The construction and reconstruction of hydraulic dams, pumping stations, and reservoirs are projected to secure sufficient water supplies for Uzbekistan's growing population, prevent destructive droughts and floods in vulnerable human settlements, and reduce extra energy usage for inefficient water pumping. Essentially, the construction of these water resource management systems are accompanied by the development of hydropower plants for the country's renewable energy expansion. The construction of centralized sewerage systems, including drainage collectors, wastewater treatment plants, and discharge facilities, is being promoted to mitigate the country's increased water and soil pollution, halt land degradation, and produce renewable freshwater sources.

The forestation of mountain, foothill, and desert zones can also be strategized as an effective measure to prevent soil erosion, increase river discharge, and improve water productivity, which, according to the United Nations Framework Convention on Climate Change (UNFCC), can be associated with the modernization of irrigation and drainage systems (footnote 25). Uzbekistan's forested land, accounting for 8.4% of the total land area in 2020, has been degraded by decades of excessive wood fuel consumption, uncontrolled livestock farming, and irrigated land expansion practices. In recent

63 World Resources Institute. 2019. Aqueduct 3.0 Country Rankings.

64 World Bank. Indicators—Water Productivity Uzbekistan (accessed 20 August 2023).

65 UNFCC. 2016. *Third National Communication of the Republic of Uzbekistan under the UN Framework Convention on Climate Change*; World Bank. 2020b. Water Services and Institutional Support Project.

66 UNDP. 2020c. Sustainable Management of Water Resources in Rural Areas in Uzbekistan; World Bank. 2019. *Uzbekistan Irrigation and Drainage Interventions to Support the Agriculture Sector*.

years, soil-protective forest plantations in the form of "agroforestry" and "silvopastoral" systems[67] have been adopted to restore degraded lands, create agroforestry jobs, attract international eco-tourists, and promote agri-food value chains, which can be supported by the application of digital technologies (World Bank n.d.a).[68] Uzbekistan, however, has institutional constraints to adopting a nd scaling up agroforestry by farmers (e.g., insecure land tenure.[69] The tree-based landscape restoration approach is being applied to lessen the human health and environmental impacts of the Aral Sea disaster. In 2010, the United Nations Development Program (UNDP) Uzbekistan Accelerator Lab launched a crowdfunding campaign, Green Aral Sea, to plant a 100-hectare forest of 100,000 saxaul saplings on the Aral's dry seabed.[70]

Uzbekistan's land, water, and air pollution problems, human health risks, and GHG emissions are being worsened by inadequate solid waste disposal practices in cities and towns, where populations are growing rapidly. The country generates an estimated 4 million tons of municipal solid waste annually, which is forecast to rise to 7 million tons by 2030, with 100 million tons accumulated over 2013–2030.[71] Most municipal solid waste is buried or dumped without preliminary processing, and only about 10% is recycled in cities. Uzbekistan had 186 official landfills and 931 illegal dumps in 2017; this excludes many small illegal dumps near human settlements in rural areas.[72] Local waste collection services are either insufficient or simply do not exist.

The Waste Management Sector Strategy, 2019–2028 says that nationwide modern solid waste management systems—that is, optimized collectors, sorting, separation, and thermal treatment facilities, designed landfill sites, and monitoring technologies—are essential for sustainable urbanization and climate change mitigation, and should be aligned with the utilization of solid waste management facilities for renewable energy generation.[73] The strategy emphasizes the need to maximize the circularity of valuable secondary resources from utilized solid waste in the country's industrial production and consumption systems with market incentive mechanisms, broadly termed a "circular economy".[74] Although the global circular economy market is expected to grow fast in the coming years there are still considerable gaps in data and knowledge about implementing circular economy models.[75]

67 Agroforestry is a collective name for land-use systems and technologies where woody perennials are deliberately used on the same land-management units as agricultural crops and/or animals, in some form of spatial arrangement or temporal sequence. Silvopastoral systems combine forestry and grazing of domesticated animals on pastures, rangelands or on-farm (FAO 2015).

68 World Bank. *In Search of a Desert Oasis: Innovative Projects Imagine a Promising Future for the Aral Sea and Central Asian Drylands*.

69 B. Djalilov et al. 2016. Exploring Constraints and Incentives for the Adoption of Agroforestry Practices on Degraded Cropland in Uzbekistan. *Journal of Environmental Planning and Management*. 59 (1). pp. 142–162.

70 UNDP. 2020a. Green Aral Sea Initiative: Planting a Forest on the Aral Seabed. *Press release*. 11 March.

71 ADB. 2020. Sector Assessment (Summary): Water and Other Municipal Infrastructure and Services.

72 M. Radkevich et al. 2022. Land Pollution by Illegal Dumps in the Tashkent Region. *IOP Conference Series: Earth and Environmental Science*. 1068.

73 President of the Republic of Uzbekistan. 2019. Presidential Decree No. 429 on Approval of the Strategy for Solid Municipal Waste Management in the Republic of Uzbekistan for the Period 2019–2028.

74 The circular economy is widely defined as a model of production and consumption, which involves sharing, leasing, reusing, repairing, refurbishing and recycling existing materials and products as long as possible. See United Nations Environment Programme. 2019. *Solid Waste Management Strategy for the Period of 2019–2028*.

75 See Circularity Gap Reporting Initiative. 2023. *The Circularity Gap Report 2023*; R. Serna-Guerrero et al. 2022. Overcoming Data Gaps for an Efficient Circular Economy: A Case Study on the Battery Materials Ecosystem. *Journal of Cleaner Production*. 374.

Spatial Planning for Sustainable Urbanization

The effectiveness of low-carbon, climate-resilient infrastructure investments in promoting green growth depends on the degree and pattern of urbanization. Urbanization can contribute to economic growth through increased productivity and employment (e.g., agglomeration economies), but this can also cause environmental quality problems and social inclusion challenges through market-driven labor migration and spatial transformation, (e.g., urban sprawl).

Spatial planning for low-carbon, climate-resilient urbanization can be seen as an enabling condition for cities to safeguard sufficient investment returns by economizing the lifecycle costs of urban infrastructure systems with emerging technologies, renewable energy, and nature-based solutions. Integrated spatial planning on a city-region scale that emphasizes the key features of "new urbanism" or transit-oriented development (such as urban density, compactness, land use mixture street connectivity, and public transport accessibility), is widely acknowledged to improve environmental conditions, decrease human health risks, promote inclusive local economic development, and reduce urban GHG emissions.[76]

World Bank data for 187 countries including Uzbekistan show that national economic productivity—GDP per capita—is exponentially correlated with the degree of urbanization–urban population to total population (Figure 2.12). The figure's upward-sloping trendline becomes even more progressive over 2000–2021, suggesting that upper-middle-income countries with higher degrees of urbanization experienced more substantial economic productivity gains. Many lower-middle-income countries are projected to follow this growth trajectory. Uzbekistan has set 60% as its national target for the degree of urbanization to be achieved by 2030. The country's urban population steadily grew from 11.4 million in 2000 to 17.6 million in 2021, an increase of 54.8% (Figure 2.13). The degree of urbanization, however, slightly declined from 51.2% in 2011 to 50.4% in 2021 because the country's rural population grew faster than the urban population and there is little change in rural-urban migration (Figure 2.13). The limited influx of the rural population into urban areas can possibly be explained by the state control of residency permits (*propiska*), the high cost of urban living, and mismatches in urban job skills, among other factors (footnote 42). It should be noted that, as the *propiska* system has been lifted since 2016, the country's urban population growth is supposed to accelerate.[77] In addition to these internal constraints, external shocks and unpredictable factors could have influenced urbanization; these include diminished urban location advantages and increased urban poverty risks during the pandemic.[78] As more cities in Uzbekistan are expansively connected by international transport corridors, the country's spatial planning needs to be adaptive to overcome urbanization challenges toward green growth in the era of VUCA—volatility, uncertainty, complexity, and ambiguity.

76 S. Lwasa et al. 2022: Urban Systems and Other Settlements. In P.R. Shukla et al. eds. *Climate Change 2022: Mitigation of Climate Change. Contribution of Working Group III to the Sixth Assessment Report of the Intergovernmental Panel on Climate Change.*

77 D. Sivaev et al. 2022. *The Time is Now: How Can Uzbekistan Leverage Urbanization as a Driver of Sustainable Development?* World Bank.

78 UNDP. 2020b. *Socioeconomic Impacts of COVID-19 in Uzbekistan: Perspectives of Mahalla Representatives*.

Figure 2.12: Relationship between Urbanization and Economic Productivity in 187 Countries, 2000 and 2021

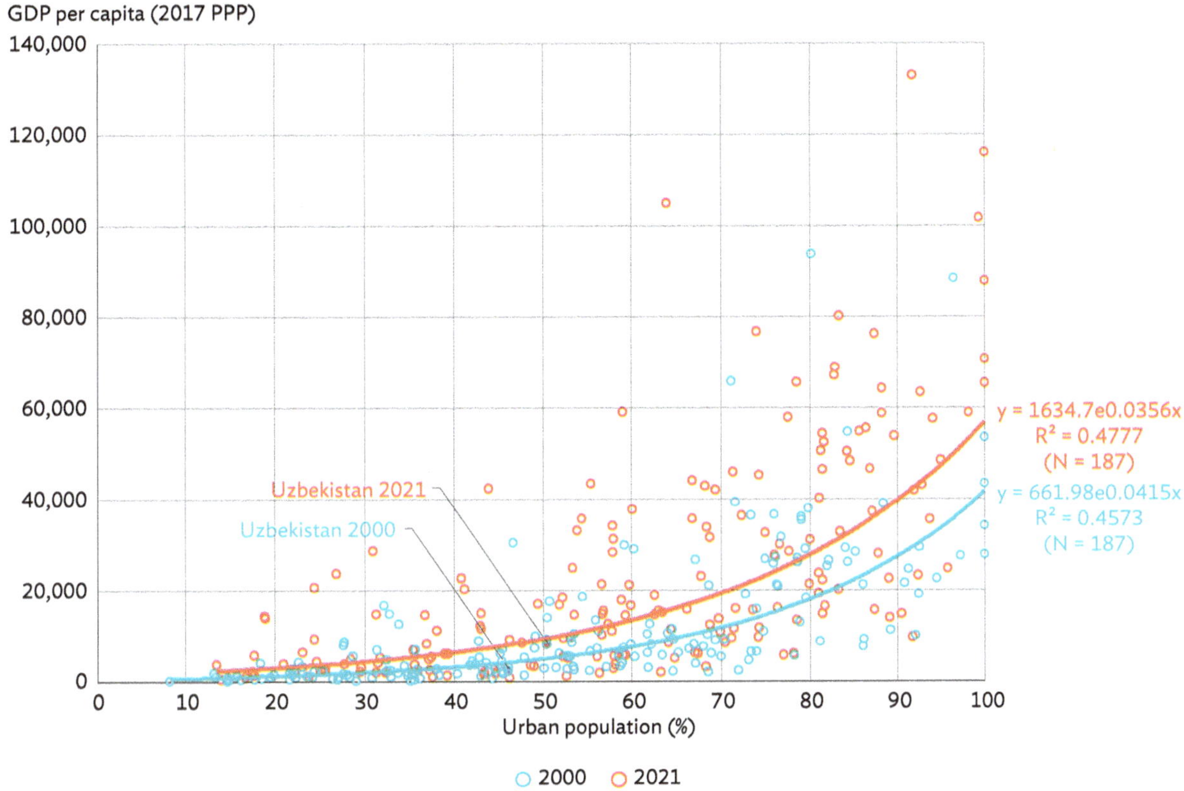

GDP = gross domestic product, PPP = purchasing power parity.
Source: World Bank. Indicators—Urban Population and Gross Domestic Product Uzbekistan (accessed 20 August 2023).

Figure 2.13: Urban Population in Uzbekistan, 2000–2021

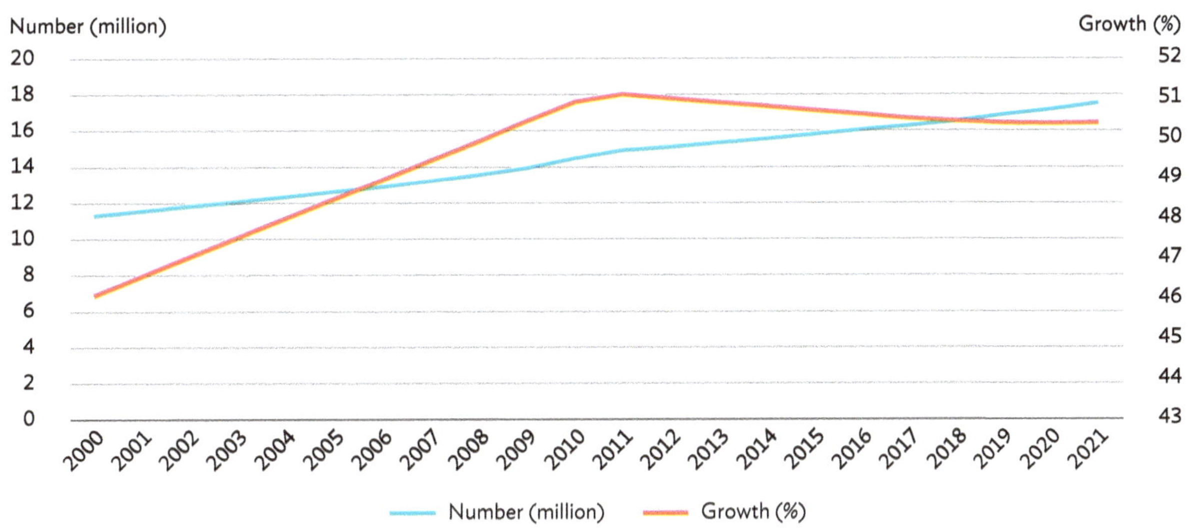

Source: World Bank. Indicators—Urban Population Uzbekistan (accessed 20 August 2023).

The pattern of Uzbekistan's urbanization presents both challenges and opportunities for taking transformative actions. The National Development Strategy for 2030, in particular, addresses the imbalance of socioeconomic development among city regions within the country (more on this below). According to ADB, the government has formally identified 119 cities with various urban population sizes and 1,071 urban settlements, statistically defined as human settlements with nonagricultural employment in rural areas (footnote 42). Because the urban population and economic production are concentrated in Tashkent, the current policy encourages decentralization and polycentric development for equitable urbanization through the reclassification of nonagricultural human settlements in rural areas and the designation of new free economic zones nationwide.

Uzbekistan's urban population rank-size distribution in 2000 and 2015 indicates a hierarchy of 58 cities, identified using the European Union's "global definition of cities and settlements" (Figure 2.14). Although Tashkent continued to play a primary role in the country's urban hierarchy over 2000–2015, the populations of many other cities grew faster—and these cities saw a more sizable expansion in their built-up areas (Figure 2.15). It is worth noting that 54 of the 58 cities increased their population density because the expansion their built-up areas was slower than their population growth. Nevertheless, the degree of urban densification is statistically unrelated to economic productivity (i.e., GDP per capita across the 58 cities) because of the inefficiency of outmoded building standards and using aged infrastructure systems for urban capacity in confined built-up areas. Hence, more liberalized urban land markets, especially residential housing markets accompanied by new road construction and rapid motorization, are likely to accelerate the expansion of lower-density built-up areas, typically resulting in urban sprawl without adequate spatial planning measures.[79]

Figure 2.14: Urban Population Rank-Size Distribution of 58 Cities in Uzbekistan, 2000 and 2015

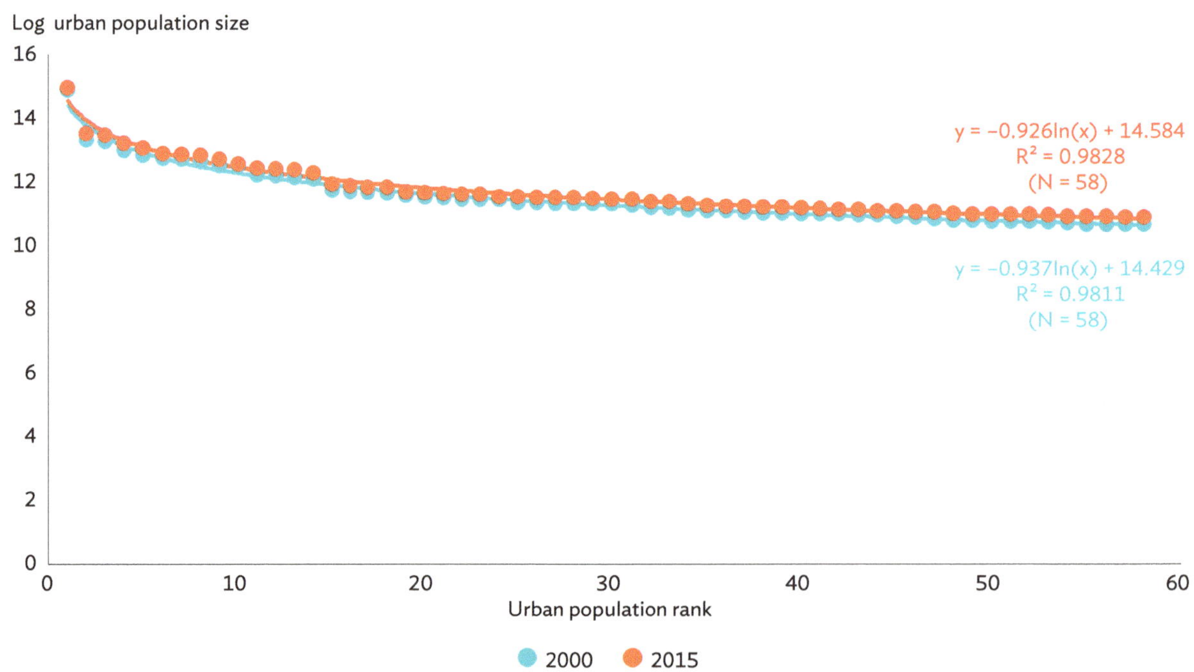

Source: Global Human Settlement Layer Urban Center Database (accessed 20 August 2023).

79 OECD. 2018. *Rethinking Urban Sprawl: Moving Towards Sustainable Cities.*

Figure 2.15: Urban Population and Built-Up Area Change in 58 Cities in Uzbekistan, 2000–2015

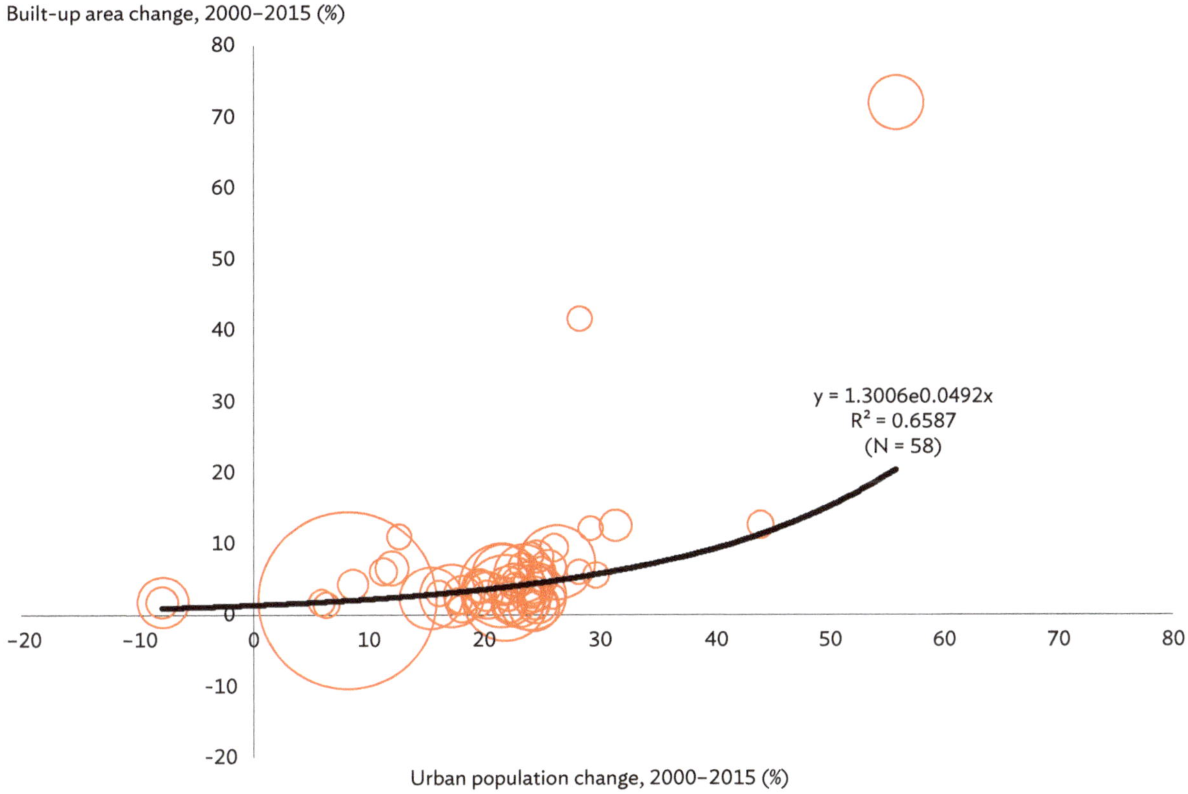

Note: The circle diameters express the urban population sizes for 2015.
Source: Global Human Settlement Layer Urban Center Database (accessed 20 August 2023).

Horizontal urban land expansion—urban sprawl—generally lessens rural green areas, intensifies energy consumption, and increases urban GHG emissions through energy-intensive sectors. These prevent the transition to green alternatives over the lifetime of built-up residential structures and infrastructure network systems. This is called carbon lock-in. International studies suggest that strategic spatial planning for vertical and compact urban development can avoid carbon lock-in and create greener growth pathways, especially during earlier stages of urbanization in lower-middle-income countries.[80]

The Global Human Settlement Layer Urban Center Database estimates that Uzbekistan's urban CO_2 emissions come disproportionately from the larger cities, although emissions declined in 56 of 58 cities over 2000–2015 (Figure 2.16). Tashkent has achieved the most significant CO_2 emissions reduction, followed by a few secondary cities, including Samarkand and Fergana. This suggests that larger cities with the capacity to mobilize substantial infrastructure investments and implement integrated urban solutions across key sectors have the greater potential for mitigating climate change. Indeed, the reduction in CO_2 emissions in the 58 cities over 2000–2015 was realized mainly by the residential sector for the energy use of residential buildings and solid waste (64.3%) (Figure 2.17). The considerable contributions of the power generation and residential sectors to the urban CO_2 emissions could decline further with the expansion of renewable energy sources and advancing green certificate programs for old-building retrofits and broader retrofit-led regeneration in densely

80 IPCC. 2022. *Climate Change 2022: Impacts, Adaptation, and Vulnerability. Contribution of Working Group II to the Sixth Assessment Report of the Intergovernmental Panel on Climate Change.* 10.1017/9781009325844.

built-up urban settings.[81] In 2017, the government revised building standards for energy-efficient urban housing and transferred district heating services for housing and communal construction. The revisions aimed to upgrade district heating systems with new technologies over 2018–2022 and to adopt the new design concept of energy-efficient closed heating systems in large city districts, such as those in Tashkent and Samarkand (footnote 42). Note that Tashkent operates Uzbekistan's largest district heating system, representing 70% of the country's overall district heating service provision.

Figure 2.16: Carbon Dioxide Emissions in 58 Cities in Uzbekistan by Population Size, 2000 and 2015

(million ton)

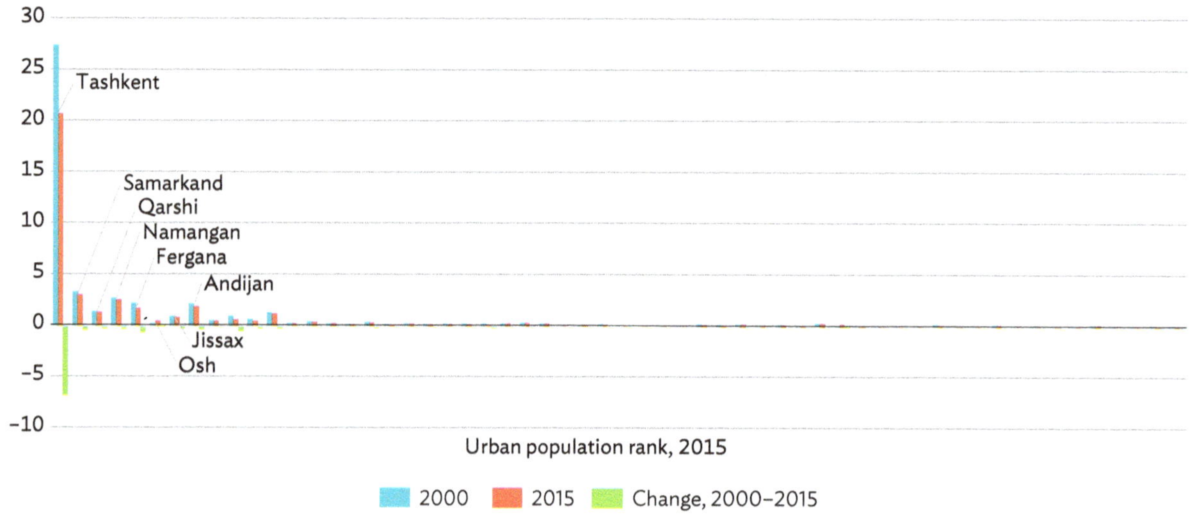

CO_2 = carbon dioxide.
Source: Global Human Settlement Layer Urban Center Database (accessed 20 August 2023).

Figure 2.17: Carbon Dioxide Emissions in 58 Cities in Uzbekistan by Sector, 2000 and 2015

(million ton)

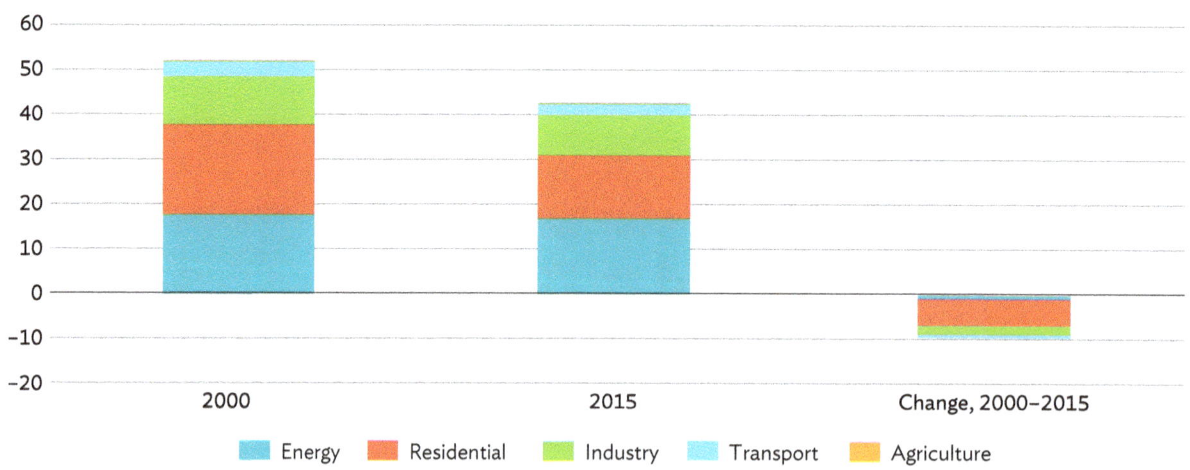

Source: Global Human Settlement Layer Urban Center Database (accessed 20 August 2023).

81 UNDP. 2021. Green Future for Construction and Housing sectors in Uzbekistan. *Press release*. 22 December; UN-Habitat (United Nations Human Settlements Programme). 2021a. *Urban Regeneration as a Tool for Inclusive and Sustainable Recovery*.

Urban CO_2 emissions from transport can decrease significantly if long-term master plans and land-use zoning codes are adopted or updated to enhance accessibility in targeted locations, such as public transport hubs, high-speed bus corridors, airport districts, tourist attractions, logistics centers, and free economic zones. The former Soviet Union's urban layouts and design norms—wide avenues, monumental vistas, identical superblocks, huge public squares, single-use zoning, and fixed building heights—did not optimize agglomeration opportunities through enhanced accessibility. These outdated standards, however, are likely to encourage more urban passenger and freight movements by road and increase the outward expansion of urban land, vehicle kilometers traveled, and energy consumption—and in turn, urban GHG emissions in transport. The weakness of local street connectivity is another urban design challenge for Uzbekistan to overcome the problem of first- and last-mile transport and to decrease vehicle kilometers traveled. Both are needed to reduce urban GHG emissions. Building well-designed tertiary roads and green walkways, as well as dedicated bike lanes and car-free precincts, are internationally advocated to promote urban passenger movements by zero-emission active transport, improve human health through physical activity, and support small retail businesses with improved street amenity (footnote 42).[82]

The creation of urban green and blue infrastructure—urban forests, street trees, green roofs, green walls, water bodies, greenways, and urban farms, for example—is recognized as climate mitigation and adaptation measures that bring co-benefits to cities, such as reducing heat stress, air pollution, and noise; enhancing biodiversity; promoting active transport and public health, and improving food security.[83] Of various green infrastructure options, urban forests and street trees are likely to have the most significant mitigation effects by sequestering carbon and reducing building energy usage. The degree of these effects will depend on their green scale, density, and pattern. Greenways are typically assigned to reduce the damage caused by urban floods on a local-district scale, but they can be extended to manage a larger volume of stormwater in broader catchment areas.

The expansion of urban green infrastructure is still moderate in many cities, despite its potential. The urban population exposed to flood risk increased by 14.0% amid urban population growth of 17.4% in the 58 cities over 2000–2015 (Figure 2.18). The total surface area of urban green infrastructure expanded at a much slower rate of 5.5% in these 58 cities over 2000–2014. To harness the potential of nature-based solutions for urban flood management, Uzbekistan's cities could adopt the sponge-city concept used in the PRC and other countries. Sponge cities are a recent urban planning model that attempts to increase cities' total capacity to absorb, filter, and release stormwater by integrating existing green spaces, water bodies, and drainage facilities into one urban water management network throughout a built-up area. Creating sponge cities usually does not require substantial new infrastructure investment, but instead calls for complex spatial planning and engineering design coordination across critical infrastructure sectors.[84]

---

82 S. Lwasa et al. 2022: Urban Systems and Other Settlements. In P.R. Shukla et al. eds. *Climate Change 2022: Mitigation of Climate Change. Contribution of Working Group III to the Sixth Assessment Report of the Intergovernmental Panel on Climate Change*; J. Murakami et al. 2021. The Capital Value of Pedestrianization in Asia's Commercial Cityscape: Evidence from Office Towers and Retail Streets. *Transport Policy*. 107. pp. 72–86.

83 S. Lwasa et al. 2022: Urban Systems and Other Settlements. In P.R. Shukla et al. eds. *Climate Change 2022: Mitigation of Climate Change. Contribution of Working Group III to the Sixth Assessment Report of the Intergovernmental Panel on Climate Change.*

84 S. Rau. 2022. Sponge Cities: Integrating Green and Gray Infrastructure to Build Climate Change Resilience in the People's Republic of China. *ADB Briefs.*

Figure 2.18: Urban Population, Flood Risk Exposure, and Green Infrastructure Changes in 58 Cities in Uzbekistan, 2000–2014 and 2015

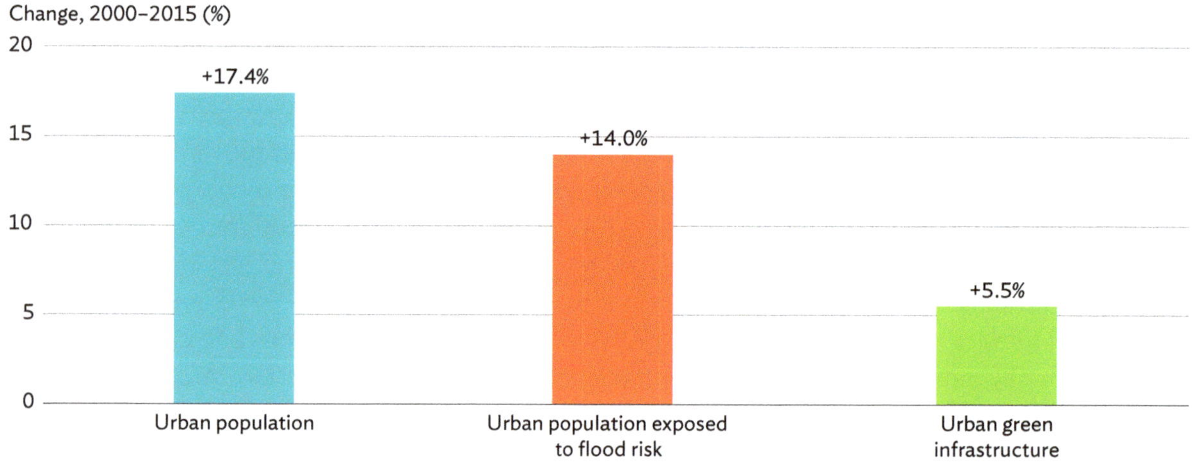

Note: Urban green infrastructure is measured by the total surface area of "high green spaces" that have seminatural vegetation features, such as street trees, lawns, parks, gardens, forests, and green roofs.
Source: Global Human Settlement Layer Urban Center Database (accessed 20 August 2023).

Scaling up urban climate projects requires several enabling conditions, including adaptive spatial planning, land-based finance, financial access, local knowledge, and multilevel governance.[85] Essentially, Uzbekistan's urban lands are state assets that date back to the former Soviet Union era, and urban development projects are carried out under strong state control. In recent years, however, private property rights have been gradually given to the country's urban land plots to promote rural–urban migration and increase urbanization. The privatization of Uzbekistan's urban and nonagricultural land aims to develop new satellite cities, optimize urban agglomerations for employment growth, and improve urban housing conditions (footnote 42). The law specifies strategic state assets not subject to urban land privatization, such as territories without layout plans; sites with mineral deposits; areas preserved for environmental, societal, and local infrastructure purposes; land plots contaminated by hazardous substances; and housing sites provided for free economic and small industrial zones.

Uzbekistan's public land auctions program are a kind of land-based finance that enables the government to generate one-time revenues to recover the upfront costs of large-scale infrastructure projects with high urban land values; these projects are typically carried out by state-owned enterprises.[86] Under the country's urban land privatization and fiscal decentralization framework, urban municipalities are supposed to receive increased "recurring" revenues—that is, more stable cash flows from property taxes, which can make municipal urban climate projects more bankable and upgrade the creditworthiness of cities for greater financial access to international capital markets.[87] For accountability, the implementation of land-based urban climate finance schemes must use evidence-based practices supported by the cadastral database that should be well-integrated with public land transaction records, property tax registers, and other digital information and performance

85 S. Lwasa et al. 2022: Urban Systems and Other Settlements. In P.R. Shukla et al. eds. *Climate Change 2022: Mitigation of Climate Change. Contribution of Working Group III to the Sixth Assessment Report of the Intergovernmental Panel on Climate Change.*
86 OECD. 2022. *Global Compendium of Land Value Capture Policies.*
87 S. Lwasa et al. 2022: Urban Systems and Other Settlements. In P.R. Shukla et al. eds. *Climate Change 2022: Mitigation of Climate Change. Contribution of Working Group III to the Sixth Assessment Report of the Intergovernmental Panel on Climate Change.*

monitoring systems across infrastructure sectors. It is crucial that the government incorporates local knowledge into its strategic public land auction program and makes spatial planning and design practices more "adaptive" for greater land value creation.[88] Global best practices commonly highlight the significance of multilevel governance as an enabling condition for mobilizing various financial resources, streamlining spatial planning measures, and synergizing transformative climate actions across different scales.[89]

Way Forward

This chapter clarified the scope of green growth in Uzbekistan's economic development and poverty reduction scenario; highlighted the country's needs for low-carbon, climate-resilient infrastructure investment in its domestic and international contexts; identified strategic investment options across the country's critical infrastructure sectors, namely, energy, transport, ICT, water and waste management and forestry and other land use; and underlined the importance of spatial planning for sustainable urbanization as an enabling condition along with recent statistics and prospects. Key takeaways are summarized as follows:

(i) **Green growth.** Green transition along with strategic investment in critical infrastructure systems is an essential piece of Uzbekistan's socioeconomic development. The scope of green growth is threefold: (a) resource use efficiency and productivity improvement; (b) environmental cost and climate risk reduction; and (c) inclusive job creation in value-added sectors.

(ii) **Economic resilience.** The country's present economy—"energy-intensive," "natural-resource-dependent," and "low value-added"—is vulnerable to climate change, natural hazards, and other external shocks in the rapidly changing global market and policy landscape. Recent external stocks, e.g., COVID-19, geopolitical tension, and energy shortage, contracted Uzbekistan's recent economic growth, heightened public awareness of environmental costs and climate risks regionwide, and accelerated the country's strategic investment policy and decisions for green growth.

(iii) **Investment readiness.** Uzbekistan has already become the largest recipient country of the Multilateral Development Bank (MDB) climate finance in the region for the ambitious national emissions reduction target and strategic transition measures by 2030. However, the country's readiness or enabling conditions to leverage substantial investments in low-carbon, climate-resilient infrastructure can still be improved across sectors.

88 J. Murakami. 2018. The Government Land Sales Programme and Developers' Willingness to Pay for Accessibility in Singapore, 1990–2015. *Land Use Policy*. 75. pp. 292–302; H. Suzuki et al. 2015. *Financing Transit-Oriented Development with Land Values: Adapting Land Value Capture in Developing Countries*. World Bank.

89 S. Lwasa et al. 2022: Urban Systems and Other Settlements. In P.R. Shukla et al. eds. *Climate Change 2022: Mitigation of Climate Change. Contribution of Working Group III to the Sixth Assessment Report of the Intergovernmental Panel on Climate Change*; OECD. 2009. *Cities, Climate Change and Multilevel Governance*; UN-Habitat. 2021b. *Multi-Level Governance for Effective Urban Climate Action in the Global South*.

(iv) **Critical infrastructure sectors.** Energy; transport; ICT; water and waste management; and agriculture, forestry, and other land use can be listed as Uzbekistan's critical infrastructure sectors for strategic investments. A systems approach is employed to assess and strategize multiscale climate mitigation and adaptation actions across interlinked critical infrastructure sectors.

(v) **Modernization.** The modernization of outdated infrastructure systems continues to be Uzbekistan's major infrastructure investment option across critical infrastructure sectors (e.g., gas pipelines and power plants, roads and railroads, water canals and gates, and treatment facilities), mainly for overall energy efficiency improvements and partially for inclusive job creation, e.g., trade, industry, and tourism, during the early transition period.

(vi) **Renewable energy.** The expansion of renewable energy sources is the country's mainstream approach to taking transformative climate actions. Uzbekistan has potential to attract substantial investments in large-scale solar PV projects with high irradiation. Renewable energy producers are also entitled to develop microgrids and trade energy units, which will be associated with green building certificates, energy storage systems, electric vehicles (EVs), digital technologies, smart grids, and demand management schemes.

(vii) **Electrification.** The electrification of critical infrastructure systems is promoted to improve energy efficiency, increase industrial productivity, and reduce GHG and air pollution emissions across key sectors (e.g., railway and water pumping). EVs are gaining market popularity in Uzbekistan. As the import of EVs increases, the country's EV sales growth calls for 2,500 public charging stations nationwide by 2025, possibly associated with solar PV systems and microgrids. The rapid expansion of EVs would generate considerable battery waste materials beyond the country's recycling capacity.

(viii) **Digitalization.** The advancement of digital technologies across critical infrastructure sectors is granted to improve integrated systems efficiency and promote inclusive growth through industrial and societal changes. Some digital divides appear to be a public issue. More information, data, and analytics will be utilized to support evidence-based investment and system operation practices. The impact of digital innovations on energy usage and emissions is still uncertain, but global tech companies are investing in renewable energies to protect hyperdata centers and broader social system operations from energy crises.

(ix) **Emerging green businesses and economies.** Uzbekistan can produce unconventional business and economic opportunities through the green transition. For example, the placement of micro-hubs can produce start-up delivery services with low-carbon mobility options. The creation of forest plantations is adopted to create agroforestry jobs, attract eco-tourists, and promote agri-food value chains. Maximizing the upstream circularity of valuable secondary resources from solid wastes is strategized as a circular economy. However, there are still gaps in data and knowledge about emerging green businesses and economies.

(x) **Spatial planning for sustainable urbanization.** The effectiveness of infrastructure investments depends on the degree and pattern of urbanization. Too hasty urban land market liberalization for the degree of urbanization may result in urban sprawl without adequate spatial planning. The pattern of urbanization is a critical opportunity for Uzbekistan. Vertical and compact development can avoid carbon lock-in and pave greener growth pathways during an earlier stage of urbanization.

(xi) **Scaling up urban climate projects.** Scaling up urban climate projects requires several enabling conditions, including adaptive spatial planning, land-based finance, financial access, local knowledge, and multilevel governance. A set of land-based finance programs, e.g., public land auction and residential property tax, would make multiscale urban climate projects more bankable and upgrade the cities' creditworthiness for broader financial access if properly interlinked with adaptive spatial planning and local knowledge.

CHAPTER 3

Agriculture Development and Food Security Policy

Nodir Djanibekov

Introduction

Since 2017, the Government of Uzbekistan has adopted ambitious and unprecedented reforms to increase agricultural productivity and competitiveness. The Agriculture Development Strategy, 2020–2030 puts forward an ambitious set of reforms to manage the transition from a state-led, cotton- and wheat-focused, inward-oriented system to a market-based, diversified, and outward-oriented one.[1] The strategy has already brought considerable improvements to agriculture, including eliminating state output targets for cotton and wheat, ending the systematic use of forced labor in cotton picking, and liberalizing horticultural exports.

Price liberalization and private investments in the ginning industry are benefiting the cotton industry. The expansion of newly established vertically integrated private enterprises called cotton-textile clusters is increasing cotton output and yields. Similarly, wheat liberalization positively impacts productivity, and state policies for utilizing comparative advantage in horticulture lifted production and exports from 2018 to 2021.

Agriculture has come a long way since state output and input monopolies, administered pricing, and stringent production plans and quotas hindered the sector's structural reform from 1991 to 2016. Despite the achievements, the early stage of agricultural reforms revealed additional challenges threatening the sector's long-term sustainable and inclusive growth. Even though smallholders contribute a large share of horticulture and livestock outputs, they are still beyond state policies to strengthen agriculture, primarily focusing on large commercial farms and agricultural enterprises. Almost no public initiatives target smallholders. This lack of attention hinders the government's efforts to generate inclusive growth.

The agricultural reforms have also failed to improve farmers' land tenure security. Farmers have little control over land allocation, crop choices, or marketing channels. They have low bargaining power and little influence on contract terms with processors and retailers. For instance, cotton growers are still compelled to sell their harvest to a single monopsonist buyer selected by the state, and farmgate pricing for cotton continues to be state-regulated. Without effective organizations through which they can seek better contract terms or have a greater stake in the agriculture sector, farmers fall under the strict control of powerful private processors (e.g., the newly established cotton-textile clusters).

1 Government of Uzbekistan. 2019. Presidential Decree 5852 on the Approval of the Strategy for the Development of Agriculture of the Republic of Uzbekistan for 2020–2030.

Further reforms are needed, particularly on the freedom to farm, land tenure security, and farmers' bargaining power. Further agricultural liberalization will advance the diversification of Uzbekistan's agri-product portfolio and export markets, increase food security, and make the sector more resilient to climate change.

Uzbekistan is one of the world's most dependent countries on irrigation water and is thus highly sensitive to climate change. Despite this vulnerability, it is an extremely inefficient user of irrigation water due to the state's poor management of agriculture and water resources. Climate change is already affecting agriculture, and its effects will accelerate, resulting in economic losses. Given the sector's role in food security and sustaining rural livelihoods, Uzbekistan must implement agricultural policies consistent with climate adaptation and mitigation strategies. Delays in switching to green agriculture run the risk that the outmoded technology used in the sector, coupled with nongreen investments, will be expensive to undo and may cut Uzbekistan off from lucrative export markets.

This chapter examines Uzbekistan's recent agricultural reforms and its current strategic policies and ecosystem for developing the sector and attaining food security. It looks at the government's efforts to diversify and strengthen the sector through reforms—and analyzes the implications of this on the economy.

The chapter answers the following questions:

(i) What have been the main elements of agri-food reforms since 2016?
(ii) What are the implications of the agri-food reforms on food security?
(iii) What should international development agencies focus on, given the current trends in agriculture?

By analyzing these focus areas and questions, the chapter offers recommendations for the sector's development and food security.

Major Agricultural Trends

Uzbekistan's current agricultural reforms are being led by the Agriculture Development Strategy, which is paving the way for reduced state involvement in agricultural and increasing private investment to enhance, diversify, and support the agri-food sector. The strategy emphasizes the rational use of natural resources and environmental care. Its main objective is to significantly improve policy to strengthen the ongoing agricultural reforms and improve the agri-food sector's competitiveness. To this end, it identifies nine priorities:

(i) Ensure food security by addressing the access to food by socially vulnerable groups, ensuring state procurement of cereals is done at market prices, gradually abolishing regulated food prices, promoting healthy diets, implementing a food security assessment and monitoring system, expanding the production of socially significant food products, and intensifying livestock production.
(ii) Improve the environment for agribusinesses and value-added chains and increasing agricultural exports by aligning the agri-food certification system to international standards and facilitating farm cooperation.

(iii) Lessen state intervention in agriculture to modernize, diversify, and sustainably expand the agri-food sector and to make it attractive for investors.
(iv) Ensure the rational use of natural resources and protecting the environment to strengthen climate change adaptation.
(v) Develop modern public administration systems by reforming the Ministry of Agriculture, establishing public-private partnership models in agricultural services, and improving communication among policy makers, agricultural producers and processors, and international donors.
(vi) Gradually diversify state spending on agriculture. Spending is currently largely focused on the irrigation sector, but it can be diversified by revising the public agricultural budget to cover more activities, increasing public funding for research and development, gradually privatizing agri-services, and reducing the tax burden on agricultural producers.
(vii) Develop research, education, and agricultural information and advisory services to increase rural human capital, agricultural innovation, and labor productivity.
(viii) Develop rural areas by reforming and decentralizing rural governments and introducing new models of rural non-agricultural businesses.
(ix) Introduce a transparent system of agriculture and food statistics that uses data from "smart agriculture" and agricultural censuses.

Through these nine priorities, the Agriculture Development Strategy set the target of 3% growth in agriculture production in 2021 and 5% in 2025, and agri-food exports reaching $20 billion by 2030. Despite the volatility of national and global agri-food markets, the government has maintained the pace of agricultural reforms. However, the coronavirus disease (COVID-19) pandemic and Russia's war in Ukraine slowed reforms and required adjustments to some of them.

Agriculture contributes about a quarter of Uzbekistan's economy and employment. Crop production and livestock almost equally account for value-added agriculture. Despite a 2.2% decrease in the total cropland area in 2019, agriculture output grew by 3.1% in that year, breaking a run of slow growth in 2017 and 2018 (Figure 3.1). In 2020, despite the pandemic, agriculture emerged as a pillar of resilience,[2] growing by 2.9%—higher than the 2.0% gross domestic product (GDP) growth. The sector grew by 4.0% in 2021. The stronger growth trend shows that it has been responsive to the economic reforms taken since 2017, the removal of market-distorting policies for horticulture, initial reforms in cotton and wheat, and repurposing some public spending on agriculture.

The total sown area increased steadily from 2011 to 2016, but it has contracted since 2017 because of a state policy to relocate crops that were being cultivationd from unproductive land (Figure 3.2). Although the cotton and wheat area has been gradually declining, these crops still have the largest sown area, at 70% of the total sown area—and they are also the largest in terms of input use. The total sown area for fruit and melons has been increasing steadily due to more land previously being used for cotton switching to fruit.[3] The total sown horticulture area has expanded since 2005 due to government measures to diversify agriculture and increase agricultural export revenue. In 2021, vegetables occupied 7% of the total sown area, melons 2%, and fruit 10%.

2 N. Djanibekov and T. Herzfeld. 2022. The Impact of COVID-19 on Agri-food Systems and Rural Areas in Central Asia and Caucasus Countries: Final Report of a Study Commissioned by FAO. *IAMO Discussion Paper*. No. 198. Leibniz Institute of Agricultural Development in Transition Economies.

3 Separating melons from fruit is a long-standing statistical classification as melons are temporary crops that can be rotated with other crops.

Figure 3.1: Uzbekistan's Agricultural Performance, 2000–2021

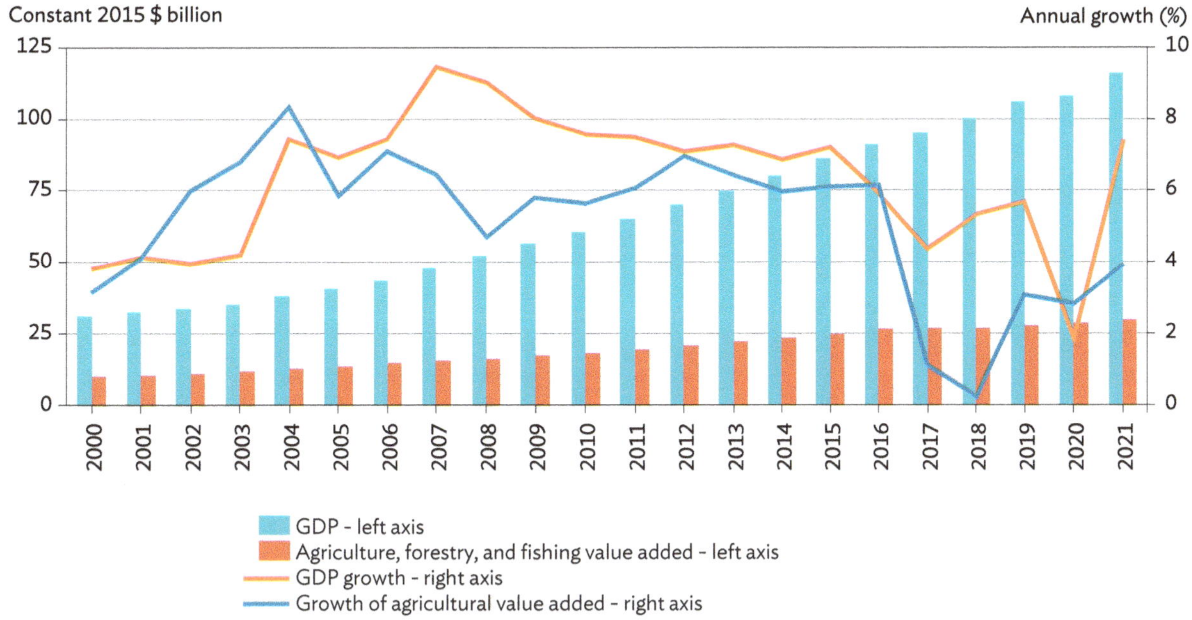

GDP = gross domestic product.
Source: World Bank. World Development Indicators (accessed 3 July 2023).

Figure 3.2: Total Sown Area and Crops by Type in Uzbekistan, 2011–2021

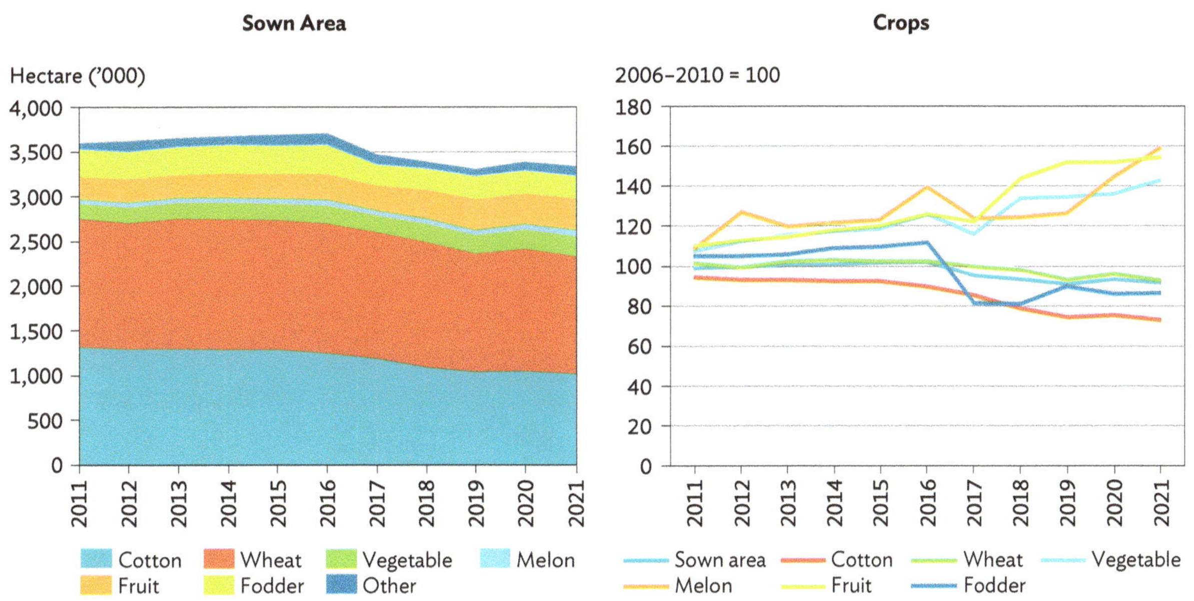

Source: Based on data from UzStat (Statistics Agency under the President of the Republic of Uzbekistan). 2022. *Statistical Yearbook on Agriculture.*

The increase in value-added agriculture is reflected in higher land, labor, and water productivity, as shown in Figure 3.3. However, the use of these inputs relative to their levels in 2000 has not declined, except for the total sown area that has lost over 10% since 2000 due mainly to government decisions to reduce the cotton area. Compared to 2017, the sown area in 2021 shrank by 2.5%, agricultural employment by 4%, and water use in agriculture by 15%. Water use in 2017 was 9% higher than the preceding 5-year average, a period of water shortage. Because Uzbekistan is vulnerable to climate-driven water scarcity, the World Bank estimates that the country's agricultural production could shrink by 6.0% to 28% for every 10% to 30% decrease in water supply.[4] Sector employment could fall by 55,000 to 250,000. Fertilizer use in total and per hectare terms has increased since 2006, mainly due to the fragmentation of large state farms into individual farms.

Figure 3.3: Land, Labor, and Water Productivity and Indices of Total Sown Land, Labor, Fertilizer, and Water Use in Agriculture in Uzbekistan, 2000–2020

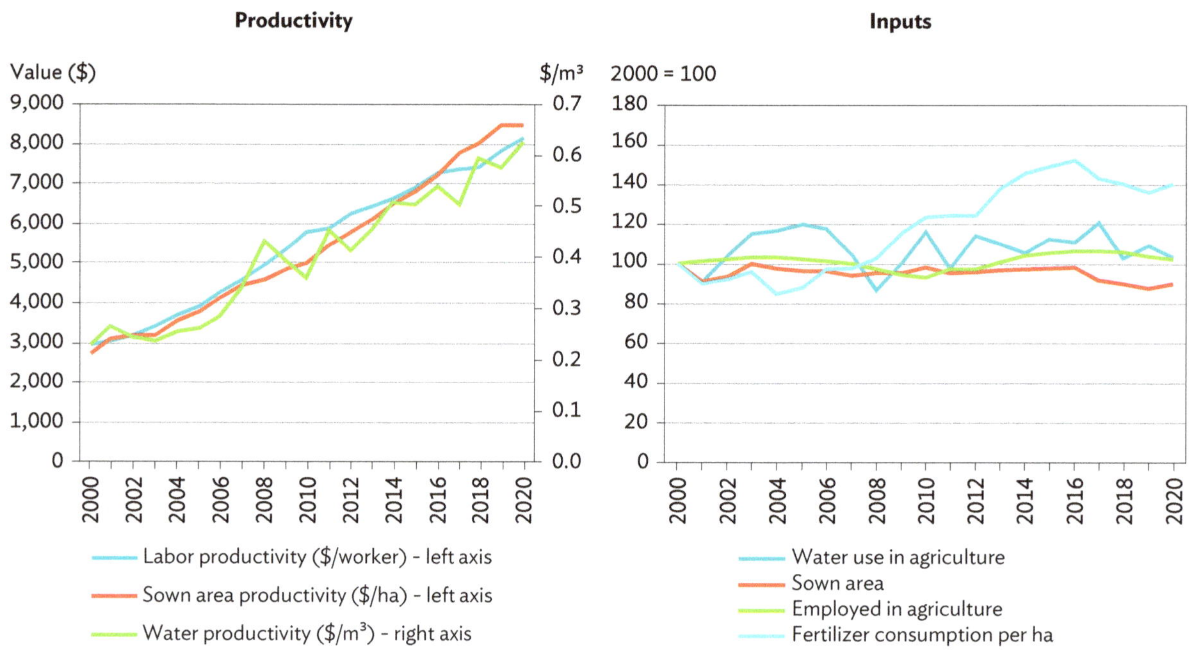

ha = hectare, m[3] = cubic meter.
Sources: Water use in agriculture from CAWater Info; agriculture value added in constant 2015 dollars and fertilizer use from World Bank. World Development Indicators; sown area and number of employed in agriculture from UzStat (Statistics Agency under the President of the Republic of Uzbekistan). 2022. *Statistical Yearbook on Agriculture.*

Farm Restructuring

Following the farm restructuring in the late 1990s, large state-operated farms were gradually fragmented into individual farms until they disappeared by 2007. Individual and small-scale (*dekhqan*) farms, including rural households, are the main producer categories. Individual farms focus on the large-scale production of mainly cotton and grains, accounting for 73% of the total sown area in 2021.[5] *Dekhqan* farms focus on horticulture and livestock (14% of the total sown area). This report treats *dekhqan* farms and rural households as a single group, which is how they are categorized in official statistics. This dualistic structure is complemented by the increasing transfer of sown areas to the cotton-textile clusters, which with other agricultural enterprises account for the remaining sown area (Figure 3.4).

4 World Bank. 2022a. Towards a Greener Economy in Uzbekistan.

5 UzStat (Statistics Agency under the President of the Republic of Uzbekistan). 2022. *Statistical Yearbook on Agriculture.*

Figure 3.4: Distribution of Sown Land Across Agricultural Producer Categories in Uzbekistan, 1992–2021
('000 hectare)

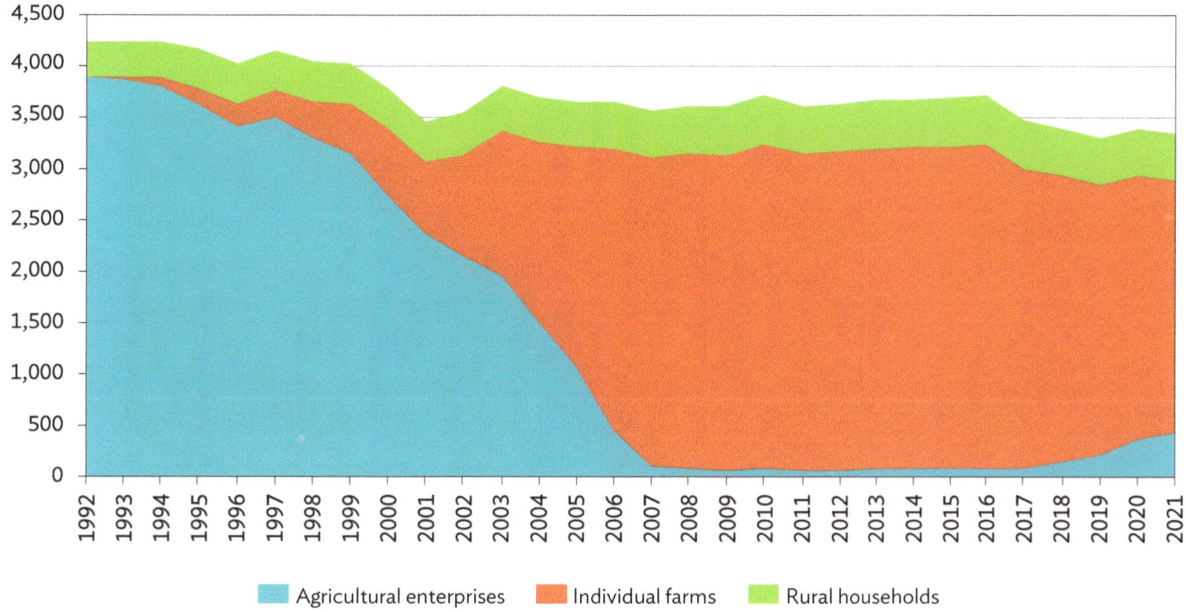

Source: Based on data from UzStat (Statistics Agency under the President of the Republic of Uzbekistan). 2022. *Statistical Yearbook on Agriculture.*

The establishment of individual farms has been accompanied by various government moves to optimize farm sizes.[6] Following the fragmentation of large state-operated farms, the government implemented several rounds of measures to optimize farm sizes by merging smaller farms into larger production units from 2009 to 2011. (Figure 3.5). This policy was motivated by the poor productivity of individual farms, particularly in meeting cotton and wheat yield targets, and the need to consolidate dispersed fields into larger production units to achieve economies of scale. In 2012, however, the government returned to "farm fragmentation" to optimize farm size and divided farms into smaller production units to improve their productivity.[7] By the end of 2018, the number of farms had more than doubled from 2011 (footnote 6). In 2019, the government reverted again to farm consolidation to increase farm sizes, reducing the number of farms by over 40%. The practice of top-down expropriations of farmland and terminations of lease contracts is common, causing a high level of insecurity over land tenure among farmers (footnote 7).

After the complete fragmentation of agricultural enterprises into individual farms in 2006 and 2007, gross agricultural output was made up of three sectors—crop cultivation by individual farms and livestock and crop cultivation by *dekhqan* farms (Figure 3.6). Livestock from *dekhqan* farms and crop production in individual and *dekhqan* farms are the biggest contributors to output. Crop production in individual farms and rural households makes up almost two-thirds of gross agricultural output. Although *dekhqan* farms accounted for 14% of the total sown area, they produced over two-thirds of agricultural output through high-value horticultural crops and livestock production. Individual farms and agricultural enterprises mostly focus on cotton and wheat production.

6 S. Zorya, Djanibekov N., and M. Petrick. 2019. *Farm Restructuring in Uzbekistan: How Did It Go and What Is Next?* World Bank.

7 N. Djanibekov et al. 2012. Farm Restructuring and Land Consolidation in Uzbekistan: New Farms with Old Barriers. *Europe-Asia Studies.* 64. pp. 1101–1126.

Figure 3.5: Number of Individual Farms and Sown Area in Uzbekistan, 1992–2021

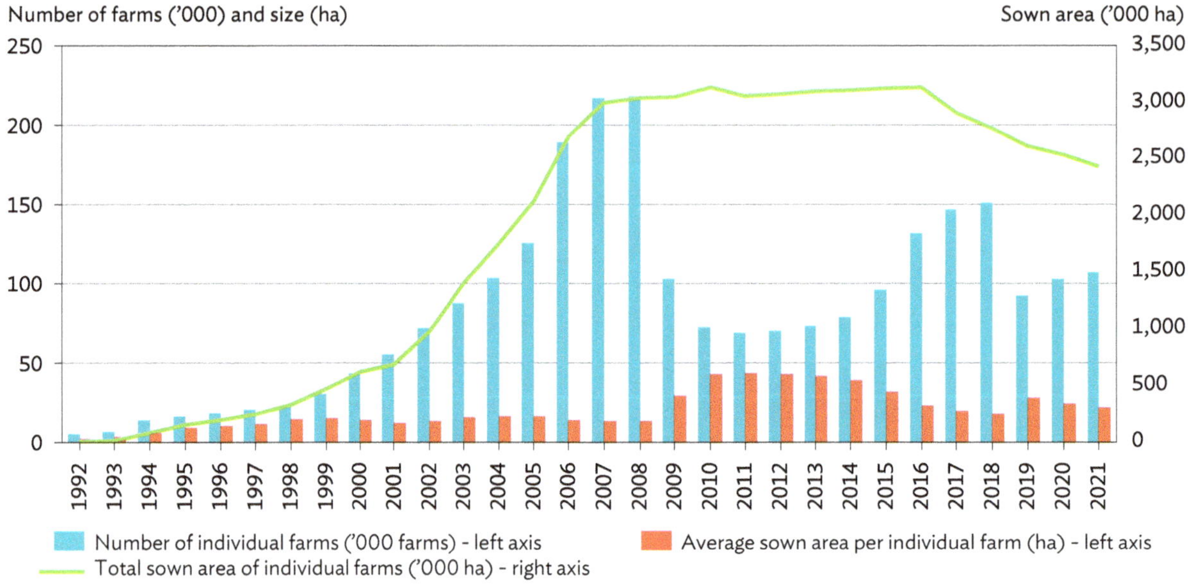

ha = hectare.

Source: Based on data from UzStat (Statistics Agency under the President of the Republic of Uzbekistan). 2022. *Statistical Yearbook on Agriculture.*

Figure 3.6: Agricultural Output by Producer Category in Uzbekistan, 1992–2021

(%)

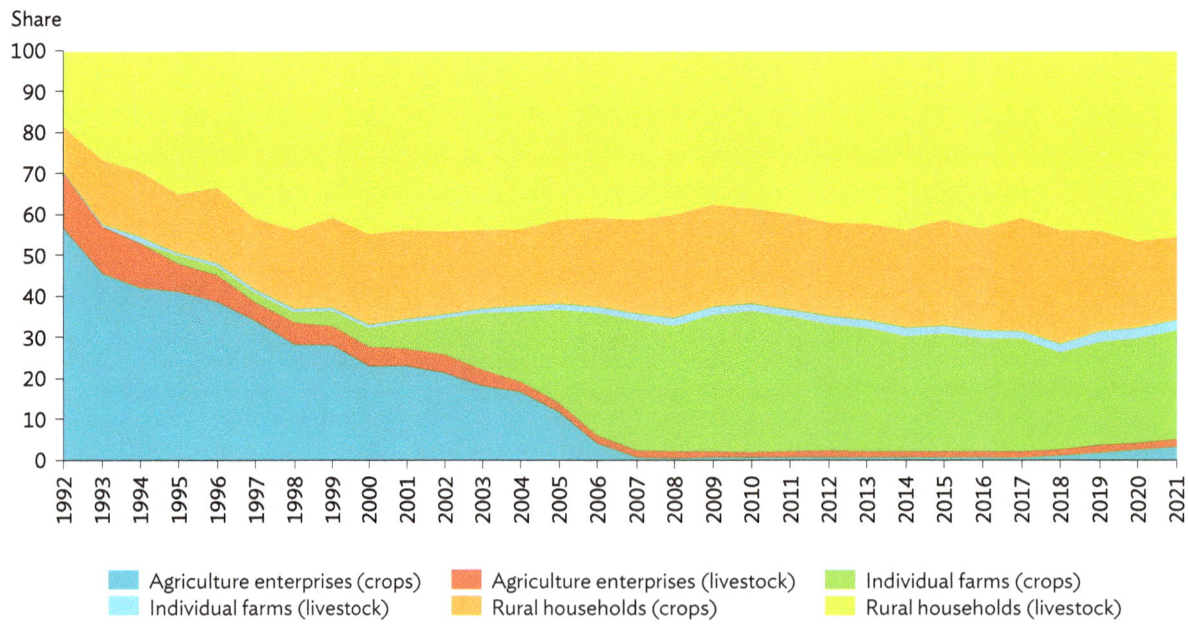

Source: Based on data from UzStat (Statistics Agency under the President of the Republic of Uzbekistan). 2022. *Statistical Yearbook on Agriculture.*

After steady growth over 2011–2016, the sown area of individual farms has been declining due to the state policy of relocating crops from unproductive and marginal land (Figure 3.7). As part of this program, the share of the cotton and wheat area in individual farms has declined. Over 2006–2011, these crops accounted for 85% of the total sown area of individual farms; by 2021, their share had declined to 77%. However, individual farms have expanded the sown area of fruit, vegetables, and melons, while the sown area of cotton, wheat, and fodder declined.

Figure 3.7: Sown Area and Major Crops in Individual Farms in Uzbekistan, 2011–2021

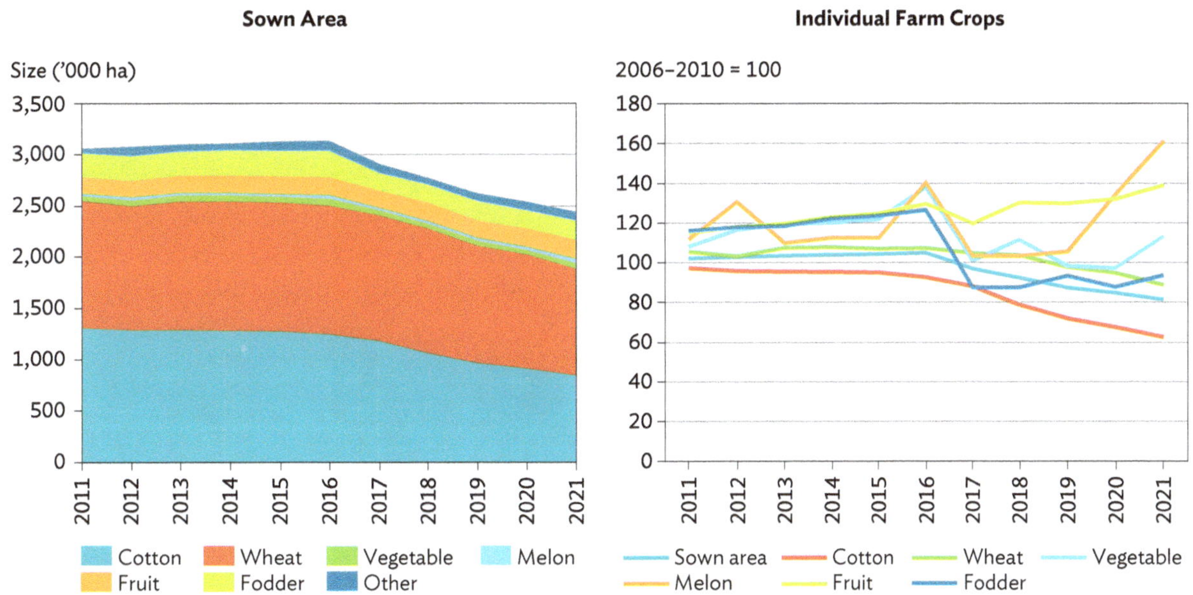

Source: Based on data from UzStat (Statistics Agency under the President of the Republic of Uzbekistan). 2022. *Statistical Yearbook on Agriculture.*

Dekhqan Farms

In 2021, 4.9 million *dekhqan* farms sowed 458,000 hectares of land. These farms are an integral element of the social and cultural fabric of rural capital. Their social capital allows them to leverage local agricultural expertise and remain resilient to shocks, such as drought or pests.[8] Members of *dekhqan* farms usually take on farm or nonfarm work in addition to working their small plots. Subsistence farming in *dekhqan* farms and by rural households makes up half of total agricultural employment. Cotton picking in the fields of individual farms is a common seasonal job for members of *dekhqan* farms.[9] The combination of small-scale farming and additional seasonal jobs enables these farms to tap various income sources.

8 E. B. Asfaw. 2020. "Dehqan" Farms: Uzbekistan's Underserved 70 Percent. *CPRO Policy Brief.* No. 2020-08. Center for Policy Research and Outreach.

9 R. Swinkels, E. Romanova, and E. Kochkin. 2016. Assessing the Social Impact of Cotton Harvest Mechanization in Uzbekistan. World Bank.

Dekhqan farms have stronger tenure security than individual farms, and *dekhqan* farms have not been affected by the government's farm-size optimization reforms over the last two decades that resulted in the insecure land tenure of individual farms (footnote 7). The sown area of *dekhqan* farms has increased along with the growth of the rural population. Unlike individual farms, *dekhqan* farms are granted land free of any responsibility to the state, such as procurement targets or land allocation plans. Thus, they are free to decide on production levels, choice of crops, agronomic processes, and when and where to sell their harvest.

Dekhqan farms can cultivate several crops within a season and diversify their crop portfolio, unlike individual farms that have a high share of sown area under cotton and wheat (Figure 3.8). *Dekhqan* farms are faster at adapting to shifting market needs and can vary planting patterns to reduce production and market risks.[10] High-value crops account for two-thirds of the sown area of *dekhqan* farms. As a general trend in Uzbekistan, the wheat area in *dekhqan* farms has been declining, and the sown area of fodder crops—a critical crop—has stagnated; however, they have expanded the sown area of vegetables and melons. The area of fruit gardens has also increased but at a lower rate.

Figure 3.8: Sown Area and Major Crops in *Dekhqan* Farms in Uzbekistan, 2011–2021

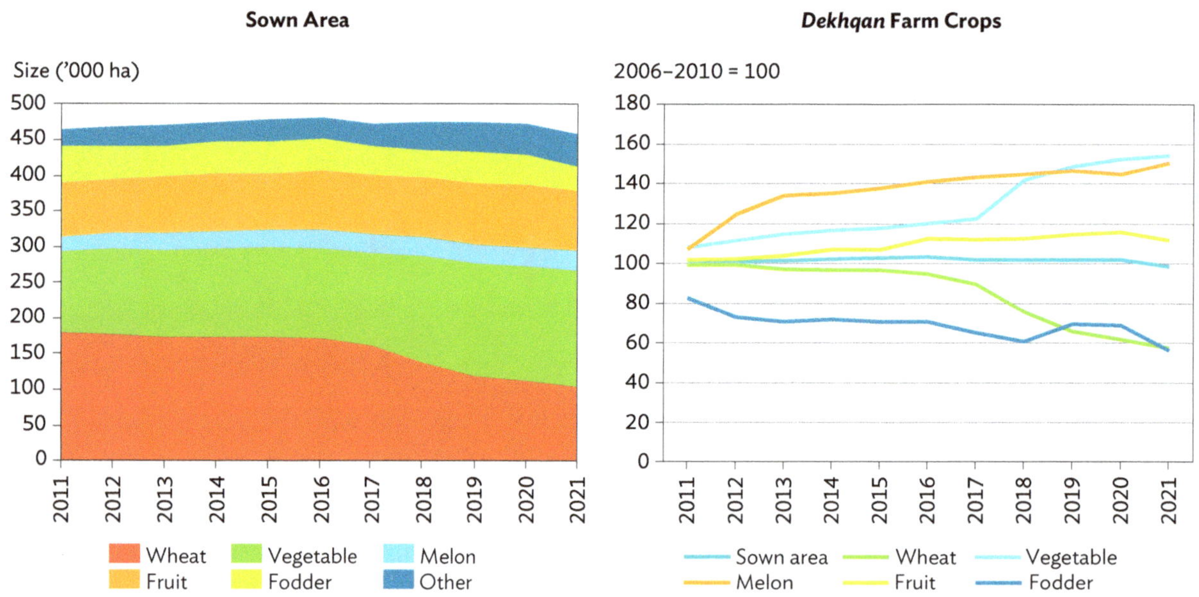

Source: Based on data from UzStat (Statistics Agency under the President of the Republic of Uzbekistan). 2022. *Statistical Yearbook on Agriculture.*

The immediate goal for many *dekhqan* farms is fulfilling their subsistence needs for essential foodstuffs that can be cultivated on their plots and selling the surplus. Most *dekhqan* farms participate in output markets, either directly or via intermediaries (footnote 8). These farms are well integrated into the rural labor market through on-farm employment (footnote 9).

10 D. F. Larson, D. Khidirov, and I. Ramniceanu. 2015 Uzbekistan: Strengthening the Horticulture Value Chain. *Uzbekistan Vision 2030 Background Paper Series.* World Bank.

Although *dekhqan* farms account for only 14% of the total sown area, their overall agricultural output is high and rising (Figure 3.9). These farms produce about 66% of the gross agricultural output and 40% of all crops, including almost 60% of horticultural crops. More visibly, these farms are the primary contributors to Uzbekistan's livestock output, accounting for some 90% of meat and milk production.

Figure 3.9: Contribution of *Dekhqan* Farms to Agricultural Output in Uzbekistan, 2021
(%)

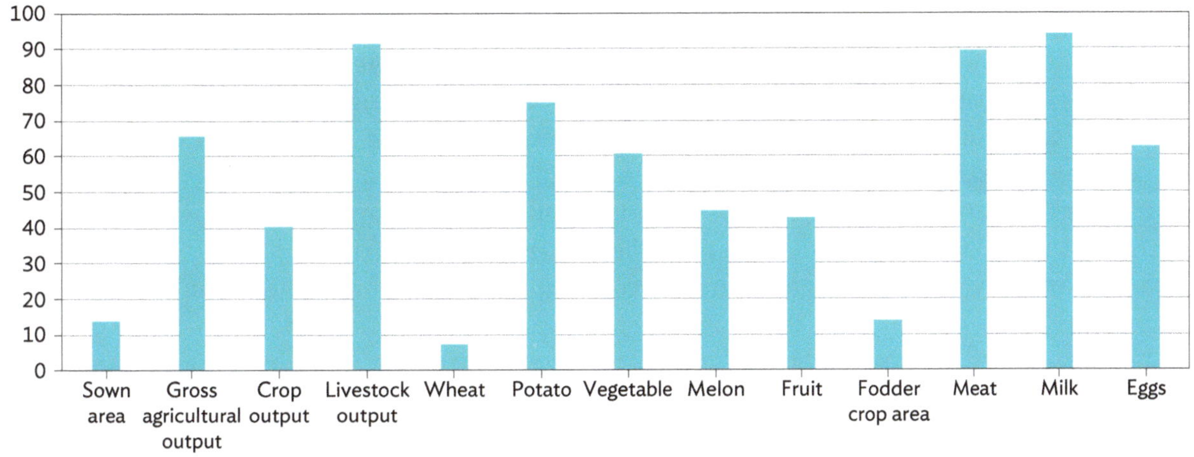

Note: Statistics on *dekhqan* farms can be weak because the quantity and accounting of granted land is not being compiled.
Source: Based on data from UzStat (Statistics Agency under the President of the Republic of Uzbekistan). 2022. *Statistical Yearbook on Agriculture*; E. B. Asfaw 2020. "Dehqan" Farms: Uzbekistan's Underserved 70 Percent. *CPRO Policy Brief.* No. 2020–08. Center for Policy Research and Outreach.

Despite contributing a large share of agricultural output and most horticulture and livestock products, *dekhqan* farms get little state support, mostly focusing on individual farms. Almost no public initiatives target *dekhqan* farms—and when they did, they were neither well-planned nor well-supported or executed. Indeed, the government has rarely engaged in smallholder production or given large public support to this segment (footnote 8). *Dekhqan* farms have little access to improved farming methods and technology, mostly developed for commercial and larger farms. *Dekhqan* farms lack access to consulting and extension services, which are directed primarily at commercial farms. Organizations engaged in collective learning and knowledge exchange are still at a nascent stage in their development (footnote 8). Because of the absence of land markets, *dekhqan* farms get access to additional agricultural lands by engaging in informal sharecropping or informal land rent arrangements with individual farms.[11]

The supply of animal feed in *dekhqan* farms is low because of a lack of available arable land to produce feed. These farms also lack access to high-quality veterinary services, high-performing genetic herds, hygienic conditions, business capabilities, and expertise to boost livestock output.[12]

11 U. Djanibekov, et al. 2013. Understanding Contracts in Evolving Agro-Economies: Farmers, *Dekhqans* and Networks in Khorezm, Uzbekistan. *Journal of Rural Studies*. 32.

12 E. B. Asfaw, 2021. State-Led Cotton Deregulation in Uzbekistan: Reforms and Effects. *Central Asian Journal of Water Research*. 7 (2). pp. 1210–1137.

Dekhqan farms gain little from market participation as they are cut off from higher-paying retailers and exports due to their low capacity to maintain consistent supply volume and quality as well as meet safety requirements. Retailers and exporters avoid the significant transaction costs associated with contracting fragmented smallholders. Although *dekhqan* farms produce large quantities of perishable horticultural and livestock products, they have almost no access to processors, storage, and packaging facilities (footnote 8). The lack of government attention to smallholders has hindered efforts to generate inclusive economic growth.

The strategy, however, recognizes the challenges of smallholders and emphasizes the importance of enhancing their productivity, market access, and standard of living. It calls for increased public investment in productivity-enhancing initiatives for smallholders. New legislation was introduced in 2021 to provide *dekhqan* farms with a formal framework for subleasing land from individual farms and other agricultural enterprises.[13] Under the law, these entities sublease—without the right of transfer to third parties—to *dekhqan* farms up to 10 hectares of agricultural land for up to 1 year. The legislation aims to formalize land transfers between individual and *dekhqan* farms. It also allows *dekhqan* farms, particularly those belonging to vulnerable families, to lease 1–2 hectares of additional land for up to 30 years.[14] This provision includes the allocation of marginal and low-productive arable lands belonging to individual farms and clusters that have been released from cotton and grain to *dekhqan* farms through open online markets. *Dekhqan* farms can convert these lands for greenhouse production.

Reforms and Policies in Cotton and Wheat Value Chains

Until 2019, cotton was one of the least reformed agriculture sectors. Central planning, the allotment of state land, and procurement pricing caused inefficiency. Cotton suffered from a monopsony of parastatal ginneries, input suppliers, and cotton exporters. Growers were taxed through government-mandated low prices for cotton and currency market controls (footnote 7). State control over cotton resulted in significant economy-wide inefficiencies and the unutilized potential of textile and high-value crop exports.

Acutely aware of these inefficiencies, the government enacted reforms in March 2020 to liberalize the cotton market and eliminate restrictions on output and pricing. The objective of the reforms is to build a competitive cotton supply chain with private ginneries and textile enterprises, with market-determined producer pricing based on international market prices. The reforms removed formal links between the public financing of agriculture and agricultural production. The backbone reform was the privatization of parastatal ginneries into cotton-textile clusters—that is, vertically integrated enterprises. State farmgate prices were replaced by new minimum farmgate prices, which set the floor that all buyers must adhere to. The reforms were intended to increase farmers' freedom of choice and cotton-textile clusters' freedom of choice. Local administration (*khokimiyat*) no longer imposed production targets on farmers and cotton-textile clusters. Commercial production contracts between cotton farmers and clusters replaced state production contracts. By inviting private investors to participate in the cotton processing sector, the government showed that it intends to shift from raw cotton exports to high-valued textile exports and diversify its cotton export markets. The strategy envisages a new wave of cotton reforms, and this is one of its major tenets.

---

13 Government of Uzbekistan. 2021. Law on *Dekhqan* Farms 680.

14 Government of Uzbekistan. 2022. Presidential Resolution 373: On Additional Measures to Increase Incomes by Supporting the Creation of *Dekhqan* Farms.

Price liberalization for cotton is expected to boost agricultural incomes and the industry's performance since the state's below-market purchasing prices gave little incentive for increasing output. The average minimum farmgate price, when measured in dollars in not only the parallel exchange rate but also the official exchange rate, has been gradually increased by over three times compared to the price cotton growers received in 2017 (Figure 3.10).

Figure 3.10: State Procurement and International Prices of Raw Cotton in Uzbekistan, 2000–2022

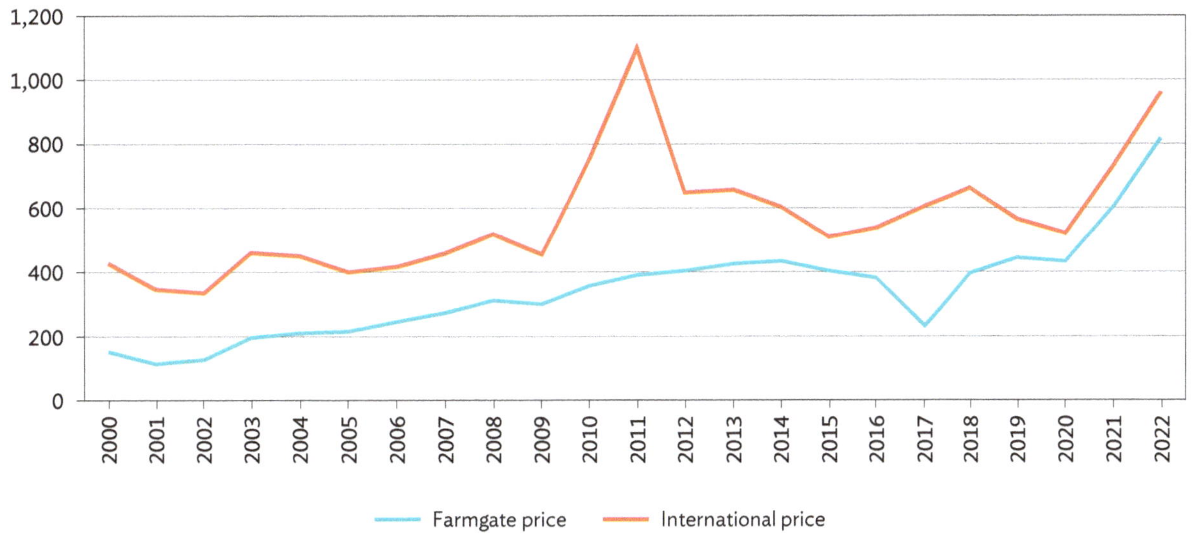

Notes: The farmgate price under the official exchange rate is the price paid to farmers converted to dollars using official exchange rates from the Central Bank of Uzbekistan. The international cotton price for raw cotton is calculated as the Cotton A Index annual prices over 2000–2021 and as average monthly prices for January–November 2022 from World Bank Commodity Price Data (The Pink Sheet) multiplied by a ratio of 0.33, which is an approximate rate of converting raw cotton to cotton fiber.
Sources: Uzbekistan's cotton prices from the Ministry of Agriculture; international prices from World Bank Commodity Price Data (accessed 23 June 2023)

Cotton-Textile Clusters

As a major part of cotton reforms, the government has started to transform cotton-textile supply chains into vertically integrated cotton-textile enterprises called clusters. These clusters are expected to provide large efficiency gains to the cotton industry by boosting processing efficiency, providing farmers greater access to inputs, and investing in new machinery and textile equipment. The clusters should use combine harvesters, increase compensation for cotton pickers, and export to international textile markets to improve export revenue. In 2022, 134 clusters were set up covering the entire area of cotton cultivation and almost 30,000 farmers (Table 3.1). Despite being called clusters, these entities do not match up to the organizational concept of western clusters in agriculture.[15]

15 J. Babadjanov and M. Petrick. *Cotton Production under the Emerging Cluster System in Uzbekistan: What Does "Cluster" Mean and What Has Changed?* Forthcoming.

Table 3.1: Number and Area of Cotton-Textile Clusters in Uzbekistan, 2018–2022

Item	2018	2019	2020	2021	2022
Number of cotton-textile clusters	13	77	97	122	134
Total sown area of cotton-textile clusters ('000 hectare)	...	668	917	1,034	1,034
Number of farms contracted by cotton-textile clusters	...	20,981	25,150	28,206	28,206
Total raw cotton output in clusters (million ton)	...	1.8	2.7	3.4	3.6

... = data not available.
Source: Based on data from the Ministry of Agriculture.

Despite this, the new paradigm legitimized the clusters' monopoly on delivering supplies and equipment services to farmers within their territory and on cotton purchases, processing, and exports. The cotton reforms have increased the responsibility of clusters to provide farmers with technical assistance and promote sustainable, climate-sensitive cotton production. The clusters must verify that cotton is not picked using forced or child labor. They also serve as financial gatekeepers. Currently, clusters have access to low-interest loans from the State Fund of Agricultural Support under the Ministry of Finance. The fund offers low-interest advance working capital to cotton and wheat farmers through the state procurement system for these two strategic crops. In 2020 and 2021, the fund made cash advances directly to farmers' bank accounts for buying inputs for cotton cultivation. However, in 2022 these advances were allocated to the clusters to buy and distribute inputs among farmers. The state covers the cost of operation and maintenance of irrigation and drainage infrastructure.

The clusters operate through the following three models.[16] First, the clusers can make contracts with local cotton-growing farmers (i.e., contract farming). Farmers retain land leases. The land is not operated directly by clusters, but farmers are contracted to grow cotton. Second, the government directly leases farmland to clusters (i.e., direct farming). Here, the state transfers land from cotton-growing farmers to clusters for crop cultivation, and the farmers become cluster employees. Third, clusters use a mix of direct and contract farming. Anecdotal evidence suggests some clusters under the direct farming or mixed models have been seizing large areas of land from cotton-growing farmers without compensating them for their land.[17]

The government designates districts where clusters must be formed, and farmers have to decide whether to join a cluster or not. The implementation of this process has not, however, been done in a transparent manner,[18] and the introduction of district-based clusters has not created competition among farmers because they are assigned to clusters within their district. The mandated specialization of clusters restricts the ability of farmers to choose crops and marketing channels. The creation of clusters has neither abolished the output limit nor the government's control over cotton pricing.

16 Government of Uzbekistan. 2021. Resolution of the Cabinet of Ministers 733 on the Approval of Regulations on the Procedure for Organizing the Activities of Cotton-Textile Clusters.
17 L. Schweisfurth. 2021. Land-Grabs: The New Red Flag for Uzbek Cotton Sector. Uzbek Forum for Human Rights. 19 February.
18 S. Zorya and S. Babaev. 2020. Cotton-Textile Clusters in Uzbekistan: Status and Outlook. *Policy Dialogue on Agricultural Modernization in Uzbekistan*. World Bank.

To prevent a cluster monopsony and to imbue competition in the cotton industry, a 2022 presidential decree granted farmers the freedom to voluntarily enter into "futures" (prefinancing) contracts with clusters in their province (*viloyat*).[19] However, the legislation's implementation for 2022's contracts was random or simply ignored.[20] Despite the aim to transition to more self-organized models of governance, the state remains the major implementer of economic reforms, particularly in agriculture.

Cotton Reform Outcomes

Cotton reforms have resulted in two major trends in the structure of cultivation, as can be seen in the official statistics. The first is that agricultural enterprises raised cotton output due to the increasing area under direct farming in some cotton-textile clusters, where they received farmland for their operations, and farmers were ordered to leave their land. The second is that cotton output increased after private investors were able to participate, and farmgate prices rose. The average raw cotton yield has increased since 2019 after stagnating from 2011 to 2018, with the yield rising in 2021 to 3.3 tons per hectare from 2018's 2.1 (Figure 3.11).

Figure 3.11: Cotton Cultivation by Agricultural Producer Category in Uzbekistan, 2012–2021

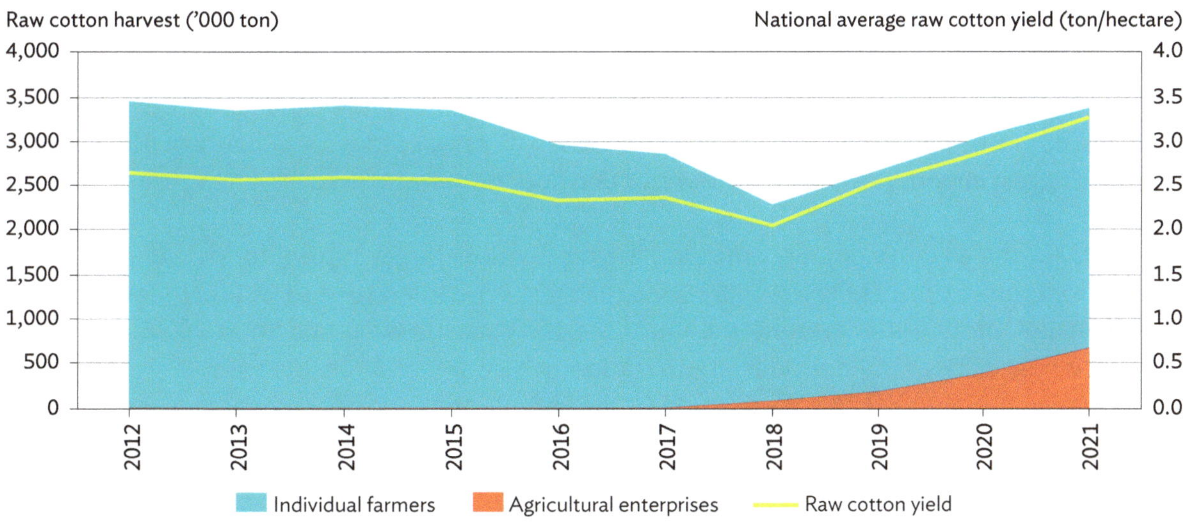

Source: Based on data from UzStat (Statistics Agency under the President of the Republic of Uzbekistan). 2022. *Statistical Yearbook on Agriculture.*

Cotton reforms have not yet strengthened the position of individual farms. Cotton growers lack effective organizations through which they can contract or own ginneries. The inability to organize alternative marketing channels puts farmers under the control of increasingly powerful private ginneries. The lack of decision-making autonomy and low bargaining power over input and output prices may be harming not just individual farms but also the cotton industry (Petrick et al. 2017). The key to cotton's sustained expansion is increased access to financing, the entry of private input suppliers, the flexibility to pick marketing channels, and a strong organization representing cotton producers' interests.

19 Government of Uzbekistan. 2021. Presidential Decree 14 on Measures to Regulate the Activities of Cotton-Textile Clusters.

20 Central Asia Labour Rights Monitoring Mission. 2022. Uzbekistan's Cotton Cannot Thrive Without Autonomy for Farmers. 9 October.

Wheat Reforms

The approach to regulating wheat has been contentious. Regulating wheat was tightly linked to the state policy of self-sufficiency, which was announced shortly after independence to achieve affordable and stable market prices, especially for low-income people. However, after over 30 years of state regulation, the increase in the national food supply has not automatically translated into improved access to food for poor people, adequate nutrient intake, nor a satisfactory quality of staple foods.[21]

The wheat self-sufficiency policy was directed at increasing wheat production by expanding the sown area and yields of winter wheat, thus lessening the country's reliance on wheat grain and flour imports. Wheat regulation was linked to the bread subsidy program in which the government controlled the distribution of domestically produced wheat and flour and set ceiling prices to reduce food costs for poor people. The government's wheat procurement policy implied that wheat-growing farmers received production targets and had to sell part of their harvest to parastatal mills at prices below the domestic market level—similar to the cotton procurement policy. Despite the low wheat procurement price effectively working as a de facto tax on wheat growers, the government's spending on wheat research resulted in high-yield domestic varieties, which lifted yields (footnote 21). An expansion of the wheat area led to exceptionally large rises in output, and new wheat varieties and crop management methods drove productivity growth.[22]

Uzbekistan can produce soft wheat varieties that are cheaper but have poor baking quality compared to hard wheat produced in the northern regions of Kazakhstan.[23] Despite the expanded wheat output, only about half of domestic wheat is used for food—the rest is for livestock fodder.[24] Because of this, Uzbekistan remains the biggest importer of high-quality wheat and flour from Kazakhstan.[25]

In March 2020, the government discontinued the production-target system for wheat and abolished state-set procurement prices.[26] However, price reforms, scheduled to start in 2021 were delayed by the pandemic. A presidential resolution announced the reforms would begin in 2022 and focus on liberalizing wheat prices.[27] Under price liberalization, wheat prices were supposed to rise by 50% for the 2022 harvest (Figure 3.12).[28] Abolishing state production targets for wheat is a complementary step to the discontinuation of subsidized bread prices in 2018 and wheat flour prices in 2019. The government does not expect the liberalization of wheat to influence the reforms on flour and bread prices. It is expected that liberalizing wheat prices will only affect the cost of a loaf of subsidized bread even though the bread subsidy was cut in 2018.[29]

21 L. Lombardozzi and N. Djanibekov. 2021. Can Self-Sufficiency Policy Improve Food Security? An Inter-Temporal Assessment of the Wheat Value-Chain in Uzbekistan. *Eurasian Geography and Economics*. 62 (1). pp. 1–20.

22 Y. Yigezu et al. 2022. Political Economy of the Wheat Sector in Uzbekistan Seed Systems, Variety Adoption and Impacts. ICARDA.

23 K. M. Kienzler et al. 2011. Winter Wheat Quantity or Quality? Assessing Food Security in Uzbekistan. *Food Security*. 3 (1). pp. 53–64.

24 Z. Lerman et al. 2016. Wheat Production and Regional Food Security in CIS: The Case of Belarus, Turkmenistan and Uzbekistan. *FAO Policy Studies on Rural Transition*. No. 2016-1. The Food and Agriculture Organization of the United Nations.

25 United States Department of Agriculture. 2018. Kazakhstan Grain and Feed Update Report. *GAIN Report KZ03*.

26 Government of Uzbekistan. 2020. Presidential Resolution 4634 on Measures for the Wide Implementation of Market Principles in the Production, Procurement, and Sale of Grains.

27 Government of Uzbekistan. 2021. Presidential Resolution 10 on the Introduction of Market Principles Ensuring Free Competition in Production and Sale of Grains.

28 Gazeta. 2022a. Grain Prices Will Be "Free" from June 1 (in Russian).

29 Gazeta. 2022b. How Reforms in Grain Production Will Affect the Cost of Flour and Bread (in Russian).

Further wheat reforms are needed as part of wider efforts to liberalize the economy. Rising food prices due to the pandemic and Russia's war in Ukraine threaten the affordability of food, which could widen inequality. Because of declining poverty in Uzbekistan, which might partly be due to the wheat self-sufficiency strategy, the government is likely to implement policies targeting underconsumption rather than underproduction. Maintaining low prices for staple foods is seen as a vital part of wheat reform to ensure stable wheat prices. Because wheat is still the most significant source of food, a strategy that maintains both the stability of supply and strives to cushion price volatility seems to be a desirable alternative.

Figure 3.12: State Procurement and International Prices of Wheat Grain in Uzbekistan, 2000–2022
($/ton)

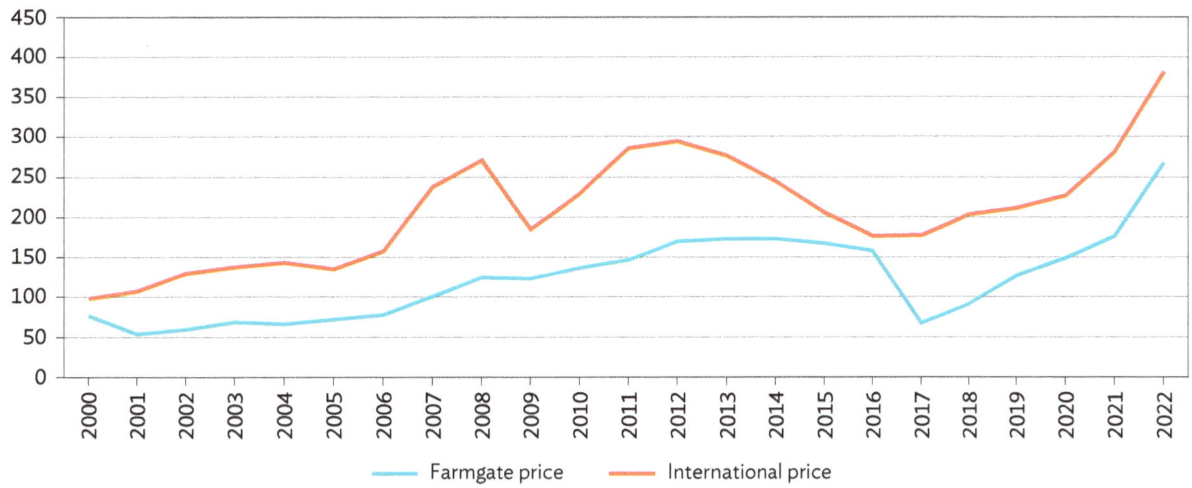

Notes: The farmgate price under the official exchange rate is the price paid to farmers converted to dollars using exchange rates from the Central Bank of Uzbekistan. The international price is the US soft red wheat price from World Bank Commodity Price Data (The Pink Sheet). The international price is calculated using annual prices for 2000–2021 and as average monthly prices for January–July 2022 from World Bank Commodity Price Data.
Sources: Ministry of Agriculture; Uzbekistan's wheat prices from L. Lombardozzi and N. Djanibekov. 2021. Can Self-Sufficiency Policy Improve Food Security? An Inter-Temporal Assessment of the Wheat Value-Chain in Uzbekistan. *Eurasian Geography and Economics.* 62 (1).

To address this and mitigate volatility in wheat prices from fluctuations in domestic production, the government plans to set up public grain reserves to replace the state procurement system to reduce Uzbekistan's heavy dependency on imported wheat grain and flour from Kazakhstan. Under the plan, the government will buy wheat for public reserves, which will also be used to stabilize the domestic wheat market. The grain reserves will play an important role in smoothing excessive price volatility in the domestic food market, given the uncertainties in the global wheat market after Russia's war in Ukraine.

Individual farms mainly produce wheat. Smallholders' share in wheat production fell from 15% in 2016 to 7% in 2021 (Figure 3.13). This period also saw the expansion of wheat clusters and cooperatives, and wheat production by agricultural enterprises increased almost tenfold, from 64,000 tons to 560,000 tons. This notwithstanding, the pace of wheat reforms has been slow, and there have been delays, resulting in poor performance in the industry. Despite ongoing wheat liberalization, low farmgate prices in state procurement reduced the incentive for farmers to improve productivity. As a direct consequence of this, wheat output hardly grew from 2016 to 2021. Indeed, 2021's harvest barely surpassed 2018's harvest, which was affected by bad weather.

Figure 3.13: Wheat Cultivation in Uzbekistan, 2012–2021

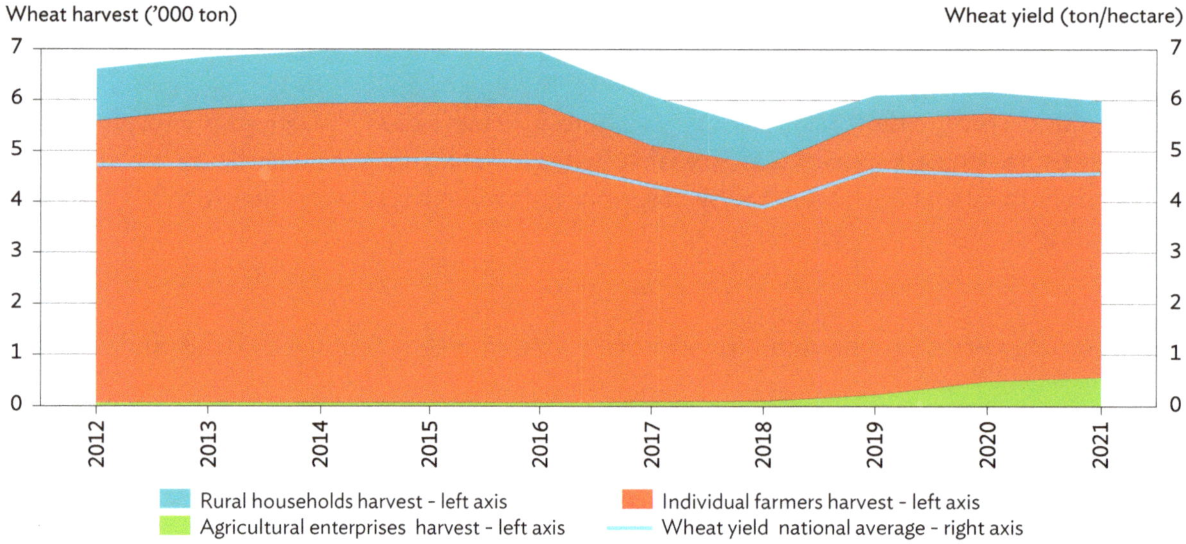

Source: Based on data from UzStat (Statistics Agency under the President of the Republic of Uzbekistan). 2022. *Statistical Yearbook on Agriculture.*

Horticulture and Livestock

Horticulture

Horticulture production in Uzbekistan is increasing in importance. Unlike strategic cotton and wheat, horticulture is highly productive and has the greatest potential for employment. Horticulture accounts for half of the country's total crop production in value terms and 40% of overall agricultural output—and all of this is cultivated on just 10% of arable land (footnote 4). A gradual shift from cotton and wheat to high-value horticulture products is already underway, and the government has set ambitious goals for increasing horticulture's export potential. A challenge is removing restrictions throughout the value chain to enable horticulture smallholders to reach their potential.

Figure 3.14 shows the sharp growth in the production of vegetables, melons, and fruit, especially since 2005. From then to 2016, horticulture underwent remarkable changes as the government increasingly recognized the potential of horticulture products. Horticulture's contribution to total agricultural output rose over this period, with vegetable production increasing by almost 190%, melon by 232%, and fruit by 175%. Bad weather hit production in 2017, but growth has since resumed. It should be noted growth has not been equal across producer categories. The production of vegetables, melons, and fruit in individual farms and agricultural enterprises during 2018–2021 rose (but fell in *dekhqan* farms), partly due to government support measures that targeted the expansion of horticulture production and exports among larger producers. *Dekhqan* farms, however, were excluded. Smallholders dominate, although larger individual farms and agribusinesses are increasingly participating in horticulture, and the scale of production is shifting to medium and small producers.[30]

[30] The official statistics' category of individual farms (*fermer xo'jaliklar*) aggregates all individual farms, including small farms and smallholders registered as individual farms. Because of this, it is not possible to assess the share of large farms in agriculture. (Source: D. F. Larson, D. Khidirov,, and I. Ramniceanu. 2015. Uzbekistan: Strengthening the Horticulture Value Chain. *Uzbekistan Vision 2030 Background Paper Series*. World Bank.)

Figure 3.14: Vegetable, Melon, and Fruit Production by Agricultural Producer Category in Uzbekistan, 1992–2020
('000 ton)

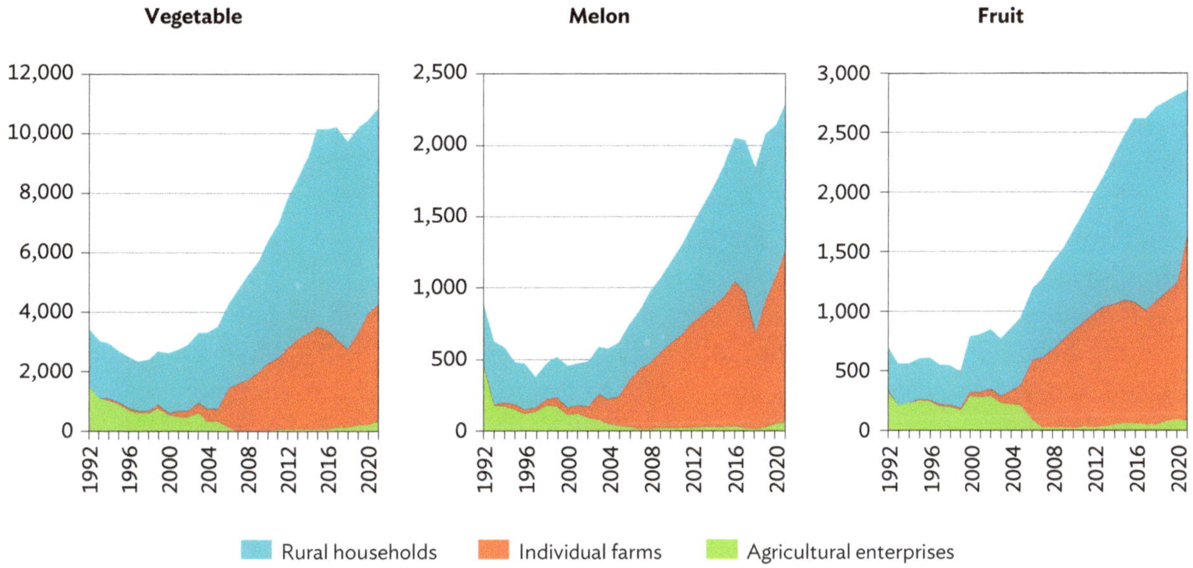

Source: Based on data from UzStat (Statistics Agency under the President of the Republic of Uzbekistan). 2022. *Statistical Yearbook on Agriculture.*

Horticulture has quickly become the second-biggest agricultural exporting sector after cotton. Uzbekistan is well-positioned to capitalize on large and expanding international markets for its horticulture products. Increased processing and exports of fresh and processed products can provide substantial opportunities for value addition. Income growth is changing diets in Uzbekistan and increasing domestic consumption of horticultural products. According to the Asian Development Bank,[31] of 2016's 20 million tons of horticultural output, only 15% was processed. In that year, of the 3 million tons of fruit produced, 69% was consumed fresh, 20% processed, and 11% exported. For vegetables, of the 10 million tons of produced, 81.0% were consumed fresh, 11.0% were processed, 4.0% were used for seeds, and 3.4% were exported.

Horticulture's fragmentation across small-scale producers limits the sector's development due to this very small size. Because of this, smallholders have limited access to financial resources and services, and they use low-cost traditional methods of production, which affects quality. Developing horticulture is impeded by small production quantities and a volatile supply of outputs to domestic and international markets. Smallholders are used to selling their produce locally through conventional retailers and markets. If they try to move into international markets, they may face increased bureaucracy and compliance procedures, as well as technological obstacles and institutional constraints. They could be delimited by their capacity to comply with international sanitary and phytosanitary regulations and food safety standards—let alone the quality and safety requirements of the more stringent export markets. The lack of access of smallholders to modern production technologies and knowledge has created a significant skills and capacity gap that needs to be bridged to achieve a modern horticulture subsector across the entire value chain. Anecdotal evidence suggests that retailers buy from smaller farms, often on the spot and without written contracts based on repeated interactions.

31 Asian Development Bank (ADB). 2021. Uzbekistan: Horticulture Value Chain Development Project—Additional Financing. Annual Safeguard Monitoring Report.

Livestock

Farm restructuring has led to livestock output being concentrated in the hands of smallholders and *dekhqan* farms. Livestock has a social safety net function in Uzbekistan, where the size of a household's herd is one of the main factors for increasing family incomes and well-being.[32] In 2021, 4.9 million *dekhqan* farms owned 12.4 million head of cattle, of which 4.3 million were cows (footnote 5). In that year, these farms accounted for 91% of total livestock production. About a quarter of the agricultural labor force is engaged in livestock as an additional source of income (World Bank 2020).

Agricultural enterprises accounted for 3.6% of livestock production in 2021. Recent agricultural reforms have not improved livestock production in individual farms and agricultural enterprises. In 2021, individual farms operated over 80% of the sown area and contributed about half of total crop output but only 5.3% of livestock production. Even so, livestock production has grown continuously since the mid-1990s (Figure 3.15) due mainly to the expansion of livestock numbers in *dekhqan* farms, which contributed 90% of the meat produced in 2021. Individual farms and agricultural enterprises produced almost equal shares, at 5% each. Meat production in individual farms and agricultural enterprises has increased sharply since 2017 (Figure 3.15). Compared to 2016 values, meat production in individual farms increased by 121%. In agricultural enterprises, the growth over 2016–2021 was even stronger, at 137%, while the meat production of *dekhqan* farms increased only by 15% in that period. The dominance of *dekhqan* farms in milk production is even stronger than for meat: in 2021, they produced 94% of the country's milk (Figure 3.15).

Figure 3.15: Meat, Milk, and Egg Production by Agricultural Producer Category in Uzbekistan, 1992–2020

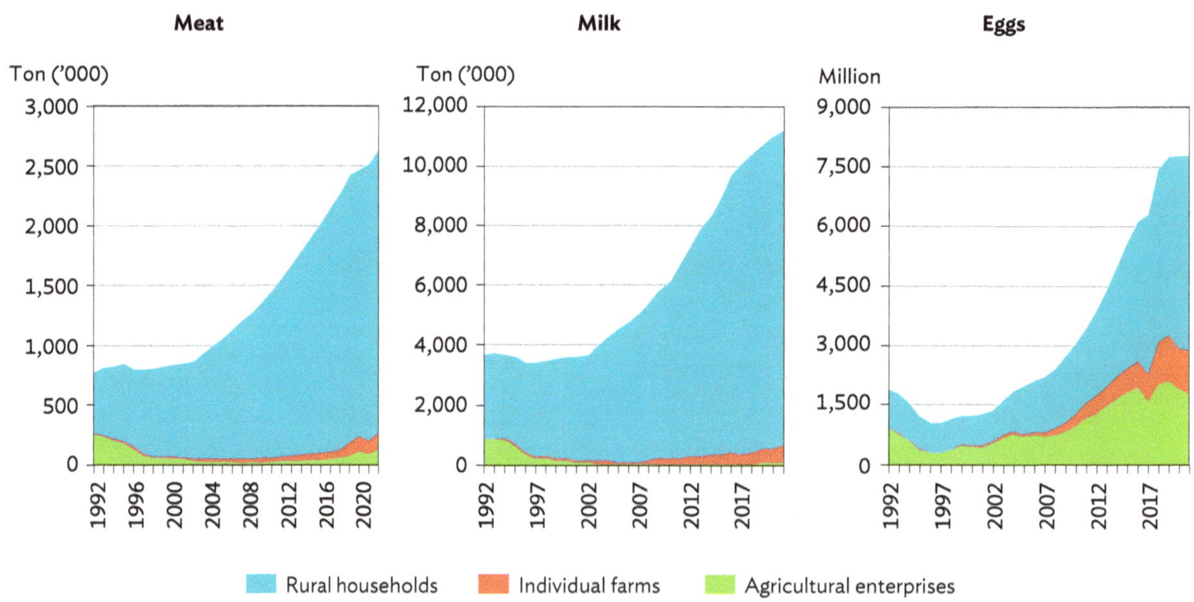

Source: Based on data from UzStat (Statistics Agency under the President of the Republic of Uzbekistan). 2022. *Statistical Yearbook on Agriculture.*

32 Z. Lerman. 2008. Agricultural Development in Uzbekistan: The Effect of Ongoing Reforms. *Discussion Paper.* No. 7.08. Hebrew University of Jerusalem.

The structure was far different in the first half of the 1990s when agricultural enterprises produced a quarter of milk production and households three-fourths. The small-scale production of milk in rural households continues to hinder the development of milk supply chains and the improvement of milk yields.[33] Since 2017, milk production has increased, as it has for meat, rising 60% in individual farms and 65% in agricultural enterprises. However, it has risen only 14% in *dekhqan* farms.

In 2021, *dekhqan* farms accounted for 63% of total egg production, agricultural enterprises 23%, and individual farms 14% (Figure 3.15). In contrast to meat and milk, which are mainly produced in *dekhqan* farms, egg production in agricultural enterprises and individual farms grew rapidly from 2009 to 2016. Individual farms saw production growth of 64% in 2016–2021. However, egg production in agricultural enterprises declined when comparing values from 2020–2021 and 2016. *Dekhqan* farms experienced a similar slowdown. From 2012 to 2017, due to increasing fodder and veterinary costs, the annual growth rate of egg production was 12%–13%, but it slowed to 7.8% in 2018 and 1.2% in 2021 due to increasing fodder and veterinary costs.

The increase in Uzbekistan's agricultural production is entirely attributable to the expansion of individual farms and the private sector, which, as noted earlier, combines *dekhqan* farms and rural households. Other countries in the Commonwealth of Independent States that transitioned to individual farming saw the same effect of these reforms on agricultural production (footnote 32). For Uzbekistan's livestock industry, smallholders have emerged as the key players in the transition process.

Expanding livestock production, particularly through intensive industrial farming, is hindered by an insufficient fodder supply. An increase in fodder output has not accompanied the steady growth of Uzbekistan's livestock herd.[34] Indeed, since 1991, the production of basic animal feeds has fallen sharply due to the expansion of the wheat area in irrigated land that was once used for fodder crops. In particular, the wheat expansion came at the cost of perennials, which were part of the cotton rotation scheme.

Smallholders own 90% of all cattle. By producing only 13% of fodder, *dekhqan* farms and rural households rely on crop byproducts from their plots, buying feedstuff and access to open pastures, neighboring canals, and farm fields for grazing their livestock.[35] Because the demand for feedstuff exceeds production, livestock keepers traditionally mix relatively rich metabolizable feedstuff, such as wheat bran, maize, and sorghum straw, with crude protein-rich feeds, such as cottonseed cake. Although cottonseed cake has been part of the traditional feed ratio, its availability has declined, resulting in the notoriously low quality of cheap grain bran and fibrous roughage—and this is one of the reasons for the poor livestock productivity.[36] The strong increase in the use of cereals for feed since 2000 may partially offset the reduced feed because of the declining area of fodder crops (footnote 35). The primary contributors to the inadequate feed output are the lack of available land, poor feed crop yields, and administrative objectives and constraints (footnote 30).

33 United Nations Development Programme (UNDP). 2010. Livestock Production in Uzbekistan: Current State, Challenges and Prospects.

34 B. I. Shapiro et al. 2022. Uzbekistan Livestock Sector Analysis: Baseline Report. *ILRI Project Report*. International Livestock Research Institute.

35 S. Robinson. 2020. Livestock in Central Asia: From Rural Subsistence to Engine of Growth? *IAMO Discussion Paper*. No. 193. Leibniz Institute of Agricultural Development in Transition Economies.

36 D. Djumaeva et al. 2009. Options for Optimizing Dairy Feed Rations with Foliage of Trees Grown in the Irrigated Drylands of Central Asia. *Research Journal of Agriculture and Biological Sciences*. 5 (5). pp. 698–08.

The Uzbek State Program for Livestock Development aims to raise the standard of livestock breeds. However, access to animal breeding services remains difficult. The obstacles include insufficient research support for pedigree breeding, low pedigree stock and frozen semen procurement from abroad, insufficient feed resources and veterinary services, lack of required hygiene norms in livestock management, and insufficient awareness about pedigree breeding (footnote 34).

The government, acknowledging the problems facing the development of the livestock sector, particularly the lack of fodder production areas, has been giving subsidies to livestock producers.[37] In February 2022, it approved a program for developing the sector from 2022 to 2026 aimed at food security by boosting livestock production, introducing new production techniques, and developing livestock value chains and cooperatives.[38] Also, in February 2002, new legislation granted additional subsidies to meat and milk producers for the next two years.[39] The legislation promotes contract farming between individual farms and rural households for livestock to "grow out" of livestock by rural households. This arrangement implies that large individual farms and clusters will be able to outsource growing processes to small family-based "growers." The legislation recommends that cotton-textile, grain, and rice clusters establish livestock feedlots for 500–1,000 head of cattle. Abandoned and unused arable lands will be leased to meat and dairy companies for fodder crop cultivation via open online bidding. Individual farms that organize grow-out contracts with smallholders and those participating in cooperatives can apply for additional irrigated lands for crop cultivation.

Agricultural and Export Subsidy Systems

The government has placed a significant emphasis on food security, rural employment, and agricultural diversification, resulting in public spending on agriculture, including subsidies, has grown in absolute and real terms. From 2016 to 2020, agricultural support accounted for an average of 2.2% of GDP, according to the World Bank.[40] In the same period, agricultural expenditure accounted for an average of 8.5% of overall government spending, equivalent to 7.8% of the agricultural value-added and 5.8% of the value of gross agricultural output. The primary focus of public farm and agribusiness support has been on the provision of finance through the State Fund for Agriculture Support. From 2016 to 2022, public agricultural spending was mainly on irrigation and low-interest credit for cotton and wheat farmers to partly compensate them for production costs and stimulate the use of inputs to increase output.

The World Bank also notes that although total direct payments to farmers have been increasing, their share in the national economy has stayed at around 1%. Subsidy payments for variable inputs account for the major share of direct support funds targeted to farmers. These subsidies are to compensate for part of the electricity costs accrued by irrigation pumps and the credit subsidies for cotton and wheat

37 Government of Uzbekistan. 2019. Presidential Resolution 4243 on Measures for the Further Development and Support of the Livestock Sector; Government of Uzbekistan. 2020. Presidential Resolution 4576 on Additional Measures for State Support of the Livestock Sector; Government of Uzbekistan. 2021. Presidential Resoution 5051 on Additional Measures for Further State Support of Livestock Sector.

38 Government of Uzbekistan. 2022. Presidential Resolution 120 on Approving the Development Program for the Livestock Sector over 2022–2026.

39 Government of Uzbekistan. 2022. Presidential Resolution 121 on Measures for the Further Development of Animal Husbandry and Strengthening the Forage Base.

40 World Bank. 2021. *Uzbekistan: Second Agricultural Public Expenditure Review.*

production (Figure 3.16). Global evidence suggests that direct farm assistance for variable inputs is minimal, at best, and there is likely a negative effect on agricultural productivity and growth.[41] Direct assistance for developing fixed capital and access to on-farm services, such as extension programs and technical assistance, have a higher impact on agricultural growth and farm productivity than subsidies (footnote 44).

Figure 3.16: Composition of Direct Payments to Farmers in Uzbekistan, 2016–2020
(billion sum)

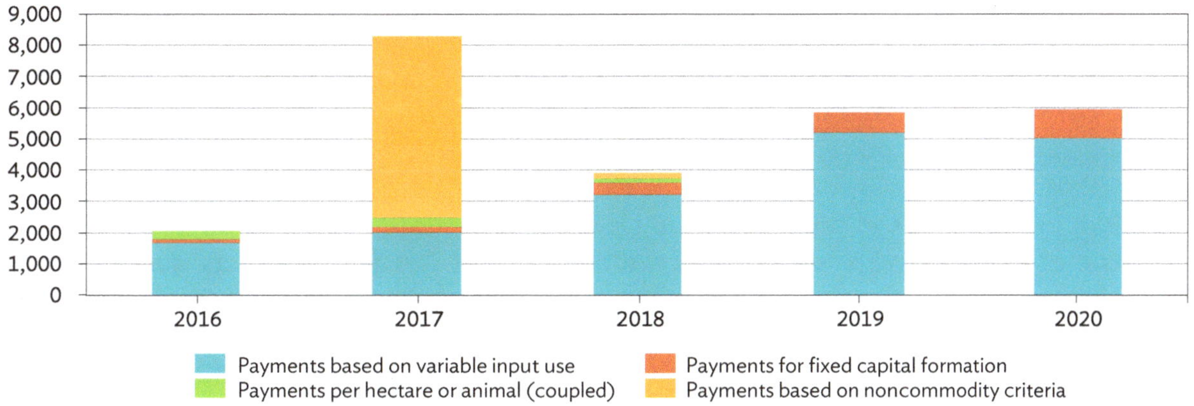

Source: Based on Table 8 in World Bank. 2021. Uzbekistan: Second Agricultural Public Expenditure Review.

New government initiatives to assist the creation of fixed capital via matching investment grants per hectare were launched in 2019; these included support for the adoption of drip irrigation to advance agriculture's modernization and climate resilience. Despite the high share of budget spending on agriculture and subsidies in total public expenditure, neither the enabling policy environment nor the allocative efficiency of the public expenditure has translated into a pattern of agricultural growth that is both climate-resilient and inclusive (footnote 44).

Many farmers and agri-food enterprises, including input suppliers and other actors along the supply chains, benefit from increasing access to direct state subsidy programs. Current direct support for farmers amounts to over half of the budgetary assistance (footnote 44). However, the institutional and regulatory framework responsible for administering direct subsidy programs lacks transparency, coordination, and coherence to the Agriculture Development Strategy (footnote 42). This has led to a relatively low degree of allocative efficiency of the subsidies and has had a negligible effect on sector productivity, incomes, and growth. Anecdotal evidence also suggests misuse of public funds and corruption.[42]

41 A. Shukurov et al. 2022. Direct Support for Farms and Agri-Food Businesses in Uzbekistan: The Need for Structural Reforms. *ISCAD Policy Brief*. International Strategic Centre for Agri-food Development.

42 *KUN.UZ*. 2022. Fake Cooperative: A Unique Method of Looting State Funds Was "Invented" in Kashkadarya (in Uzbek). 19 October.

Direct support programs for agriculture include various schemes targeting crop production, animal husbandry, irrigation, processing, transportation, and other processes and sectors along the agricultural production process. The structure of available direct subsidies is adjusted regularly as new support schemes are launched or existing ones are terminated by government resolutions. This ad hoc and inconsistent policy environment is not supportive of long-term planning and investment in agriculture (footnote 42), and direct support programs for agri-foods involve multiple ministries and state agencies that complicate the coherence of actions and do not necessarily connect them to the national objectives of agriculture development.

No mechanism exists for evaluating the allocation efficiency and impact of active assistance programs. Consequently, the complicated framework of farm and agribusiness assistance and the lack of monitoring capacities and mechanisms do not allow for determining which programs function effectively and which should be amended or canceled. The lack of management control and monitoring may breed corruption and power abuse at all levels of system management (footnote 42).

In addition, new priorities in the Agriculture Development Strategy call for the development of a broader set of direct payment schemes for a wider range of agri-food products, such as fruit and vegetables, and more assistance to small farmers. Yet, the public support program is still directed toward large producers, such as cotton and wheat farmers and clusters. Although a trend in recent years has been to make more funds available for horticulture and smallholders, these funds are just a tiny part of the overall public assistance supply (footnote 42).

Since 2017, Uzbekistan's agricultural export policy has become much more open, particularly the liberalization of fruit and vegetable exports. In June 2017, the government removed the monopolistic function of Uzagroexport JSC on exports of fruits and vegetables.[43] The sale of 25% of foreign currency revenue from exports of all items was eliminated in August 2017, marking another milestone in export liberalization.[44] Uzagroexport's practice of setting recommended minimum prices for export contracts was abolished in August 2018.[45] The reason for this was that since farmers were not allowed export to their harvests at lower prices than those set by Uzagroexport, agricultural products were often wasted. In May 2018, hundreds of tons of vegetables were abandoned in the Fergana Region because centrally set export prices were too high and farmers were not allowed to export at lower prices.

In 2019, for the first time since independence, fruit and vegetable exporters received subsidies to cover up to half of the cost of shipping by rail when sending goods to countries outside the Commonwealth of Independent States. The effect of these subsidies, however, was limited because exports were bound to deliveries via rail and shipments by road and air were not included. Because of this, in May 2020, export transportation subsidies were extended, and shipments by road and air were included as the pandemic raised transportation costs for exporters.[46] In October 2021, a 1-year compensation system was introduced to cover half of the transport costs for exports of high-value products to European markets.[47]

43 Presidential resolution 3077, 21 June 2017, on Measures for the Further Support of Domestic Exporting Organization and the Improvement of Foreign Economic Activities.

44 Presidential resolution 3157, 28 July 2017, on Additional Measures to Stimulate Domestic Exporting Enterprises.

45 Government of Uzbekistan. 2018. Presidential Decree 5495 on Measures to Cardinally Improve the Investment Climate in Uzbekistan.

46 Government of Uzbekistan. 2020. Presidential Resolution 4707 on Measures for Further Support of Export Activities.

47 Government of Uzbekistan. 2021. Presidential Decree 6306 on Additional Measures to Stimulate Exporting Enterprises.

In January 2017, the government set up UzAgroExportBank JS to fund investment projects for improving agricultural production and exports, especially fruit and vegetables. As part of the measures to help exports, the participation costs of exporters in international exhibitions were partially reimbursed.[48] Legal entities that exported fruit and vegetables were allowed to do so without getting advance payment, opening a letter of credit, getting a bank guarantee, or having an insurance policy that covered export contracts' political and commercial risks.[49] In November 2022, this measure was extended to individual entrepreneurs exporting horticultural products.[50]

Since 2019, exporters buying fruit and vegetables from agricultural associations have been subsidized to cover half of the costs of training association members in new production technologies, monitoring agri-engineering activities, and marketing research of foreign markets. The subsidies are provided by the state budget from the Export Promotion Agency under the Ministry of Investments and Foreign Trade and international financial institutions.[51] In May 2019, the State Fund of Support to Entrepreneurial Activities was launched to subsidize interest expenditure on pre-export credits but not for exports of primary agricultural products, such as cotton lint.[52] Since August 2019, the Export Promotion Agency has been covering the export costs of agricultural certification.[53]

In October 2020, the State Fund of Support to Entrepreneurial Activities extended credit compensation for pre-export financing to 2021. The Export Support Fund was added to the Export Promotion Agency to consolidate government efforts to expand exports of agri-food products.[54] The year 2020 ended with the government introducing new subsidies for boosting horticultural exports. The measures implied that exporters could apply for the full coverage of costs for implementing standards, getting conformity certificates, and product promotion to foreign markets.[55] A new set of subsidy measures that included low-interest credits to promote exporters was adopted in May 2021.[56] The preferential credits secure competitive advantages for Uzbek agricultural products in global markets. Under this measure, exporters can receive preferential credits for working capital at a 4% interest rate.

The liberalization of horticultural exports in 2017 resulted in the sector's rapid export growth in 2018, when its share in total agricultural exports rose to 66% from 48% in 2017 (Figure 3.17).

48 Government of Uzbekistan. 2017. Presidential Resolution 2740 on Establishing JS Commercial Bank UzAgroExportBank.

49 Government of Uzbekistan. 2018. Presidential Resolution 3978 on Additional Measures to Increase the Efficiency of Promoting Fruit and Vegetable Products on Foreign Markets.

50 Government of Uzbekistan. 2022. Presidential Resolution 417 on Ensuring Inviolability of Property Rights of Individual Entrepreneurs when Exporting Fruit and Vegetable Products.

51 Government of Uzbekistan. 2019. Presidential Resolution 4239 on Measures to Develop Agricultural Cooperation in the Fruit and Vegetable Sector.

52 Government of Uzbekistan. 2019. Presidential Resolution 4337 on Measures to Expand Mechanisms of Financing and Insuring Export Activities.

53 Government of Uzbekistan. 2019. Presidential Resolution 4406 on Additional Measures for Deep Processing Agricultural Products and Further Developing the Food Sector.

54 Government of Uzbekistan. 2020. Presidential Decree 6091 on Measures for the Further Expansion of Financial Support for Export Activities.

55 Government of Uzbekistan. 2020. Cabinet of Ministers Resolution 826 on Approving a Regulation on Procedure for Providing Financial Assistance to Exporting Organizations by the Export Promotion Agency under the Ministry of investment and Foreign Trade.

56 Government of Uzbekistan. 2021. Presidential Resolution 5087 on Additional Measures to Improve the Entrepreneurship Support System and Business Climate.

Figure 3.17: Uzbekistan's Export Value of Fruit and Vegetables, 2010–2020

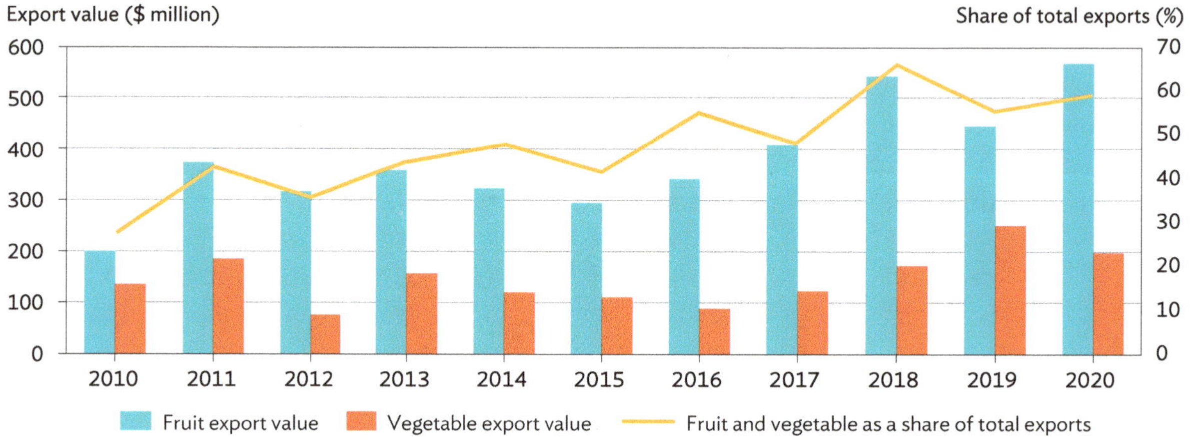

Source: Based on the Food and Agriculture Organization of the United Nations. FAOSTAT.

Despite export-oriented subsidies and new development projects in horticulture, the value of fruit exports declined in 2019, as did vegetable exports in 2020. Furthermore, exports of fruit and vegetables focused on traditional products, while the potential for producing higher-value niche products like berries and nuts was overlooked. New crops suiting Uzbekistan's agri-climatic conditions, such as kiwi, asparagus, and avocado, could lift export revenue by reaching high-income consumers in international markets. In 2021, exports of frozen fruit and vegetables quadrupled compared to 2020, and they shifted to higher-priced items.[57]

Food Security

The COVID-19 pandemic and Russia's war in Ukraine significantly affected food security in Uzbekistan.[58] Impacts included higher trade costs, food inflation and unemployment, and a fall in remittances. As a result, the buying power of low-income households has been falling, affecting private consumption and exacerbating poverty. The poverty rate decreased from 28% in 2000 to 11% in 2019, based on the official definition of the low-income population. According to World Bank estimates, the most severe types of poverty were practically eradicated by 2018[59] by which year the poverty rate, using the threshold typical of lower-middle-income countries, was 9.5%. Even though severe poverty is increasingly uncommon in Uzbekistan, progress on more ambitious well-being standards has substantially slowed over the past decade, particularly considering Uzbekistan's national income level and growth rate.[60] Since 2017, income growth has quickened but grew fastest in the population with the highest incomes. Income growth has been substantially lower for the lowest 40% of welfare distribution, and in 2018, 79% of poor people were in rural areas and thus dependent on agriculture, according to the Listening to the Citizens of Uzbekistan baseline survey (footnote 60). Thus, the effectiveness of economic growth on poverty reduction in Uzbekistan is declining (footnote 60).

57 East Fruit. 2021. Uzbekistan: Top 10 Major Fruit and Vegetable Events of 2021 (Part 2).

58 Organisation for Economic Co-operation and Development (OECD). 2022. Weathering Economic Storms in Central Asia: Initial Impacts of the War in Ukraine.

59 W. Seitz. 2019. Where They Live: District-Level Measures of Poverty, Average Consumption, and the Middle Class in Central Asia. *Policy Research Working Paper*. No. 8940. World Bank.

60 World Bank. 2022b. Toward a Prosperous and Inclusive Future: The Second Systematic Country Diagnostic for Uzbekistan.

Because of the pandemic, which disrupted commerce and supply systems, higher food prices and declining family incomes stalled the fall in poverty and food insecurity that had been mostly on track. Had there been no pandemic, an improvement in food security indicators would have likely been achieved. COVID-19 caused the global poverty rate to rise to 15% in 2020, with the damaging effects continuing into 2021.[61]

According to the official measure, 43% of total income is concentrated in the wealthiest quintile and 5% in the lowest quintile. Both indicators show moderate and sustained long-term trends in inequality (footnote 61). The 2020 national household budget survey showed the Gini coefficient of income was 0.36 and the Gini coefficient of per capita spending 0.34. This indicates that inequality in 2020 was about the same as in 2003, when it was assessed at 0.35 in a comparable survey. Statistics Agency income distribution estimates over the long term also indicate modest and constant levels of inequality.

Although incomes regularly increased from 2015 to 2019, the rise was much slower than the growth of per capita GDP—and income growth among poor people was substantially slower. Over this period, inflation-adjusted GDP per capita expanded at an annual rate of 4.8%; while median income grew 1.4%; while the income of the lowest quintile rose at almost half the average rate, or 0.7% (footnote 61).

The primary objective of Uzbekistan's food policy is to provide food security via domestic production and through the food self-sufficiency policy (footnote 19). Domestic production of eggs and dairy products, vegetables, fruit, and melons cover domestic food demand. However, sugar, vegetable oils, meat, grains, and potatoes are imported (Table 3.2). The coverage of food supply for domestic food production has increased for meat, eggs, fish, vegetables, and fruit, but declined for cereals and vegetable oils.

Table 3.2: Coverage of Food Supply by Domestic Production in Uzbekistan, 2010–2019
(%)

Food Item Aggregate	2010	2011	2012	2013	2014	2015	2016	2017	2018	2019
Cereals excluding beer	83	83	79	83	85	82	80	83	63	74
Starchy roots	99	100	99	94	105	103	101	93	97	96
Sugar and sweeteners	1	1	2	2	2	2	2	2	2	3
Oil crops	99	99	99	98	97	94	95	94	87	84
Vegetable oils	79	73	71	72	61	61	57	54	54	56
Vegetables	103	103	101	103	102	102	102	102	105	106
Fruits excluding wine	111	120	116	115	113	119	135	128	123	119
Meat	87	90	93	96	98	101	102	93	107	94
Eggs	100	99	100	100	100	100	100	106	116	146
Milk excluding butter	100	100	100	100	100	100	100	100	100	100
Fish, seafood	55	54	56	55	73	68	87	90	90	90

Source: Based on the Food and Agriculture Organization of the United Nations. FAOSTAT. (accessed 16 July 2023).

61 World Bank. 2022b. *Toward a Prosperous and Inclusive Future: The Second Systematic Country Diagnostic for Uzbekistan.*

Uzbekistan's average dietary energy supply adequacy shows the country has improved its food supply. From 2010 to 2012, the average dietary energy supply exceeded the food energy requirement by over 20%. Since 2016, there has been slight growth in this measure, from 136% to 138%, pointing to increased imports of high-quality wheat grains and flour from Kazakhstan that offset a recent decline in domestic wheat production.

Despite a high average dietary energy supply adequacy, the prevalence of both moderate and severe food insecurity slowly rose over 2014–2021 (Figure 3.18). Over 2019–2021, about a quarter of the population was affected by moderate (18%) and severe (5.6%) food security. The prevalence of severe food insecurity became more pronounced in 2018, a period of rapid economic reform.

Figure 3.18: Moderate and Severe Food Insecurity Among the Uzbek Population, 2014–2021 (%)

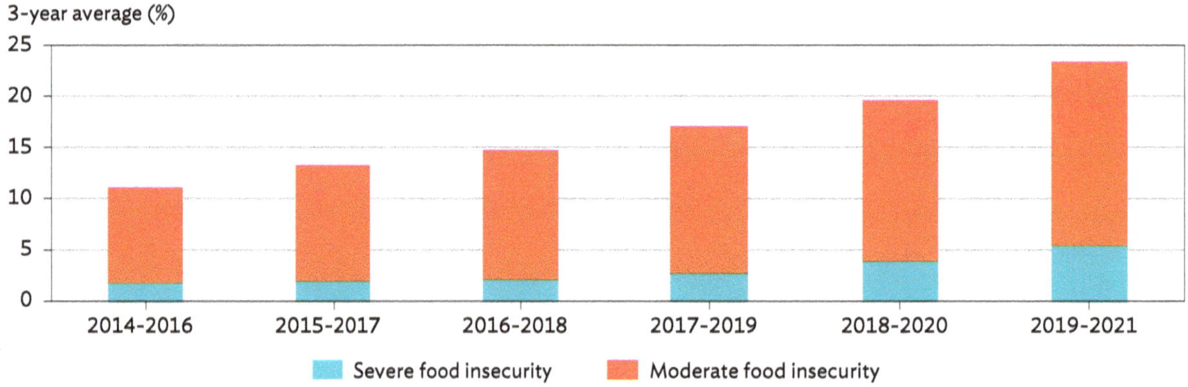

Source: Based on the Food and Agriculture Organization of the United Nations. FAOSTAT (accessed 16 July 2023).

Grain and grain products, vegetable oil, and sugar make up more than 60% of Uzbekistan's food imports. Russia's war in Ukraine put Uzbekistan at risk of food insecurity. Uzbekistan imports around 30% of its food from the Russian Federation and 2% from Ukraine.[62] The actual figure may be higher, given the significant amount of food from these countries entering Uzbekistan through Kazakhstan. Rising food prices have been another aftershock as reduced food imports, including wheat, vegetable oil, and sugar, and rising fuel prices, pushed up food prices (Central Asian Bureau for Analytical Reporting 2022). To stabilize retail prices, Uzbekistan has set aside large reserves of flour, vegetable oil, and sugar.

The quality of diets is a challenge. About a third of the adult population has hypertension, a fifth is at high risk of a heart attack or stroke, and about half is overweight or obese.[63] A global study researching

62 United Nations Development Programme. 2022. Uzbekistan Raises Alarm over Food Insecurity Triggered by Ukraine War. Caravanserai. 8 April.

63 World Health Organization (WHO). 2021. Uzbekistan Is Making Healthy Diets a Cornerstone of National Policy with the Help of WHO. 11 January.

diet-related deaths found that in 2017 Uzbekistan had the highest rate of diet-related deaths.[64] Noncommunicable diseases, which are closely associated with unhealthy diets are responsible for 79% of deaths in Uzbekistan, and cardiovascular diseases are the main cause of premature mortality. The government, acknowledging the need to reduce health risks, took measures in 2021 that should significantly improve food safety and the quality of nutrition.

Way Forward

Uzbekistan's agriculture sector can increase value-added and production through improved farming methods, more efficient use of fertilizer and water, and better land allocation. Since 2017, the government has implemented bold, historically unprecedented reforms to increase agriculture production and competitiveness. The adoption of the Agriculture Development Strategy resulted in substantial reforms, including the abolition of state output objectives for cotton and wheat, the termination of the systematic use of forced labor in cotton harvesting, and the liberalization of horticulture exports. Farmgate prices for wheat and cotton were boosted to close the gap with global market prices.

The reforms taken to liberalize agriculture will certainly bear fruit through diversifying the agriproduct portfolio and export markets, enhancing food security, and making farmers resilient to the changing climate. The success of these reforms will depend on the matching changes in the institutional environment. The following recommendations are offered for future agriculture reforms, particularly those aimed at making the sector more viable and inclusive:

(i) **Freedom to farm.** The abolition of cotton and wheat output quotas should be accompanied by legalizing "freedom to farm." The crop placement system should be abolished to enable farmers to make market-based decisions on how they use their land. The introduction of additional mandates, such as those on high-value crops or diversification, should be avoided to free farmers from production constraints—that is, giving them more decision-making autonomy. Freedom-to-farm reforms should focus on allowing farmers to decide what and how to produce and where to sell at what price.

(ii) **Empowering farmers.** The liberalization of cotton and wheat ignored farmers' interests and the benefits of competition within supply chains. The monopolistic clusters do not compete for the selection of farmers in the market, while farmers lack the bargaining power to negotiate more favorable contractual terms and farmgate prices. The reputation and credibility of the cotton cluster system suffers from a lack of transparency.[65] The rapid expansion of supermarkets in urban areas and the development of the restaurant and catering sector requires that farmers should be at an advantage in contractual settings with bigger retailing chains. One solution could come from setting up an influential organization that can defend and present the interests of farmers. Currently, they do not have independent organizations to advocate their interests or collectively negotiate

64 GBD 2017 Diet Collaborators. 2019. Health Effects of Dietary Risks in 195 Countries, 1990–2017: A Systematic Analysis for the Global Burden of Disease Study 2017. *The Lancet*. 393 (10184). pp. 1958–1972.

65 K. Lasslett, U. Niyazova, and D. Stanczak. 2020. *Out of the Cauldron, into the Fire? Risk and the Privatisation of Uzbekistan's Cotton Sector*. Uzbek Forum for Human Rights and Ulster University.

for more favorable conditions. The Council of Individual Farms, *Dekhqan* Farms, and Household Plot Owners is responsible for monitoring and exercising public supervision over the execution of contractual responsibilities of agricultural producers rather than truly representing farmers' interests.

(iii) **Abolish land allocations.** The government and cotton-textile clusters should not impose production targets on farmers, such as setting minimum yields on the basis of land quality. Along with freedom to farm, abolishing crop allocation and production targets will allow farmers to diversify their crop portfolio, which will help reduce agriculture's vulnerability to climate change. Terminating land lease contracts should not be contingent on achieving any form of output goals by farmers.

(iv) **Support to smallholders.** Well-being of smallholders increases when access to land, financing, and training are tailored to their needs. Capacity-building programs focusing on technical and business skills, technological research, and demonstrations of high-yielding crop varieties, livestock breeds, veterinary services, and fertilizer applications can contribute to the modernization of smallholders and support their growth. Improving the public sector's responsiveness to the needs of smallholders will be crucial for creating more sustainable and inclusive development.

(v) **Alternative agricultural input and service channels.** Because agricultural services such as water, machinery, know-how, and marketing options, are largely centralized within cotton cluster systems, it is crucial to establish alternative channels to improve farmers' access to commercial inputs and credit outside of farmers' contracts with cotton clusters. Alternative service channels will be particularly important for smallholders and farmers producing noncotton crops.

(vi) **Reallocation of public subsidies.** Rather than sharply increasing overall spending on agriculture, the primary objective of public funding for the sector should be to support high-quality, high-impact initiatives to increase climate-resilient production over the long run. Support for traditional, energy-intensive irrigation systems and subsidized credit for growing cotton and wheat continue to dominate public spending on agriculture, while spending on education, research and advisory services, and other general support services programs remains low. Subsidies should be redirected toward the supply of public goods and to improve the delivery of services, such as land registers and advisory services, as well as enhancing agricultural research and extension capacities. This will require better monitoring of the use of public funds to increase the efficiency and impact of existing public assistance programs in agriculture. Smallholders should also get a greater share of available funds.

(vii) **Voluntary agricultural cooperatives.** The government should focus on creating an environment that favors collective action and local self-help initiatives among farmers. Trust in government-directed collective action is being lost because of the rapid proliferation of monopolistic cotton clusters and the top-down introduction of cooperatives without the consent and voluntary participation of farmers.[66] Inclusive agricultural services cooperatives might help the smallholders in particular to reach new markets and improve their bargaining power. These cooperatives could promote shared equipment, machinery services, irrigation water, output marketing, financing, and input access.[67]

66 D. Niyazmetov, I. Soliev, and I. Theesfeld. 2021. Ordered to Volunteer? Institutional Compatibility Assessment of Establishing Agricultural Cooperatives in Uzbekistan. *Land Use Policy*. 108.

67 N. Djanibekov and A. Wolz. 2014. Development Problems in Central Asia: The Example of Agricultural Service Cooperatives. *IAMO Annual 17*. Leibniz Institute of Agricultural Development in Transition Economies.

(viii) **Promote horticultural exports.** The government should establish an environment conducive to the greater production and exports of horticultural products by addressing the sector's most significant constraints, such as investments in food safety, quality control systems, research and development, and supporting export promotion in fast-growing markets in Asia and Europe. Expanding horticulture will depend on a conducive environment for private investments in cold chain and storage systems, and postharvest processing.

(ix) **Rural nonfarm economy.** Increasing rural incomes and employment through agricultural reforms will need actions beyond the sector. Private investment in upstream and downstream businesses, as well as private intermediation with export markets, has the potential to generate new rural employment and expand government revenue. A significant transformation of agriculture will require reforms that revitalize the rural nonfarm economy.

(x) **Evidence-based policy making.** The absence of high-quality and frequently collected data remains one of the biggest obstacles to be able to fairly assess the effects of recent agricultural reforms. The design of agricultural policies, such as state support schemes, often relies on subjective expert opinions and political interests. Priority should therefore be given to ensuring the timely availability of data for analysis and policy design—not just about production sectors but also for other levels of the chain, such as rural incomes, expenditure and consumption, employment, and processing and exports. Given the debate over the best approach to direct support programs for farms, an evidence-based system will contribute to the more efficient use of agricultural subsidy schemes.

(xi) **Piloting new policies.** The positive benefits of these suggested reforms should be tested and proved in pilot districts. Implementing reforms experimentally through pilots will allow policy makers to rigorously assess available options and select successful ones for nationwide implementation. Experimenting with historically unprecedented changes will allow for the less costly testing of policy reforms as well as abandoning less efficient initiatives through experiments.

CHAPTER 4

Private Sector Development, Privatization, and Access to Finance

Begzod M. Djalilov, Adham Kuchkarov, Ajay Bhandoola, and Elbek Rikhsiyev

Introduction

Uzbekistan embarked on reforms beginning 2017 with its first National Development Strategy (NDS), 2017–2021.[1] The overarching goal of the national economic reforms was to transform from a state-controlled to a market economy by expanding the private sector's role. The reforms created an enabling environment for private investments and influx of development finance into the country. Uzbekistan improved its score in the Ease of Doing Business from a score of 61.7 in 2016 to 69.9 in 2020.[2] Implementation of the first NDS yielded immediate results—currency convertibility; sequenced price and market liberalization in wheat, cotton, and energy; streamlined procedures of setting up new business; and increased transparency in legislation governing entrepreneurship. In addition, in 2017–2022, the reforms to create an enabling environment for the private sector had yielded tangible outcomes:

(i) A notification system was established replacing 33 types of licensing and permits.
(ii) The number of taxes was reduced from 16 to 9.
(iii) The number of tax audits dropped from 13 to 3.
(iv) Value-added tax declined from 20.0% to 12.0%.
(v) The social tax rate decreased from 25.0% to 12.0%.
(vi) Import customs duties payment for about 3,500 goods and excise tax on about 1,100 goods were abolished.
(vii) Import customs duties were substantially reduced for over 3,000 goods.

1 Government of Uzbekistan. 2017. *National Development Strategy of Uzbekistan, 2017–2021* (accessed 4 December 2023). In particular, (i) governance and public administration covers improvements to e-government services and the quality and efficiency of public services; (ii) rule of law and judicial system covers stronger independence of the judiciary, and guaranteed protection of the rights and freedoms of citizens; (iii) economic development covers liberalization, competitiveness, and modernization; intensive development of agriculture; institutional and structural reforms to reduce the state's presence in the economy; further strengthening of private ownership, small businesses, and private entrepreneurship; socioeconomic development of the regions; and attraction of foreign direct investment by improving the investment climate; (iv) social development covers improved social protection and health care, women's social and political activity, affordable housing, transport system, education, culture, and the state youth policy; and (v) security, tolerance, and foreign policy covers stronger sovereignty of the state, creation of a security belt around Uzbekistan, and promotion of interethnic harmony and religious tolerance.

2 World Bank. 2020. *Doing Business Archive* (accessed 4 December 2023). In 2021, the World Bank discontinued the Ease of Doing Business Report.

With the completion of the first NDS, Uzbekistan adopted the second NDS for 2022 to 2026,[3] which prioritizes (i) human capital development, (ii) prosperity through sustainable economic growth, (iii) water saving and environmental protection, (iv) rule of law and people-oriented governance, and (v) pursuit of secure and peaceful country policy. Sustainable economic growth is to be pursued through the continuation of structural reforms with focus on further liberalizing the economy and expanding the role of the private sector.

This chapter discusses private sector participation in the economy, state-owned enterprises (SOEs), privatization, and small and medium-sized enterprises. It highlights cross-cutting areas—gender and financial inclusion, digital economy and private sector, and access to finance—relevant to private sector development in Uzbekistan.

Private Sector Participation

The Government of Uzbekistan aims to foster private sector participation by (i) expanding public–private partnership (PPP) agreements to $14 billion; (ii) increasing the trade volume in stock market to $7 billion; and (iii) divesting state assets amounting to $100 billion, including SOEs and state-owned banks (SOBs) until 2026.[4] Energy infrastructure leads in attracting private sector through PPPs. In 2021, private participation in Uzbekistan's infrastructure was the second-highest in the world (Figure 4.1).

Figure 4.1: Private Participation in Infrastructure, 2021
(% of gross domestic product)

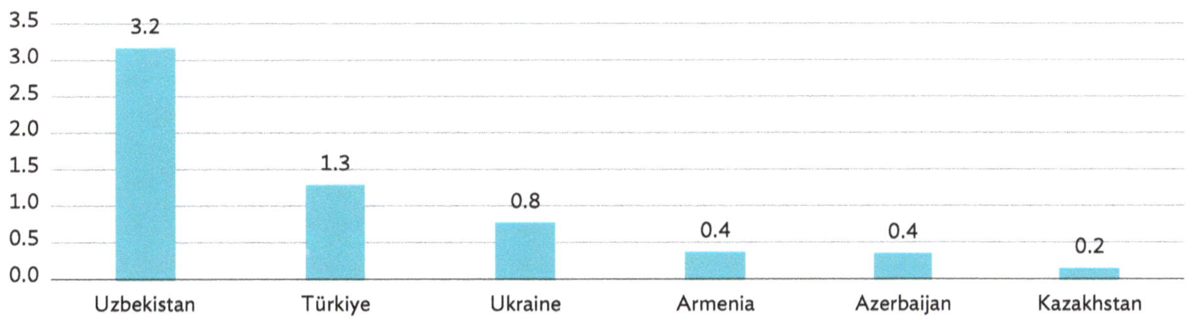

Source: World Bank. 2021. Private Participation in Infrastructure (PPI): 2021 Annual Report (accessed 4 December 2023).

In 2022, PPP transactions, including projects at post-contract award stage, contract signing stage, and tender stage, amounted to about $12.5 billion with regulatory and other measures. Energy is the largest focus of PPP at $12 billion, out of which 65% are renewables. This is followed by $5 billion in transport projects mainly for road and airports to build trade and tourism infrastructure.

3 Government of Uzbekistan. 2023. *National Development Strategy of Uzbekistan, 2030* (accessed 4 December 2023).

4 Government of Uzbekistan. 2022. *Presidential Decree No. 60. About Development Strategy of New Uzbekistan for 2022-2026* (accessed 4 December 2023).

The key issues in expanding PPPs in Uzbekistan are as follows:

(i) **Process.** There are two different views on how to do PPP: the new way of proper bidding that takes time and follows process; and direct negotiation mechanism, which is quicker, sometimes more expensive, but usually comes with financing. The direct negotiation mechanism is what has been used historically for the government and SOE projects as it usually comes with an associated Export Credit Agency financing. There are justifications for both approaches. For example, there was a need to rapidly build infrastructure for Samarkand for a series of high-level conferences that were to be held in 2022. Whichever approach is taken, there should be transparency in the process.

(ii) **Project finance expertise.** The Public–Private Partnership Development Agency was operating at 20% less than its approved number of staff at the time of interviews in 2023. Nearly all of the initial team of trained experts had left the agency and joined financial institutions. In banks, however, there was limited project finance capacity and nearly all PPP financing came from international banks. There is a need to train a number of PPP and project finance specialists if the government's targets in increasing PPPs are to be met. Retention mechanisms should also be put in place.

The stock market had an estimated capitalization amounting to $200 million in 2022. The government authorities had conducted preparatory works to develop the stock market infrastructure, set up regulations, and ease trading, including providing transparency for intial public offering (IPO) listings. To develop domestic investors through the People's IPO program, three IPOs of UzAuto, UzMetKombinat, and Qishloq Qurilish Bank were selected. However, there was limited success from the first UzAuto IPO due to perceived high pricing and pricing policies, for example, in bidding. While this is a standard practice in more developed markets, the Tashkent Stock Exchange is yet at an early stage of development.

There is limited investor appetite domestically and internationally as it is a very nascent market and will take some time and a track record for interest. This is well demonstrated by the UzAuto IPO, which is a well-known brand and of relatively higher interest; however, the dates of the UzAuto IPO was moved three times due to limited interest before finally being held in February 2023. UzAuto had hoped to sell at least 5% of its shares during the initial offering but sold merely 0.29% of its shares. The company raised about $5 million instead of $90 million that it had hoped for. The key issue was pricing and a lack of domestic investor appetite.

To develop the stock market, in addition to investor sentiment and experience, the following areas require attention:

(i) There is limited information technology infrastructure, which is necessary for quick settlements and a number of other areas. Some of the payment mechanisms should be through the central bank, not a commercial bank. While there is good legislation for investor protection and repatriation, best international practices—for example, more independent directors—in corporate governance should be adopted.
(ii) There is a need for international global custody and clearing companies, as this is a base requirement for many international investors.

(iii) To foster investor appetite and confidence in regulations and the performance of companies in the stock market, the companies need to have good governance and be financially sustainable to offer a chance for a good return for investors. To achieve investor gains, there is a need to initially price assets at attractive rates.

Divestment of Public Assets

Uzbekistan has had effective privatization cases, the acquisition of Ipoteka Bank by the OTP Group of Hungary in 2023 being a good example. This transaction is expected to transform Ipoteka Bank and make a significant change to the market as OTP Group are international experts especially in retail banking (Box 4.1).

Box 4.1: Privatization Case Study in Uzbekistan

In Uzbekistan, state-owned banks (SOBs) account for nearly 80% of total banking assets and serve to allocate directed credit. The dominance of SOBs has contributed to the low level of financial intermediation, meager profitability, market distortions, and operational inefficiencies, necessitating broad structural reforms to operate on commercial terms and free from political influence. At the request of the Government of Uzbekistan in 2017, the International Finance Corporation (IFC) embarked on a comprehensive advisory project to prepare Ipoteka Bank, the country's fifth largest with a market share of 10% and a wide network throughout the country, for privatization. In its approach, IFC leveraged the World Bank Group's experience in state-owned enterprise (SOE) transformation and privatization support, and the World Bank's regulatory and sectoral work in the banking sector of Uzbekistan, development of a banking strategy, as well as corporate governance reforms. The ambitious Ipoteka Bank institutional transformation project was delivered over 5 years in three phases: (i) establishing commercial banking foundations, (ii) business model and implementation support, and (iii) finetuning the transformed institution and ensuring its capacity for profitable and sustainable operations.

In December 2022, IFC and the government witnessed the successful signing of a long-awaited landmark privatization deal between Ipoteka Bank and a leading Central and Eastern European banking group. The privatization deal was the first for the Uzbek banking sector and was expected to serve as a demonstration effect for other SOBs that are planning similar privatization. This project was a key step toward a more efficient, inclusive, and transparent banking sector—a critical enabling factor for transitioning to a market-oriented economy.

Based on discussions with key members of the IFC Transformation Team—Ipoteka Bank management and staff, consultants, and government entities that have been involved in the transformation since 2017—the following were the key success factors for Ipoteka:

- **Governance, risk, and strengthened support functions.** Ipoteka Bank developed and adopted modern corporate governance policies and was the first and only bank in Uzbekistan with majority independent board and an independent chairman. The other successful important achievements were strengthened risk management, improved channel productivity, a transformed human resources, and a bold transition from a product-centric to a client-centric model.

- **Commercial business pivot.** Ipoteka Bank revamped its business model by diversifying away from the corporate segment composed of a few large SOEs, to retail and small business lending, which was a crucial part of the bank's strategy.

- **Reskilling staff.** By a combination of retraining existing staff and attracting new staff, the capabilities of Ipoteka Bank were enhanced.

- **Attracting investment.** As a result of the transformation, Ipoteka Bank raised $300 million funding through a successful Eurobond issuance and attracted investments from international financial institutions.

Source: Asian Development Bank (Central and West Asia Department).

In preparing for the divestment of public assets to attract strategic investors for privatization, three main considerations are required:

(i) **Attractive macroeconomic environment and investor protection.** Uzbekistan has a stable high economic growth, and investor protection laws have been put in place.

(ii) **Making the company investor-ready.** In addition to legal issues, the following need to be addressed:
(a) **Governance.** Have a strong board and independent directors, ideally an independent chairperson.
(b) **Business plan.** Address the move from the earlier capital allocation and price-fixing era to a competitive business environment, ideally using technology.
(c) **Management.** Investors may bring in a few strategic management players such as the chief executive officer or chief financial officer, but the company itself needs to have enough local management to effectively manage the company.
There may be plans in place for a bank that also receives advice from international financial institutions; however, the sale proceeds for the bank might be less than 10% of the total amount needed for the ideal target of $100 billion. To achieve this target, similar to Ipoteka Bank, a focused plan is needed for each SOE identified for sale. Consideration should be given to engaging special transformation consultants who are available on the market and can work with the companies to make them ready for investors.

(iii) **Targeted sale process.** The final part of the divestment is to address the sale process and attract international investment bankers and financial advisors to Uzbekistan to be able to work with each of the companies to start targetting strategic industry buyers. The best investment banking firms have a sound due diligence process for company and the owners, in this case the government. Some of the investment banks need to obtain special approvals to work in the Commonwealth of Independent States due to the geopolitical challenges. Their due diligence can be addressed through a structured and proactive process of inviting them to participate. This will benefit the SOEs by getting the best investment bankers who can then find the best long-term strategic buyers.

Aside from Ipoteka Bank, four other banks, namely, SQB (Industrial and Construction Bank), Asaka Bank, Aloqa Bank, and Turon Bank are to be privatized with the assistance of international financial institutions. They are undergoing transformation on multiple levels to make them more attractive for investors and are being transformed from traditional SOBs to commercial market-oriented banks with strong governance, risk, and business practices. Ipoteka Bank was the first successful transaction, when OTP Bank of Hungary acquired 100% of the state stake in January 2023. As for IPOs, Xalq Bank, Microcreditbank, Aloqa Bank, and the National Bank of Uzbekistan are potential IPO candidates in 2024 and 2025.

State-Owned Enterprises

In Uzbekistan, SOEs dominate the major sectors, combining regulatory, operational, and social protection functions.[5] The government has granted SOEs preferential treatment in accessing markets, government guarantees, tax and customs benefits, low input prices, and concessional or directed loans through SOBs, while private sector firms remained subject to tax and regulatory burdens.[6] Nearly 3,000 SOEs in Uzbekistan accounted for a half of the country's gross domestic product (GDP), about 36.0% of budget revenues, 18.0% of employment, and 20.0% of exports in 2020.

Bertelsmann Stiftung transformation index ranked Uzbekistan behind its peers in effectiveness of antimonopoly policies.[7] The banking sector is concentrated and dominated by 12 SOBs out of 33 commercial banks, accounting for 80.0% of capital and assets, 85.0% of total credit, and 65.0% of deposits in 2022. The government began reducing directed lending in 2019. Prior to this change, SOBs' credit to SOEs at below-market rates represented more than 50.0% of loans, crowding out private sector financing. Subsidized lending by SOBs is available for social programs, but their performance evaluation is inadequate and affects the overall profitability of state-owned banks.

State-owned enterprises, in most cases, follow national accounting standards in producing financial statements, limiting fairness and accuracy in representing SOEs' financial positions. The reforms to set an annual public debt ceiling and to disclose extrabudgetary funds in the budget have not been enough to establish a coherent framework for disclosing guarantees on SOE borrowings, contingent liabilities, budgetary subsidies, and directed lending. This trend increases fiscal risks. SOEs' corporate governance, accountability, and performance monitoring mechanisms are inadequate and inconsistent with the Organisation for Economic Co-operation and Development principles of (i) independence of supervisory boards, (ii) competitive selection of executives, (iii) compliance with International Financial Reporting Standards and international auditing standards, and (iv) risk management. In addition, women occupied only 11.0% of management positions in SOEs in 2022, reflecting limited diversity and gender parity. The quality of services and products of SOEs (public utilities) lack performance measures, inadequate investment in infrastructure, limited financial resources, and weak institutional capacity, leading to deterioration. For instance, Uzsuvtaminot, which is a state-owned water utility company, has been providing services below full cost, leading to financial losses and dependence on government subsidies. Other public utilities and service-oriented SOEs such as Uzbekiston Pochtasi (postal services company) and Toshshahartransxizmat (transport company) require transformation to enhance their performance.

5 Asian Development Bank (ADB). 2023. Uzbekistan: Economic Management Improvement Program, Subprogram 2 (accessed 4 December 2023).

6 E. Ramirez Rigo et al. 2021. State-Owned Enterprises in Middle East, North Africa, and Central Asia: Size, Role, Performance, and Challenges. Middle East and Central Asia Departmental Paper Series. International Monetary Fund (accessed 4 December 2023).

7 World Bank. 2022. Toward a Prosperous and Inclusive Future: The Second Systematic Country Diagnostic for Uzbekistan (accessed 4 December 2023).

To expedite the transformation and privatization of SOEs, the government set up the State Assets Management Agency in 2019. The Anti-Monopoly Committee was established to promote competition and nondiscriminatory access to markets, unbundle integrated monopolies, and increase regulatory and enforcement powers. With the transformation strategy for 2021–2025, SOEs and SOBs are required to (i) have independent supervisory board members, (ii) comply with the International Financial Reporting Standards for audited financial statements, and (iii) implement key performance indicators and modern corporate governance standards. Similarly, with the banking sector reform strategy for 2020–2025, SOBs are required to improve their performance and reduce ownership of banking assets from 85.0% in 2019 to 40.0% by 2025. A few SOBs—Agrobank and Xalq Bank (People's Bank)—are kept for state programs. Compounded with the state property management law and privatization law approved in 2022, the government targets expediting SOEs' equity offerings via local capital markets.

Privatization

The government has taken a gradual and prudent approach in privatizing state assets. In the past, small assets, including land and properties, were frequently privatized compared to the slow privatization of large assets. In 2022, the government scoped the state assets for more intensified privatization using streamlined criteria in selecting state assets for privatization.[8] Two approaches in privatization were taken:

(i) **Direct privatization.** To ensure transparency in privatization of small assets not exceeding $10 million, an electronic auction platform is used. Privatization of larger assets, however, warranted a more strategic approach by SOEs and associated regulating ministries to source investment partners, including foreign direct investors. Partnering with strategic investors can ensure sustaining growth of privatized companies. International financial institutions such as IFC were contracted as an advisor to prepare for privatization, as when IFC advised the government on the privatization of petrochemical company Ferghanaazot.

(i) **Initial public offerings.** The government identified 21 IPOs to be introduced to the stock market in 2022–2023 (Table 4.1). Authorities undertook measures to ready the stock market for the sale. There is a need for similar readiness from companies, and education of domestic and international markets to move the market capitalization of $200 million in 2022 to $7 billion by 2026. Companies also need to improve governance and competitiveness, which are both critical aspects in for success in privatization.

8 Government of Uzbekistan. 2022. *Presidential Decree 168 On Additional Measures to Further Reduction of State Participation in the Economy and Expediating Privatization* (accessed 4 December 2023).

Table 4.1: Initial Public Offerings of Selected State-Owned Enterprises

1.	Agrobank ATB	12.	Universal Insurance JSC
2.	Alskom JSC	13.	Uzagrosugurta JSC
3.	Dori-Darmon AJ	14.	Uzauto Motors JSC
4.	Halq Bank JSC	15.	Uzavtosanoat JSC
5.	JSC Uzbekistan Post	16.	Uzbekgeofizika JSC
6.	JSC Alokabank	17.	Uzbekinvest JSC
7.	Kurilishmashleasing JSC	18.	Uzbekistan Airways JSC
8.	Microcreditbank ATB	19.	Uzbekneftgaz JSC
9.	National Bank of Uzbekistan JSC	20.	Uzmetkombinat JSC
10.	O'ztemiryo'lkonteyner AJ	21.	Uztransgaz JSC
11.	Qishloq Qurilish Bank ATB		

JSC = joint stock company.
Source: Government of Uzbekistan. 2022. Resolution of the Cabinet of Ministers No. 446 About Initial and Secondary Public Offerings of Large State-owned Enterprises in Stock Market (accessed 4 December 2023).

Corporate governance reforms comprise two elements:

(i) **Management boards.** While theoretically there should be separation of SOEs from the government, in Uzbekistan, the SOE management board is composed of senior government officials. The board chairmen in large SOEs are, in most cases, with the rank of Minister or First Deputy Minister. There are numerous staff movements between the government and SOEs; hence, the management of SOEs is not composed of professional managers or industry experts. The focus is on bureaucracy and administration rather than business and innovation because of limited industry knowledge. There has also been more focus on KPIs, which are tracked with business plans that determine the variable remuneration. However, the quality and monitoring of the KPIs are uncertain. The long-term success of management boards is determined by market forces, which will come after privatization.

(ii) **Supervisory boards.** While there are regulations on independent directors and some good examples of implementation of independent directors, there is no penalty nor reward for compliance. This leads to sporadic implementation and often no autonomy for the Supervisory Board. It is common for senior government officials to occupy the positions of directors without relevant skills or training. While there is some training on good environmental, social, and governance practices and a few SOEs have independent directors, greater improvement is warranted.

Several SOEs have preferential access to resources such as energy, subsidized funding, and other market subsidies without which the basic competitiveness of these SOEs may be questionable. A few SOEs are virtual monopolies and do not have experience in managing competition. Although some sectors are changing, notably the financial sector, there is still a need to create a more market-driven approach to create a vibrant private sector.

The government supports small and medium-sized enterprises (SMEs) through policy measures. The contribution of SMEs to the economy is expanding. In 2017–2023, the number of SMEs surged from 225,635 to 523,600. In 2019–2020, SMEs accounted for 54.0% of GDP, which declined briefly to 52.0% in 2022 due to firm closures caused by the coronavirus disease (COVID-19) pandemic.[9] However, as of March 2023, these enterprises still accounted for over a half of Uzbekistan's GDP and employed almost 80.0% of the workforce. In 2022, 97.0% of all firms in agriculture and 75.0% in construction were SMEs, while the most significant sectoral shares of newly registered SMEs in the first half of 2022 were trade (37.0%) and industry (19.0%), indicating a positive trend of firm growth in higher-productivity, export-oriented sectors. In 2022, SMEs' share of investments was 48.0% concentrated in the Tashkent and Samarkand regions.

The NDS 2030 continues the direction of reforms implemented during 2017–2021, with a focus on improving the business environment through free market mechanisms, ensuring healthy competition and the inviolability of private property, and supporting entrepreneurship. In 2021, SMEs accounted for 20.0% of exports and 45.0% of imports. However, in 2022, the share of SMEs in exports increased to 30.0%, while their share in imports rose to 49.0%. The SMEs play a critical role in achieving the Sustainable Development Goals (SDGs), particularly SDG 8 (decent work and economic growth) and SDG 9 (industry, innovation, and infrastructure).

During 2017–2021, structural reforms were implemented to support entrepreneurship in Uzbekistan. These reforms included simplifying business registration, reducing unnecessary regulation of business activities, streamlining and reducing taxes, establishing industry clusters and zones, providing targeted subsidies, eliminating customs duties for all exported goods and services, reducing customs fees for certain imported goods, simplifying the licensing system and export procedures, and reducing the number of state-owned enterprises. Despite these wide-ranging reforms, SMEs in Uzbekistan still face several constraints that impede their growth, productivity, and competitiveness, and the creation of diversified and higher value-added jobs. These constraints include a lack of diversified financing sources and instruments, a bank-dominated financial sector and its reliance on collateral-based lending, institutional barriers, lack of a strategic approach to SME development, low financial literacy and financial management skills, low digitalization, and insufficient technical human capital.

Uzbekistan's financial sector is dominated by banks, with the top five controlling about 70.0% of banking system assets as of 2023. The financial market is still in its early stages, with fragmented regulatory infrastructure and all market segments lacking depth and liquidity. The SMEs are constrained in accessing finance. State-owned banks mostly channel funds from the government to priority sectors and SOEs at below-market rates. This has constrained the availability of commercial financing for the private sector, including SMEs and individuals.

9 ADB. 2023. *Uzbekistan: Small and Medium-Sized Enterprises Development Program (Subprogram 1)*. Forthcoming.

In addition, banks have limited product innovation, particularly for SMEs' requirements. The lack of hard collateral in a still collateral-dominated bank lending system, lack of credit history, and high informality of microenterprises and SMEs further limit SMEs' access to formal bank credit. Commercial banks provide microcredit at concessional rates but have high collateral and documentation requirements and provide only noncash credit, e.g., letters of credit. Microcredit organizations offer simplified processing and cash credit without collateral but their maximum loan size is small. Leasing as an alternative source of SME finance is limited, partly because leasing firms lack long-term funding, and many potential customers are unaware of how leasing works and its potential benefits. Reforms in the legislative and regulatory framework are being made to enable nonbank finance and capital market financing. An ecosystem for venture capital is also being developed to open equity financing for SMEs. Major banking sector reforms are currently underway, aimed at restructuring and privatizing the largest state-owned banks. The limited financial reporting and financial management skills of SMEs continue to constrain the role of financial markets in supporting SME investment and productivity.

The State Fund for Support of Entrepreneurship Development supports SMEs through partial credit guarantees and interest rate subsidies on loans. The fund has recently undergone governance reforms, including the establishment of a new organizational structure with a Management Council consisting of at least seven board members, including three independent board members; and the operationalization of an audit committee, risk management committee, and internal audit service. Additionally, a risk analysis and monitoring and evaluation department has been established. These reforms, along with the transformation of the fund into a joint-stock company to enable capital contributions by nongovernment entities, aim to support sustainable business expansion.[10]

Eastern Europe and Central Asia had the second-lowest percentage finance gap after Latin America in 2016.[11] Within Central Asia, Uzbekistan is among the countries with the lowest finance gap (Table 4.2). Implementation by SOBs of state programs to support SME development with available state finance was the key reason for the lower finance gap (Table 4.3). However, nonperforming loans (NPLs) in state financing programs are higher than in the lending programs to larger enterprises. This trend illustrates a need to revamp the state programs to ensure the sustainability of SOBs and state programs.

Table 4.2: Micro, Small, and Medium-Sized Enterprises Financing Gap Among Central Asian Countries, 2016

Country	Number of MSMEs	Current Supply	MSME Finance Gap	MSME Finance Gap/GDP (%)
Uzbekistan	95,231	1,732,099,219	11,789,541,678	18
Kazakhstan	1,290,000	9,509,760,067	47,071,024,239	26
Kyrgyz Republic	298,500	91,889,281	1,403,743,130	21
Tajikistan	155,291	239,528,518	1,451,766,421	18

GDP = gross domestic product; MSMEs = micro, small, and medium-sized enterprises.
Source: World Bank. 2017. MSME Finance Gap 2017 (accessed 4 December 2023).

10 As of September 2023, the State Fund's capital was SUM346 billion, and its liabilities were SUM5.2 trillion. From the beginning of its operations in 2017 to 1 March 2023, the State Fund has issued 13,039 guarantees totaling SUM10.5 trillion. The total amount of loans issued by partner banks amounted to SUM26.7 trillion (leverage of 1:20).

11 World Bank. 2017. MSME Finance Gap 2017 (accessed 4 December 2023).

Table 4.3: Commercial Banks' Credit to Micro, Small, and Medium-Sized Enterprises in Uzbekistan
(SUM billion)

2020	2021	2022
48,389	59,552	69,770

Source: Central Bank of Uzbekistan. 2023. Statistical Bulletin, January–December 2022.

In addition to access to finance, international financial institutions such as the Asian Development Bank (ADB) help Uzbekistan with SME programs to streamline regulatory, policy, and institutional frameworks; diversify formal financial instruments; ease barriers to trade and competitiveness; increase digitalization; and align skills development with market needs.

Financial Inclusion

Gender

In Uzbekistan, businesses owned by women grew by 79% in 2017–2022 (Figure 4.2). Women had stable access to credit, averaging 67% of total women having access to credit, up by 2 percentage points of men's share accessing credit resources for the same period.[12]

Figure 4.2: Share of Businesses Owned by Women in Total Business Entities in Uzbekistan
(%)

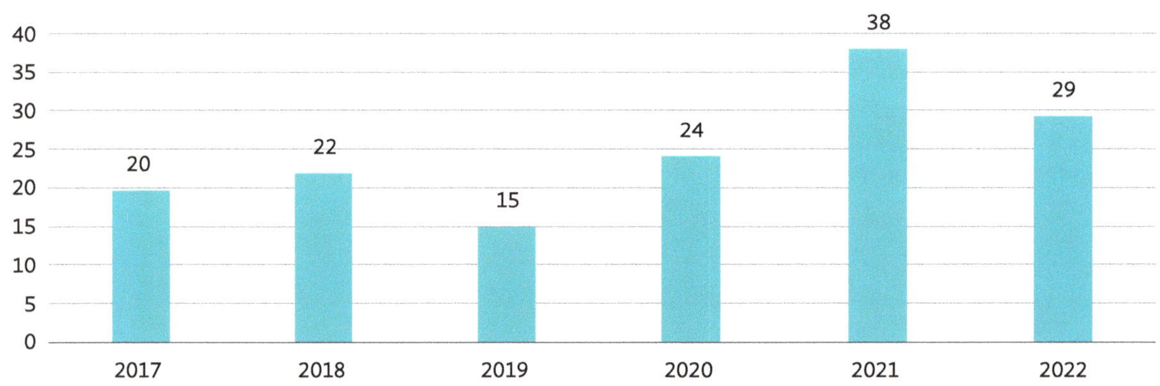

Source: Statistics Agency under the President of the Republic of Uzbekistan. 2023 Gender Statistics: Economic Resources (accessed 4 December 2023).

Uzbekistan adopted its first National Financial Inclusion Strategy (NFIS) 2021–2023 in June 2021.[13] ADB supports the development of a new NFIS for 2025-2030 through the Inclusive Finance Sector Development Program. The NFIS provides a comprehensive approach to improving financial inclusion. It defines national financial inclusion objectives, identifies a prioritized set of actions to achieve those objectives, and outlines the main opportunities and obstacles that policymakers should consider during implementation. The NFIS focuses on five main policy areas for reform actions: basic financial services, access to finance for SMEs, digital financial services, financial consumer protection, and financial literacy.

12 Statistics Agency under the President of the Republic of Uzbekistan. 2023. Gender Statistics: Economic Resources (accessed 4 December 2023).

13 World Bank. 2023. From Livestock to Lifelong Savings: Improving Financial Inclusion in Uzbekistan (accessed 4 December 2023)

The NFIS is consistent with Uzbekistan's gender equality policy. The medium-term priorities in gender equality are as follows:[14]

(i) Create an atmosphere of intolerance toward oppression and violence against women.
(ii) Ensure women's rights and legitimate interests.
(iii) Assist women with job placement, support their entrepreneurial activity, and identify talented young women for focused career development.
(iv) Continue policies directed at gender equality by increasing the social and political activity of women.
(v) Establish systemic measures to provide housing for women in need of housing, improve living and working conditions, and increase income.
(vi) Provide socio-legal assistance, psychological assistance in difficult social situations, and targeted support to women.
(vii) Foster women's participation in the economy and social protection.

Uzbekistan is advanced in digital infrastructure. In 2021–2022, 14 e-wallets were registered and 47 payment systems were operational. There are instant, high-value, and low-value payment systems, and there is no manual physical check payment system. The amount of physical cash in the economy has declined and the number of digital banking users has increased (Figure 4.3). UzCard is one of the most successful products providing SMEs with access to the banking system and alternate channels. The other popular payment applications are Click, Oson and Payme wallets, and HUMO. However, only a small proportion of Uzbekistan's population buys goods online, subscribes to services, earns cashback, and invests.

Figure 4.3: Digital Banking Users in Uzbekistan, 2018–2022

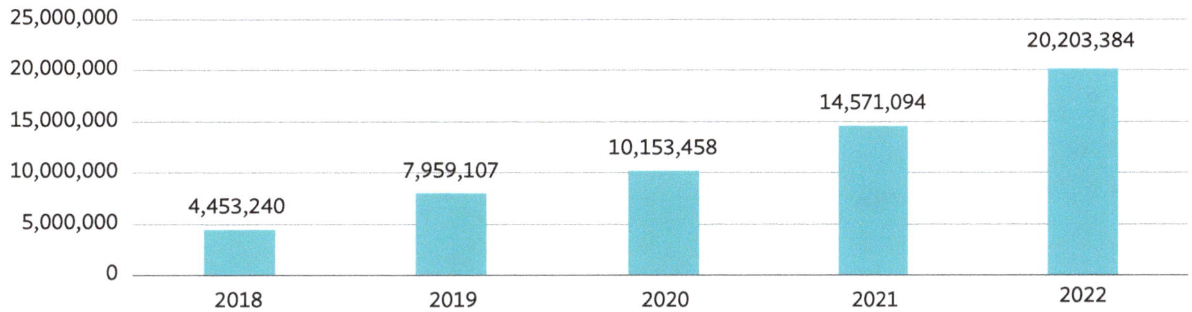

Source: Central Bank of Uzbekistan. 2023. Indicators of Payment System (accessed 4 December 2023).

The fintech startup system is underdeveloped with only 63 startups as of September 2022.[15] The main reason for the few startups is lack of funding. The startups are funded by large groups, e.g., Payme belongs to TBC Bank, where fintech is a small part of the funding and the focus is payments. There is a limited venture capital startup ecosystem and in its absence, funding is limited. The government is putting in place a sandbox and fintech association as well as several regulations to expedite the development of the fintech ecosystem.

[14] Government of Uzbekistan. 2022. Presidential Decree No. 60. About Development Strategy of New Uzbekistan for 2022–2026 (accessed 4 December 2023).
[15] V. Dobrynin. 2022. The Digital Divide and Super Apps: How Uzbek Fintech Market is Structured.

Banks

As of December 2022, the banking sector in Uzbekistan comprised 33 banks, with the 12 SOBs accounting for over 80.0% of the sector's loans. The top six largest SOBs comprised over 60.0% of loans as of December 2022.[16] The government controls over 90.0% of the shares of the SOBs via the Ministry of Economy and Finance, and various other agencies and companies (Table 4.4).

Table 4.4: Banks with State Ownership in Uzbekistan as of 2022
(%)

No.	Bank	SRA	UFRD	Others
1	JSC Agrobank	52.2	46.3	1.5
2	JSC Asakabank	10.7	88.2	1.1
3	JSC UzPromstroybank (SQB)	13.1	82.1	4.8
4	JSC Xalq Bank	22.4	77.6	0
5	JSC TuronBank	8.7	90.1	1.2
6	JSC Qishloq Qurilish Bank	74.5	23.9	1.6
7	JSC AloqaBank	3.8	75.4	20.8
8	JSC UzMilliybank (National Bank of Uzbekistan)	40.7	59.3	0
9	JSC Mikrokreditbank (MKBank)	70.8	28.2	1

JSC = joint-stock company, SRA = Strategic Reforms Agency, UFRD = Uzbekistan Fund for Reconstruction and Development.
Sources: Government of Uzbekistan. 2023. Presidential Decree No. 83 About Expediating State-owned Enterprises Reforms (accessed 4 December 2023); Statistics Agency under the President of the Republic of Uzbekistan.

Figure 4.4 shows the growth trajectory of loans of SOBs and private banks, which reflects faster growth in SOBs' loan portfolio. Among others, transfer of loans held in the Uzbekistan Fund for Reconstruction and Development to several SOEs, as well as loans and related equity to SOBs, contributed to the faster growth in SOBs' loan portfolio.

Figure 4.4: Total Loan Portfolio of Banks in Uzbekistan, 2017–2022
(SUM billon)

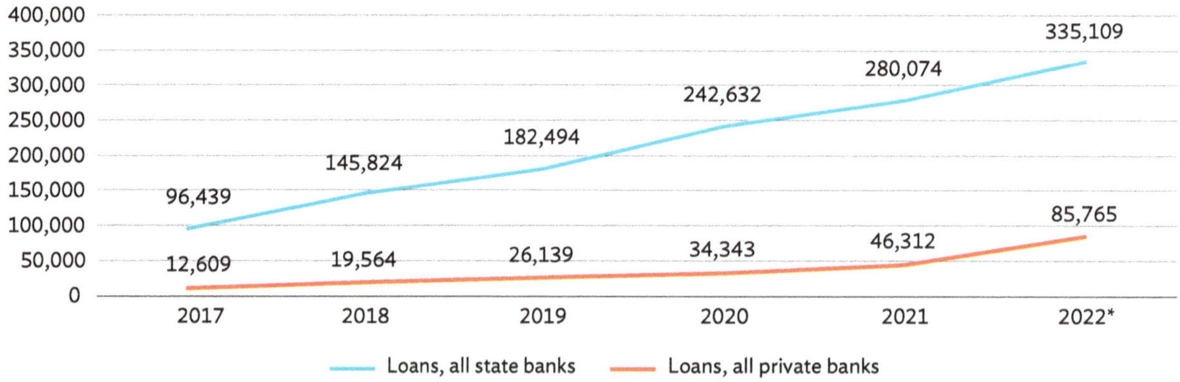

Source: Central Bank of Uzbekistan. Indicators of Banking System (accessed 4 December 2023).

[16] Central Bank of Uzbekistan. Indicators of Banking System (accessed 4 December 2023).

Returns on assets and equity, however, are lower for SOBs than private banks (Figures 4.5 and 4.6). There are two main reasons for this. One is that there are still several historic low-priced loans for state-owned companies.[17] Two, new facilities are much closer priced to market but some of the large historic loans still have lower pricing.

Figure 4.5: Return on Assets of Banks in Uzbekistan, 2017–2022
(%)

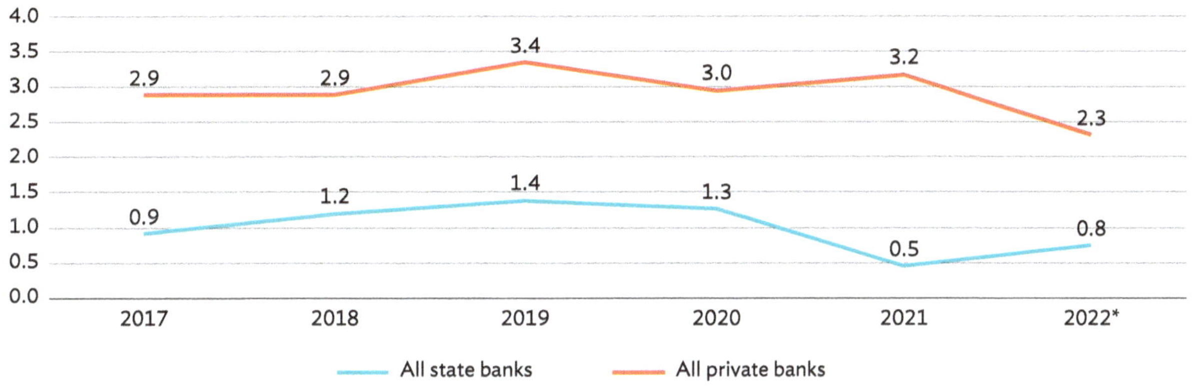

Source: Central Bank of Uzbekistan. Indicators of Banking System (accessed 4 December 2023).

Figure 4.6: Return on Equity of Banks in Uzbekistan, 2017–2022
(%)

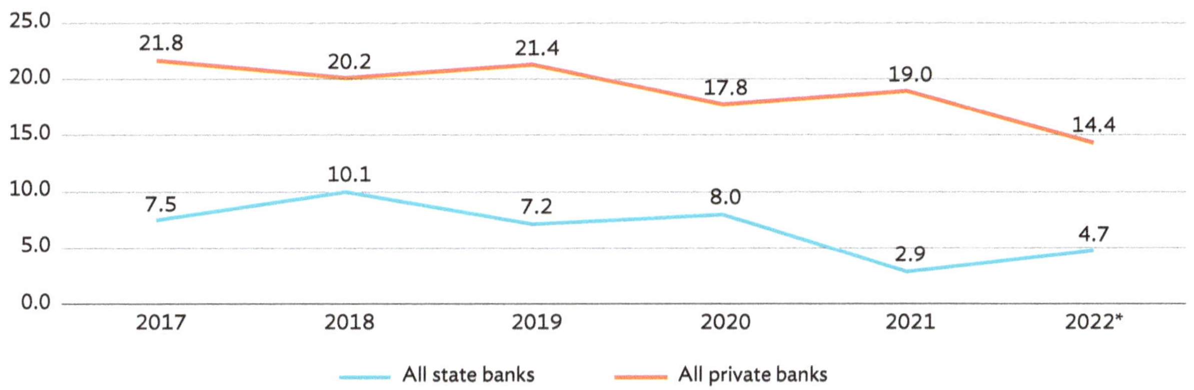

Source: Central Bank of Uzbekistan. Indicators of Banking System (accessed 4 December 2023).

The other key trend in the banking sector is the reduction in returns on assets and equity; however, this is generally attributable to NPL growth.The NPLs in the entire banking sector have increased substantially from 2018 onward (Table 4.5). Some of this it attributable to management of loans during the COVID-19 pandemic for which there was a moratorium in 2020, but the impact was felt in 2021 and partially in 2022.[18] The impact started to subside in 2022.

17 Based on discussions with bank officials and consultants.
18 Based on discussions with bank officials and consultants.

Table 4.5: Nonperforming Loans of All Banks in Uzbekistan, 2018–2022

Year	Nonperforming Loans
2018	1.2
2019	1.3
2020	2.1
2021	5.2
2022	3.6

Source: Central Bank of Uzbekistan. Indicators of Banking System (accessed 4 December 2023).

(i) **State-owned banks.** The priority policy in the banking sector is acceleration in privatization of state-owned banks. Consistent with the 2020–2025 banking sector reform strategy, the authorities target to reduce the state's role in the banking sector by expanding the share of nonstate banks in banking system assets. The strategy sets the following key self-reinforcing targets:[19]

(a) Expand the share of nonstate banks in total system assets from 15.0% in 2020 to 60.0% in 2025.
(b) Increase the share of private sector borrowers in the system loan portfolio from 28.0% in 2020 to 70.0% in 2025.
(c) The charter capital of at least three banks with state ownership must be subscribed by foreign strategic investors with required experience, knowledge, and reputation.

The expansion in banking sector assets should be achieved by attracting strategic investors to SOBs and divesting others in the stock market. The National Bank of Uzbekistan, Agrobank, and Microcreditbank will remain as SOBs as they are of strategic importance to the country to meet the needs of the population in financial services. The rest of the SOBs are expected to be privatized through IPOs or strategic investors.

(ii) **Private banks.** Private banks in Uzbekistan are small with an average equity of $61 million as of 2022, most of which serve the private sector on commercial terms. Private banks operate in a market niche with efficient operations and high profitability, and are not major players in the market segments, which are dominated by state-owned banks. Unlike SOBs, private banks fund their operations through retail deposits at higher market rates. Private banks charge market rate for loans and are more profitable than SOBs (Figures 4.5 and 4.6). They have lower NPLs and higher profitability and no obligation to participate in state programs with potentially higher NPLs. Private banks are more progressive in offering innovative solutions to their clientele. For example, TBC Bank integrated e-payment solutions by owning Payme. Meanwhile, neobanks (operating solely online) are also transforming the sector both for technology and interest rate. TBC Bank is already active and a new digital bank, Smart Bank, was granted a license in December 2022.

19 Government of Uzbekistan. 2020. Presidential Decree No. 5952 About Reforming Uzbekistan's Banking Sector, 2020–2025 (accessed 5 December 2023).

Nonbank Financial Institutions

Nonbank credit organizations consisted of microcredit organizations, leasing companies, pawnshops, and one mortgage refinancing company as of 2022. The assets of 63 microcredit organizations and 64 pawnshops are modest, equivalent to 0.3% of banking sector assets. To foster the role of nonbank financial institutions, Uzbekistan (i) set formal procedures to establish and commence nonbanking credit institutions, (ii) defined types of permitted and prohibited activities, (iii) set the legal basis for protecting the rights of consumers of microfinance institutions and pawnshops, and (iv) cleared the regulatory and supervisory system of nonbank credit institutions by adopting the law on nonbank credit organizations and microfinance activities in 2022.[20] In addition, the government aims to create an enabling environment to increase the share of nonbank financial institutions in the total volume of lending from 0.35% in 2020 to 4.0% in 2025.[21]

Uzbekistan had 47 insurance organizations in operation as of 2021 with over 6.8 million contracts, up by 15.2% from 2021.[22] The insurance penetration ratio (gross written premiums to GDP) reached 0.52% and pricing is exceptionally low for the risks covered.[23] Voluntary insurance accounted for 71.0% of total insured amount, while the rest was compulsory insurance as of 2021. The top 16 insurance products include compulsory motor insurance, compulsory employer's liability insurance, contractor's voluntary all-risk insurance, credit risk insurance, and property insurance. The life insurance sector is nascent, comprising about 10.0% of gross written premiums.

Uzbekistan's insurance sector faces several challenges. It operates under obsolete regulations and supervision, constraining the efficient management and transfer of risks, inexpensive and effective coverage, and ensured protection of insurance policy holders' rights. Insurance entities have modest penetration and institutional capacity for assessing financial risks using statistical methods, and inadequate information technology.[24] These challenges limit the insurance entities from having robust business models and having the ability to meet their long-term financial liabilities.

In terms of system reform, areas for potential policy interventions to rapidly develop Uzbekistan's insurance market with private sector participation are (i) setting up clearly defined rules and conditions for indemnity payments, (ii) increasing financial literacy, (iii) strengthening consumer protection legislation, and (iv) fostering competition by enabling resources for innovation in insurance entities' expansion of product mix and distribution channels. The insurance entities need to improve their risk management, mitigate the accumulation of high risk, and expand reinsurance. In light of climate change, incorporating climate change impact into the insurance policy portfolio will likely be a requirement in the sector.

20 Government of Uzbekistan. 2022. Law on Non-bank Credit Organizations and Microfinance Activities in Uzbekistan (accessed 5 December 2023).
21 Government of Uzbekistan. 2020. Presidential Decree No. 5952 About Reforming Uzbekistan's Banking Sector, 2020–2025 (accessed 5 December 2023).
22 Statistics Agency under the President of the Republic of Uzbekistan. 2022. Insurance Market in the Republic of Uzbekistan for 2021.
23 Based on data and interviews with Insurance companies and industry bodies.
24 World Bank. 2022. Uzbekistan Financial Sector Reform Project (accessed 5 December 2023).

CHAPTER 5

Unlocking the Productivity Potential Through Enhanced Education

Daryll Naval and Kiyoshi Taniguchi

This chapter focuses on the education aspect of human capital development in Uzbekistan. Education plays a pivotal role in nurturing human capital by imparting knowledge, developing skills, driving innovation, and fostering personal growth. Increased investment in education is needed for Uzbekistan to achieve its goal of becoming an upper-middle-income country by 2030. However, for this to happen, developing the country's human capital will be critical, and investments in this need to be long-term and cover the entire life cycle (Figure 5.1).

Figure 5.1: Human Capital Life Cycle

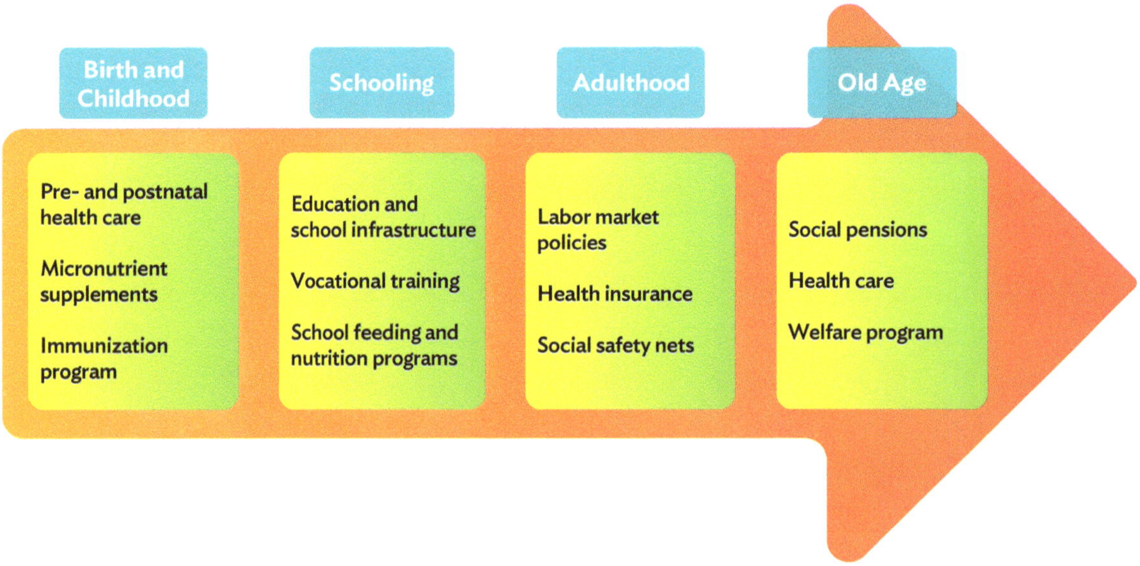

Source: Authors.

The crucial role of human capital in sustainable economic growth is well described in the literature, which emphasizes the interconnectedness of social and economic development. For instance, investments in education and human capital play a dual role in fostering long-term economic growth and reducing income inequality.[1] It is also well-documented that higher levels of education lead to

1 R. Barro. 2000. Inequality and Growth in a Panel of Countries. *Journal of Economic Growth*. 5. p. 532.

increased productivity, higher wages, and overall economic growth.[2] A landmark study analyzing historical policy changes over the past half-century in the United States shows that direct investment in health and education of children from low-income families has historically had the highest impact on social welfare because these policies paid for themselves through additional taxes and reduced transfers.[3] Beyond economics, research suggests that investments in human capital—particularly education—will be vital for enhancing climate adaptation.[4] Investments in human capital, therefore, have far-reaching effects on economic growth, societal progress, and sustainable development.

However, designing long-term human capital policies and developing suitable institutions are complex. The outcome of investments in human capital is intangible, and time lags often occur between when investments are made and the realization of their benefits. This contrasts with infrastructure investments, where project benefits are tangible and quickly realized. This is partly why significant underinvestment in human capital continues, especially in developing countries, such as Uzbekistan, which stand to gain the most from these investments.

Human Capital Opportunities and Risks

The World Bank's Human Capital Index (HCI), launched in 2018, presents a novel perspective on human capital by assessing the impact of education and health on future workforce productivity. It covers 174 countries, including Uzbekistan. The HCI measures the degree to which a child will become an effective employee by age 18 compared to a complete education and full health benchmark.[5] It has three components that quantitatively capture key life-stage outcomes: survival, school, and health.

The 2020 HCI shows that globally, children born in 2020, on average, can expect to be 56% as productive when they grow up as they could be if they complete education and full health. In Uzbekistan, this value is slightly higher at 62%. This is lower than the average for Europe and Central Asia but higher than the average for lower-middle-income economies.[6] It is interesting to note that Asian economies rank high on the HCI, with Singapore placing first with 88% followed by Hong Kong, China (81%) then Japan and the Republic of Korea (both 80%). Economies in Africa generally ranked toward the bottom, with Chad last (39%).

Table 5.1 compares the HCI and its components in Uzbekistan with countries within and outside Central and West Asia before the coronavirus disease (COVID-19) pandemic. Uzbekistan's HCI score of 0.62 is the second-highest in the region after Kazakhstan (0.63).

---

2 G. Psacharopoulos and H. Patrinos. 2018. Returns to Investment in Education: A Decennial Review of the Global Literature. *Education Economics*. 26 (5). pp. 445–458.

3 N. Henderson and B. Sprung-Keyser. 2020. *A Unified Welfare Analysis of Government Policies*. Harvard University Working Paper. Cambridge. M.A.

4 W. Lutz, R. Muttarak, and E. Striessing. 2014. Universal Education Is Key to Enhanced Climate Adaptation. *Science*. 346 (6213). pp. 1061–1062.

5 The index value ranges from 0 to 1, with a higher value indicating that today's children will be more developed and prepared for the future.

6 World Bank. 2020. *Uzbekistan: Human Capital Index 2020*.

Table 5.1: Human Capital Index in Uzbekistan and Selected Countries, 2020

Country	Survival Component		Education Component		Health Component		Human Capital Index 2020
	Probability of survival to age 5	Expected years of school	Harmonized test scores	Learning-adjusted years of school	Fraction of children under 5 not stunted	Adult survival rate	
Central and West Asia							
Armenia	0.99	11.3	443	8	0.91	0.89	0.58
Azerbaijan	0.98	12.4	416	8.3	0.82	0.88	0.58
Kazakhstan	0.99	13.7	416	9.1	0.92	0.84	0.63
Kyrgyz Republic	0.98	12.9	420	8.7	0.88	0.85	0.60
Tajikistan	0.97	10.9	391	6.8	0.82	0.87	0.50
Uzbekistan	0.98	12.0	474	9.1	0.89	0.87	0.62
Other							
China, People's Republic of	0.99	13.1	441	9.3	0.92	0.92	0.65
India	0.96	11.1	399	7.1	0.65	0.83	0.49
Indonesia	0.98	12.4	395	7.8	0.72	0.85	0.54
Philippines	0.97	12.9	362	7.5	0.7	0.82	0.52
Viet Nam	0.98	12.9	519	10.7	0.76	0.87	0.67

Note: Prepandemic scores.
Source: World Bank. 2020. Uzbekistan: Human Capital Index.

The following highlights Uzbekistan's performance on the HCI components:

(i) **Probability of survival to age 5.** Ninety-eight out of 100 infants born in Uzbekistan will survive to age 5, almost the same as the other countries in Table 5.1.

(ii) **Expected years of schooling.** Students in Uzbekistan can expect to complete 12.5 years of schooling by their 18th birthday. This is slightly lower than most of the other countries.

(iii) **Performance in harmonized test scores.** Students in Uzbekistan scored 474 (625 = advanced, 300 = minimum level of achievement). Although Uzbekistan achieved a high score on this compared to the other countries, it was behind Viet Nam (519), which scored on par with high-income Sweden, the Netherlands, and New Zealand. Given Uzbekistan's economic capabilities, this highlights the country's potential to improve its harmonized test scores.

(iv) **Learning-adjusted years of school.** Factoring in what children actually learn, the expected years of schooling in Uzbekistan is only 9.1 years, well below Viet Nam's 10.7.

(v) **Share of children under 5 not stunted.** Out of every 100 children in Uzbekistan, 89 are not stunted, but 11 are at risk of lifelong cognitive and physical limitations. This rate is similar to most other countries in Central and West Asia and slightly higher compared to the countries outside this region in Table 5.1.

(vi) **Adult survival rate.** Eighty-seven out of 100 people aged 15 and over will survive until 60, almost the same as the other countries.[7]

[7] This statistic is an indicator for the various health risks that a child born today would potentially encounter as an adult, based on existing conditions.

Figure 5.2 shows Uzbekistan's ranking on the HCI and gross domestic product (GDP) per capita in relationship to three other countries in the region. Generally, countries with high GDP per capita tend to have higher levels of human capital development, indicating a positive correlation. This is because countries with greater economic resources can spend more on education and health. Although Uzbekistan has a relatively high ranking on the HCI, its GDP per capita is below that of other countries with comparable HCI rankings, such as Kazakhstan. This could be because of time delays in realizing the full benefits of human capital investments, as it can take over 4 decades for increased investments in human capital to be fully reflected in the capabilities of the workforce.[8] Thus, over time, as Uzbekistan's workforce becomes more productive and contributes to the economy, GDP per capita is expected to gradually catch up with or surpass countries at similar HCI rankings. It is important to recognize the feedback loop between income and investments in human capital, as higher income and economic growth are expected to bring more investments in human capital. Clearly, continual investments in developing human capital will be vital for Uzbekistan's sustained economic progress.

Figure 5.2: Human Capital Index vs. Gross Domestic Product in Uzbekistan and Three Central Asian Regional Economies

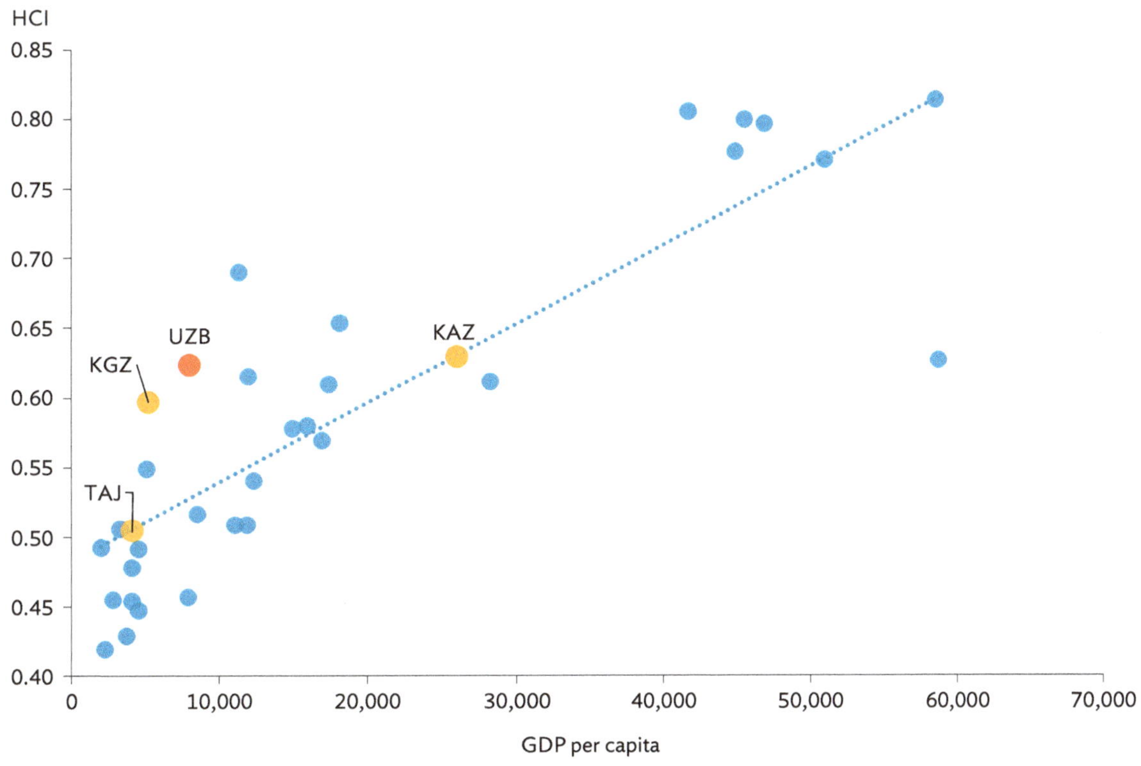

HCI = Human Capital Index, GDP = gross domestic product, KAZ = Kazakhstan, KGZ = Kyrgyz Republic, TAJ = Tajikistan, UZB = Uzbekistan.
Notes: GDP per capita in terms of purchasing power parity (constant 2017 international dollar). Not all labels on data points shown.
Sources: Values for HCI from World Bank. 2020. Human Capital Index; GDP per capita from World Bank. World Development Indicators (accessed August 2023).

8 M. Collin and D. Weil. 2018. The Effect of Increasing Human Capital Investment on Economic Growth and Poverty: A Simulation Exercise. *Policy Research Working Paper*. No. 8590. World Bank.

Reaping the Benefits of the Demographic Dividend

Uzbekistan has been in a steady demographic transition since 1990, a period that has seen a significant increase in the working-age population (15–64), from 11.6 million to 22.7 million in 2023. The rising working-age population, coupled with a declining birth rate, has led to a substantial decline in the total dependency ratio, from 78.1% to 55.1% over the period (Figure 5.3).[9] Because of this transition, Uzbekistan has reached the demographic dividend stage—a critical turning point for the country. According to the United Nations Children's Fund (UNICEF), with a larger share of the working-age population, Uzbekistan stands to gain from increased disposable income, driving greater consumption, production, and investment.[10]

Figure 5.3: Population by Age Group and Dependency Ratio in Uzbekistan, 1990–2100

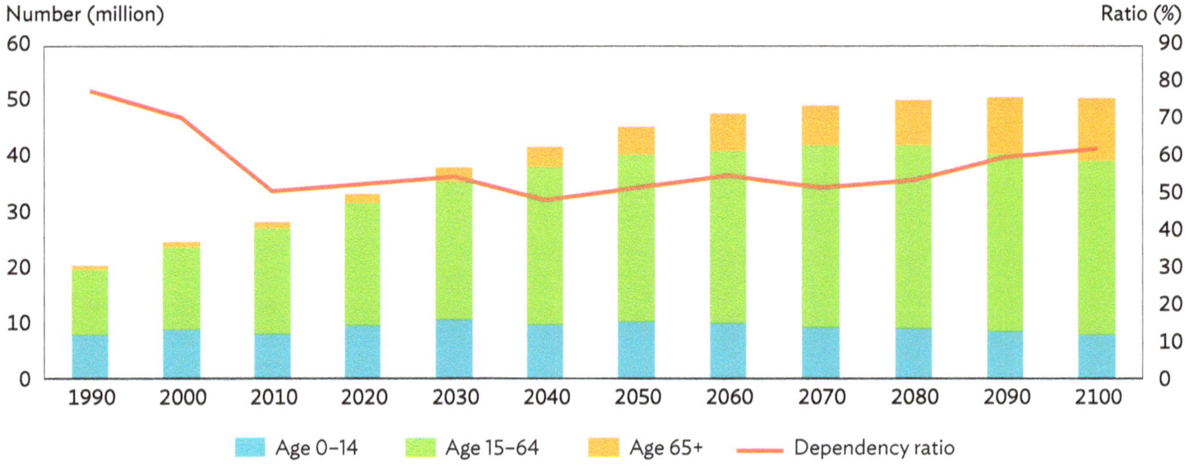

Notes: Population data for 1990–2010 are based on estimates; 2020–2050 estimates are based on medium-variant projections as of 1 July of the year. Dependency ratio is the ratio of dependents—people younger than 15 or older than 64—to the working-age population (aged 15–64).
Source: United Nations Department of Economic and Social Affairs, Population Division. 2022. World Population Prospects 2022 (accessed July 2023).

Beyond 2040, however, a different trend is expected to emerge as the working-age population is projected to decline as the proportion of older people grows at a faster pace. The dependency ratio is expected to increase from 48.6% in 2040 to 62.4% by the end of the century (Figure 5.3). This shift can also be seen in Figure 5.4, which shows Uzbekistan's population pyramid. By 2050, a significant portion of the population is projected to consist of those born in the 2020s—and they are expected to reap the greatest benefits from current investments in human capital.

9 The total dependency ratio compares the combined population of young individuals (ages 0–14) and older people (over 65) to the working-age population.

10 United Nations Children's Fund (UNICEF). 2018. *Generation 2030: Uzbekistan Investing in Children and Young People to Reap the Demographic Dividend.*

Figure 5.4: Population Pyramid of Uzbekistan

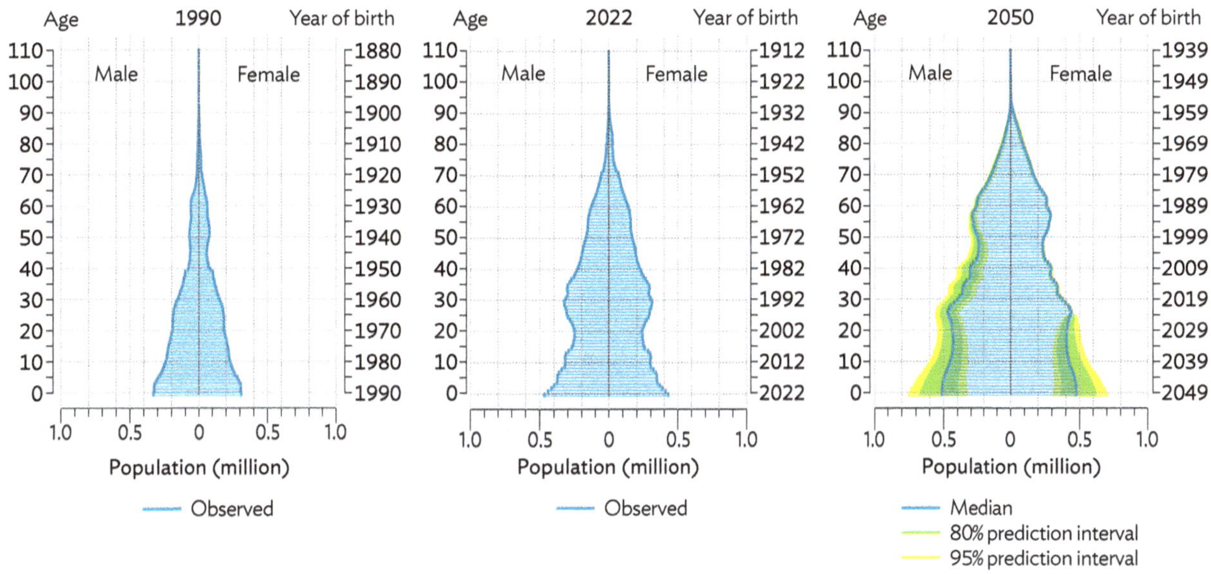

Source: United Nations Department of Economic and Social Affairs. World Population Prospects 2022: Uzbekistan (accessed 5 March 2024).

It is imperative that Uzbekistan takes advantage of this limited window to reap its demographic dividend by ensuring there are enough productive jobs and by nurturing the development of skills to meet future demand. Investments in human capital will also be essential for ensuring that both the current and future workforce are healthy and skilled to take on productive jobs. The experiences of other countries that have achieved remarkable economic growth highlight the crucial role played by the demographic transition from rising working-age populations. A notable example is the People's Republic of China, where about a quarter of economic growth during 1980–2010 can be attributed to this.[11] Thus, the years leading up to 2040 will be pivotal in determining whether Uzbekistan can leverage its demographic dividend to stimulate growth and development. Investing in human capital will be key to achieving this.

Uzbekistan has one of the world's highest rates of public spending on education.[12] Despite the generous budgetary support, the education system faces the challenges of outdated teaching methods, limited access to quality education in rural areas, and the need for curriculum reform to align with evolving labor market needs. Regional educational disparities need to be addressed to ensure equal opportunities for all.

11 F. Cai and Y. Lu. 2016. Take-Off, Persistence and Sustainability: The Demographic Factor in Chinese Growth. *Asia and the Pacific Policy Studies*. 3 (2). pp. 203–225.

12 World Bank. 2018a. *Growth and Job Creation in Uzbekistan: An In-Depth Diagnostic*.

Investments in Education

Education System Financing

Although the state budget is the primary source of funding for education, additional financial resources are raised through, among other things, fees, parental contributions, donations, support and generating income at the school level, as well as from international donors. Education is compulsory and free from preschool to primary and secondary education (aged 4–15, or 11 years of education). All universities charge tuition fees to students who do not meet the threshold for receiving a state grant based on their entrance test results.[13]

Apart from the state budget, extra-budgetary funds are in place. One such fund is for building and equipping educational facilities, primarily targeting general education schools, professional colleges, academic lyceums, and medical institutions. Another fund focuses on developing materials and technical infrastructure for higher education institutions. Both funds are managed by the Ministry of Finance (footnote 13).

The state budget for public education in Uzbekistan is divided into three levels: central, regional, and local budgets. The central budget primarily allocates funds to support higher education, educational establishments, and academic lyceums associated with higher education. The regional budget finances vocational colleges and academic lyceums operating independently from higher education institutions. Most expenses for capital investment are covered by regional budgets. Local budgets finance the day-to-day operational costs of preschools, specialized schools, and general schools (footnote 13).

Government Expenditure on Education

Because a large portion of the population is of working age, as well as youth, the education system is essential for socioeconomic development and political transformation. Raising education outcomes and creating productive jobs depend on increasing government spending on education.

The government puts a significant emphasis on education and health care, with an average allocation of 5.9% of GDP for education and 2.5% of GDP for health care over 2013–2022 (Figure 5.5). Government spending on education, as a percentage of GDP, exceeds that of countries with similar incomes, regional peers, and, remarkably, Organisation for Economic Co-operation and Development countries.[14] However, even as the education budget had risen to 5.6% of GDP in 2022, the budget has been declining in recent years, from 7.0% in 2019 to 4.8% in 2021. It is worth mentioning that while allocations to the education budget as a percentage of GDP fluctuated quite considerably over this period, the health budget was fairly stable.

13 Government of Uzbekistan. 2019. *Education Sector Plan of Uzbekistan, 2019–2023*.
14 UNICEF. 2021. *Uzbekistan Education Sector Analysis: 2021*.

Figure 5.5: Education and Health Expenditure in Uzbekistan, 2013–2022

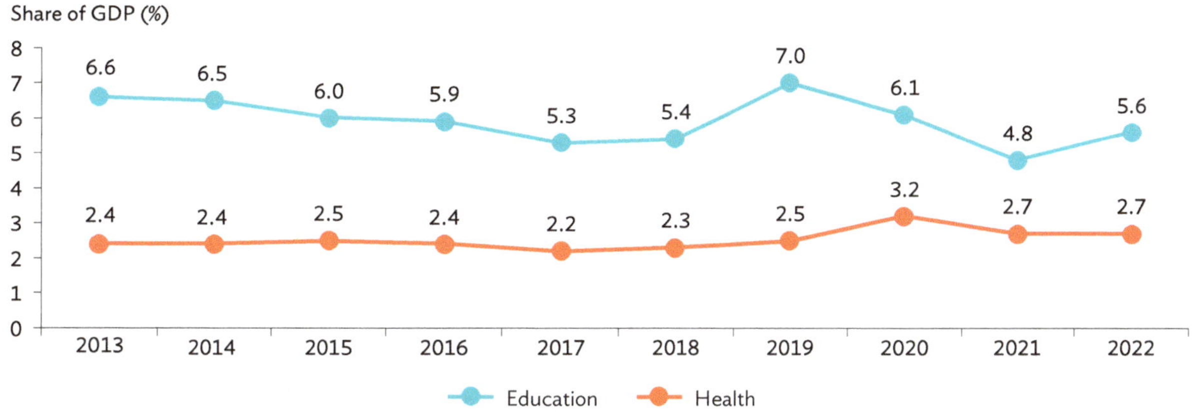

GDP = gross domestic product.
Source: UNICEF. 2021. *Uzbekistan Education Sector Analysis: 2021*.

The distribution of education spending across different education levels was relatively stable from 2018 to 2022 (Figure 5.6). Primary and secondary education comprises approximately 68% of the total education budget, preschool accounts for 20%, and higher and secondary special education is 15%. Public spending on preschool education has risen considerably, in line with government efforts to increase enrollment rates and develop early childhood education (Box 5.1). The allocation for preschool education increased from SUM3.0 trillion in 2018 to SUM8.6 trillion in 2022 (footnote 14). In terms of share of total education expenditure, this represents an increase from 15% in 2018 to 18% in 2022 (Figure 5.6).

Figure 5.6: Composition of Total Education Expenditure in Uzbekistan, 2018–2022
(%)

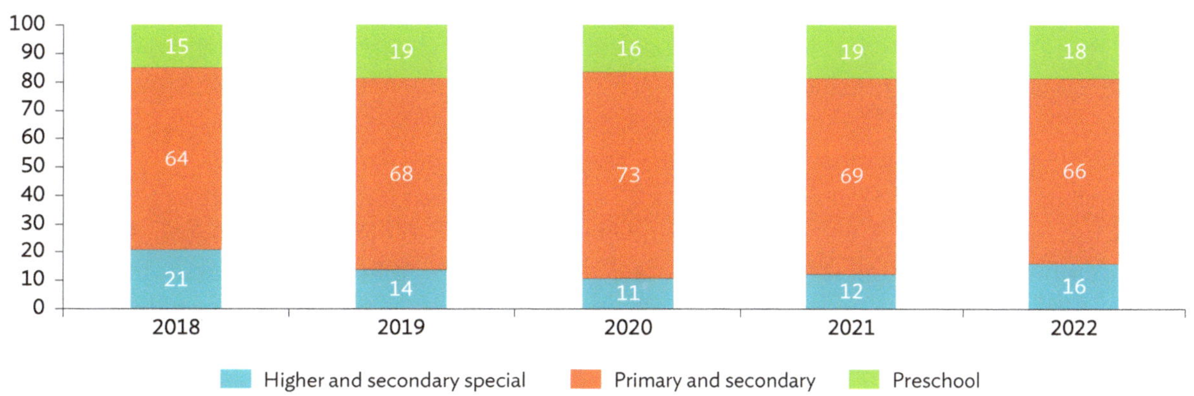

Source: UNICEF. 2021. *Uzbekistan Education Sector Analysis: 2021*.

Box 5.1: Improving Early Childhood Education in Uzbekistan

Since 2017, the Government of Uzbekistan has been working intensively to improve preschool education. It created the specialized Ministry of Preschool Education and adopted the Concept for the Development of Preschool Education until 2030, the legal basis for implementing reforms in preschool education.

The government is expected to pay particular attention to attracting private capital to develop preschool education through public–private partnerships, increasing the percentage of children in preschool education to 80.8% by 2030, and boosting the coverage of 6-year-old children in the preschool training system to 100% by the end of academic year 2024/25.

The Law on Preschool Education, 2019 aims to gradually phase in universal access to preschool education and ensure at least 1 year of preschool education before entering school in line with Sustainable Development Goal 4.2. The law envisages the following:

Setting up preschools through public–private partnerships, particularly family preschools for more than 12,000 new nonstate preschools established from 2018 to 2021.

- Increasing enrollment rates from less than 30.0% in 2017 to 69.4% in 2022.
- Introducing a new curriculum, Ilk Kadam, based on a competency-based approach that is in line with the revised Early Learning Development Standards being implemented in all preschools since 2018.
- Upgrading the education management information system piloted and scaled up in 2018 and 2019.
- Establishing a preschool education quality assurance framework and mechanism for self-assessment and external evaluation.
- Launching digital platforms such as Bebbo for parents and the Learning Passport for providing information and training for parents, teachers, and other caregivers.
- Undertaking several studies and providing information to support evidence-based planning and programming.

Sources: Eureporter. 2023. Uzbekistan: State Guarantees Developing a Sustainable Education System. 7 April; UNICEF. 2022. *Towards Achieving Universal Early Childhood Education in the Republic of Uzbekistan*.

Uzbekistan's commitment to preschool education was recognized during the UNESCO Conference on Early Childhood Care and Education in Tashkent in 2022. Uzbekistan is among the countries committed to spending a minimum of 10% of their total education budgets on preprimary education. The government has said that it wants to bring preschool staff salaries and working conditions to the level of primary education teachers.[15]

The government is substantially increasing spending on higher education, which rose from SUM1.0 billion in 2018 to SUM5.5 billion in 2022, lifting higher education's share in total education expenditure from 5.2% to 11.6% over this period (footnote 15). It is important to note, however, that spending on higher education is well below the 20% benchmark followed by several other countries, including Austria, where a remarkable 35.5% of the education budget is for higher education (footnote 13).

As a direct consequence of the increased education budget at all levels, expenditure per student has risen notably (Figure 5.7). In 2022, the lowest expenditure per student was in primary and secondary education, totaling SUM4.6 million; the highest was in higher education, totaling SUM9.5 million. It is important to note, however, that the increased expenditure per student in higher education may have been influenced by comparatively lower enrollment rates at this level.

15 United Nations Educational, Scientific and Cultural Organization (UNESCO). 2022. UNESCO Member States Commit to Invest at Least 10% of Education Budget on Early Childhood Education. Press release. 18 November.

Figure 5.7: Expenditure per Student in Uzbekistan, 2012–2022
(sum million, current prices)

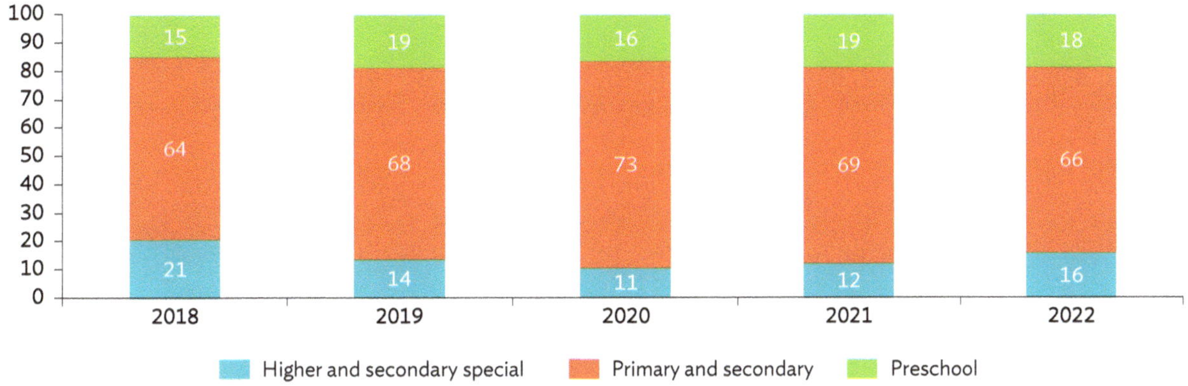

Sources: Data from 2012 to 2016 are from Government of Uzbekistan. 2019. *Education Sector Plan 2019–2023*; 2018 to 2022 data are from UNICEF. 2021. *Uzbekistan Education Sector Analysis: 2021*.

Significant regional differences in expenditure per student exist, which could be because of differences in teacher pay, student–teacher ratios, utility expenses, and operational efficiency. General secondary education makes up most of the education budget, but there are significant regional differences in the costs per student. For instance, Navoi spends SUM3.7 million per student, 73% more than Tashkent City's SUM2.2 million.[16]

Until 2018, education had the biggest share of total budget spending at the regional level, although there were notable variations in spending levels. Before the pandemic, the proportion of regional budgets allocated to education ranged from 30.9% in Tashkent to 48.0% in the Fergana region (Figure 5.8). Because of COVID-19, regional governments had to redirect budget allocations predominantly toward health care, resulting in the share of education in regional budgets falling significantly, from an average of 42.6% in 2018 to 14.6% in 2020, with the lowest share in Kashkadarya (9.5%). With the pandemic passing, regional budgets will likely revert to their prepandemic spending trends, resulting in education once again being the biggest expenditure item.

Figure 5.8: Share of Education in Regional Budgets in Uzbekistan, 2018 and 2020
(%)

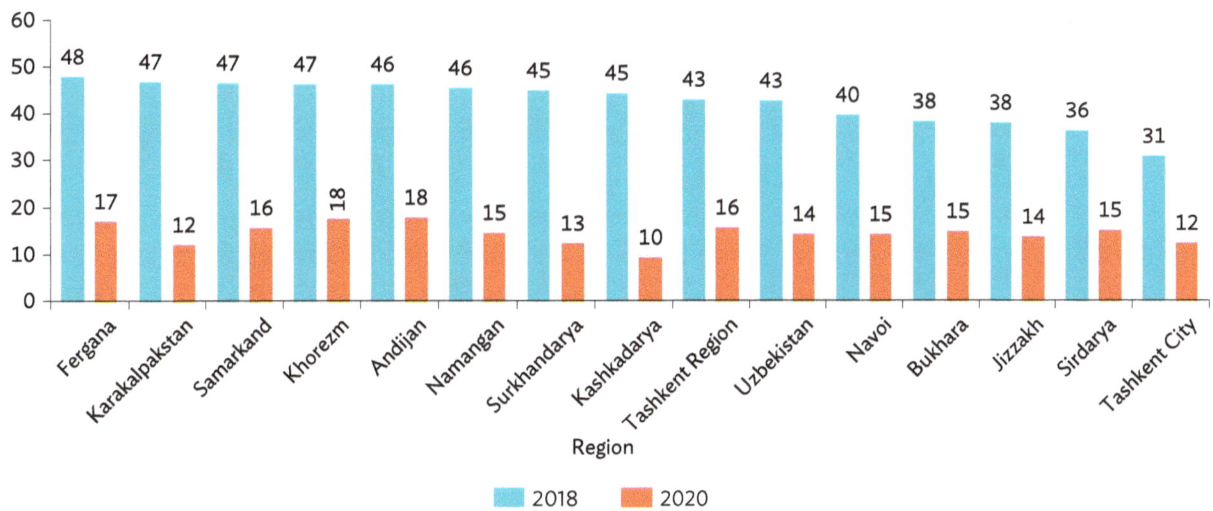

Source: UNICEF. 2021. *Uzbekistan Education Sector Analysis: 2021*.

16 World Bank. 2022. *Uzbekistan Public Expenditure Review. Better Value for Money in Human Capital and Water Infrastructure.*

Despite significant government spending on education, there was a forecasted financing gap of SUM44.3 billion over 2019–2023 encompassing preschool, general secondary, and higher education (Figure 5.9). The impact of the pandemic is expected to have widened this gap due to significant learning losses and increasing learning inequalities. The financing gap in preschool education is expected to be narrowed with the government's strong push for preschool education.

Figure 5.9: Education Financing Gap in Uzbekistan, 2019–2023

(%)

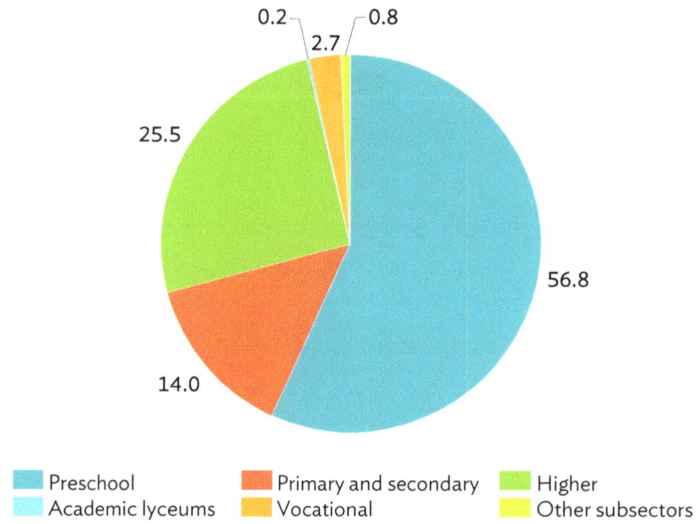

Source: Government of Uzbekistan. 2019. *Education Sector Plan (ESP) of Uzbekistan 2019–2023*.

The financing gap manifests itself in various ways, one of which is evident in inadequate teacher pay. Even though 80% of spending on preschool and basic education goes to salaries, teachers are low-paid. From the first quarter of 2017 to the first quarter of 2023, nominal teacher salaries in public education increased by 4.4%, lower than the overall wage growth of 5.0% in this period. Although teacher salaries more than tripled from SUM1.1 million to SUM2.9 million in the period, teachers are among the country's most underpaid professionals, as Figure 5.10 shows. The government has pledged to increase teacher salaries to SUM11.5 million by 2025.[17, 18] The low pay hurts teacher morale and, consequently, the quality of teaching.

Not surprisingly, many teachers go into private education or leave the country for better economic opportunities. Anecdotal evidence suggests some private schools and study centers in Tashkent City offer monthly salaries in the range of $600–$1,000.[19] In the Russian Federation, labor migrants earn the equivalent of about $615, nearly three times the income of teachers in Uzbekistan.[20] The disparity becomes even more apparent when comparing teacher salaries with neighboring countries: teachers in Uzbekistan earn 3.5 times less than teachers in Kazakhstan and 6.5 times less than teachers in the Russian Federation.[21]

17 *KUN.UZ*. 2021a. Salary of Teachers Will Be Increased to $1,000 by 2025—Shavkat Mirziyoyev. 6 November.
18 $1 = SUM11,535 (1 July 2023).
19 N. Uralova. 2022. Uzbekistan's Teacher Exodus is a Multi-Layered Problem. Central Asian Bureau for Analytical Reporting.
20 *Sputnik Tajikistan*. 2021. How Much Do Migrants Earn in Russia: Survey Results (in Russian). 9 December.
21 *KUN.UZ*. 2021b. Teachers in Uzbekistan Earn 3.5 Times Less than Teachers in Kazakhstan, 6.5 Times Less than Teachers in Russia. 22 November.

Figure 5.10: Average Monthly Salary of Employees in Uzbekistan, January–March 2023
(SUM million)

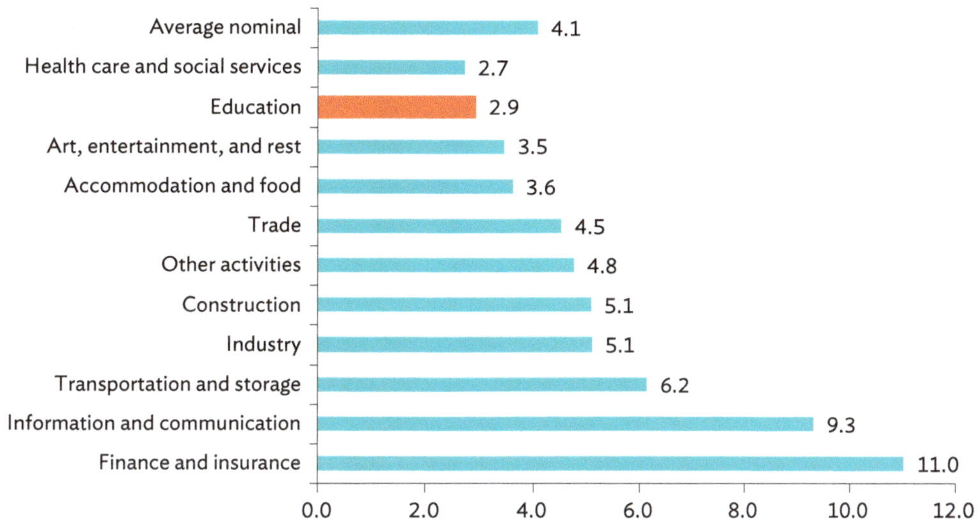

Source: Statistics Agency under the President of the Republic of Uzbekistan. Labor Market Statistics (accessed July 2023).

Teacher salaries in public schools differ across education levels, with preschool teachers receiving notably lower pay than teachers at higher levels of education. According to available data, preschool teachers earn 68% less base income than primary school teachers and 50% less than secondary school teachers (footnote 13).

Pay discrepancies disproportionately favor men. In academic year 2021/22, 68% of teachers in public schools were women. Nevertheless, for teachers educated at universities where income and status tend to be higher, women represented only 44% of teachers and professors.[22] This is highest in the Bukhara Region, at 52.9%, and lowest in Sirdarya, at 30.9%.[23]

The shortage of teachers and school facilities, coupled with rising enrollment, has led to the widespread implementation of double shifts in schools. Nationally, 74% of public schools run double shifts, although there is considerable regional variation. For instance, the prevalence of double shifts ranges from 40% in Buxoro to 87% in Karakalpakstan (Figure 5.11). Furthermore, given the large number of students in urban areas, the proportion of schools that operate double shifts in these areas is 78% compared to rural (73%) and remote (69%) areas. This disparity highlights the uneven distribution of educational resources and infrastructure across and within regions. Double shifting, however, does not always lead to smaller student-to-classroom ratios. The share of public schools having a ratio greater than the national average size of 20 students is 37% during the first shift and 12% during the second shift. This is significantly higher in Tashkent City, at 66% for the first shift and 29% for the second. In Karakalpakstan and Jizzakh, only 20% of the schools have a density of high students, particularly for the first shift (footnote 15).

22 N. Saida. 2022. Closing the Gender Gap in Uzbekistan's Universities. *The Diplomat*. 9 August.
23 Statistics Agency under the President of the Republic of Uzbekistan. Education (accessed July 2023).

Figure 5.11: Proportion of Schools in Uzbekistan by Region Using Double Shifts
(%)

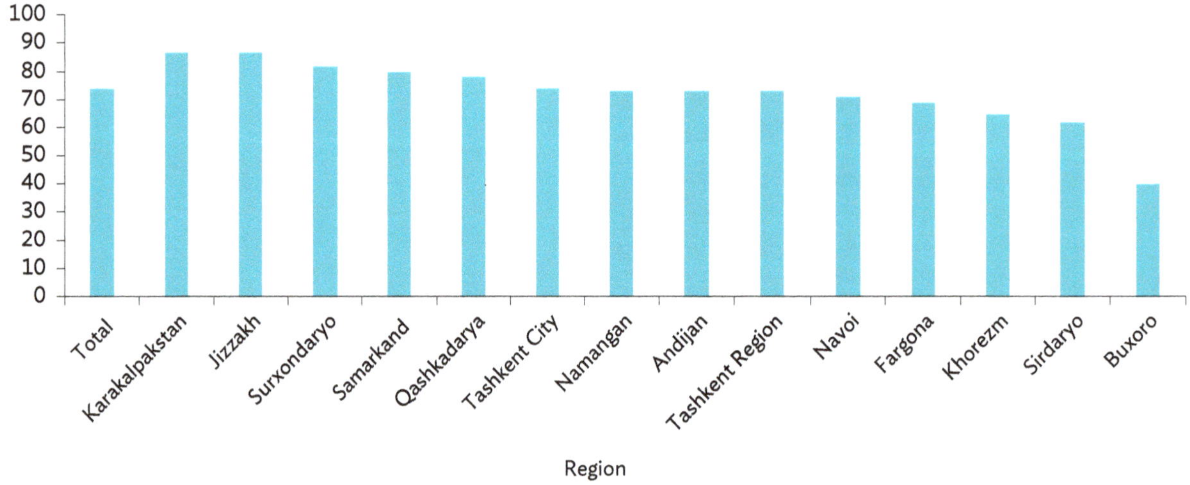

Source: UNICEF. 2021. Uzbekistan Education Sector Analysis: 2021.

The quality of school infrastructure and access to water, sanitation, and hygiene are concerns. For instance, at the preschool level, 43% of public schools need repairs. This is significantly higher in Tashkent City (52%) and Namangan (53%). Only 83% of schools have basic access to clean drinking water and 78% to basic sanitation facilities (footnote 15). These shortfalls need to be tackled to provide students with the safe and conducive learning environments that are essential for their well-being and academic development.

Student Participation Rates

Access to basic education is good, with the population receiving 12.5 years of education on average.[24] Girls and boys attend primary and secondary schools at comparable participation rates. However, access to early childhood education and higher education remain low despite significant investments to these levels.

Figure 5.12 shows the structure of Uzbekistan's education system. Children aged 3–6 can enroll in preschool education. One year of compulsory preschool education at age 6 was introduced in academic year 2019/20 in the Republic of Karakalpakstan, regions, and Tashkent City. General secondary education is compulsory in primary (grades 1 to 4) and secondary (grades 5 to 9) levels.

After completing pre-university education, students can take a bachelor's and then a master's degree. With the expansion of general secondary education from 9 to 11 years, the education structure now offers three pathways to students for their pre-university education:

(i) 11 years of general secondary education (pathway 1 in Figure 5.12);
(ii) 9 years of general secondary education plus 2 years in an academic lyceum (pathway 2); and
(iii) 11 years of general secondary education plus 0.5 to 2 years in a vocational college (pathway 3).

---

24 Data on mean years of schooling of the population over 25 years old is from Statistics Agency under the President of the Republic of Uzbekistan. Social Sphere, Minimum Indicators of Guarantees of Children's Rights (accessed July 2023).

Figure 5.12: Uzbekistan's Education System

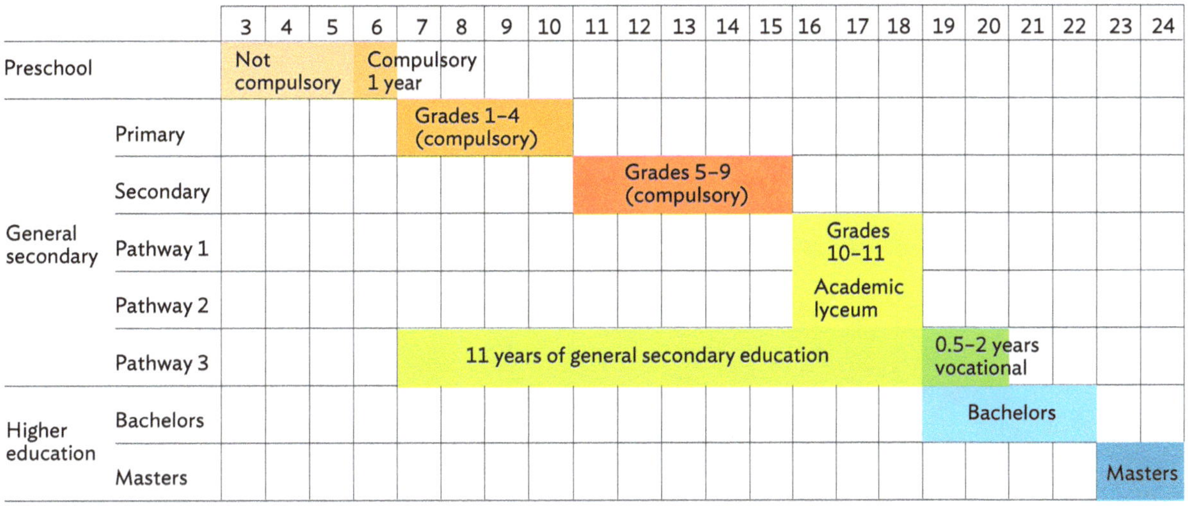

Source: Government of Uzbekistan. 2019. *Education Sector Plan (ESP) of Uzbekistan 2019–2023*.

Investing in high-quality early childhood education is essential for tackling learning poverty and nurturing human capital. Research indicates that prioritizing early years, including preschool education, yields substantial returns for individuals and economies.[25] Quality early childhood education contributes to improved productivity in subsequent educational stages because children who have attended early childhood education have higher attendance rates at later levels, achieve better academic outcomes, and are less prone to repeating or dropping out.[26] A study conducted in Uzbekistan further underscores the significance of attending preschool, as it serves as a stepping stone toward higher education and enhances the likelihood of securing employment and better future prospects.[27]

The gross enrollment rates (GERs) in preschool education in Uzbekistan have risen sharply on recent investments in early childhood education. The GER was below 30% until 2018 (Figure 5.13). With the recognition of early childhood education as a crucial component for school readiness and child development, Uzbekistan has taken significant steps to strengthen this level of education, including setting up the Ministry of Preschool Education in 2017, approving a concept for advancing preschool education by 2030, and implementing the Preschool Education Law. As a result, the preschool GER rose from 28% in 2018 to 44% in 2021. Despite these positive developments, participation in early childhood education remains a challenge, particularly among girls, low-income families, children with disabilities, and those living in rural areas.

The government has set an ambitious target of achieving 80% enrollment for ages 3–6 in preschool education by 2030. Achieving this target will mean ensuring the availability of preschool spaces for some 2 million children by that year. However, as of 2021, there were only 850,000 spaces. Not only will capacity need to be more than doubled but access to the increased spaces needs to be ensured for all segments of the population (footnote 15).

---

25 J. Heckman et al. 2015. Early Childhood Development. *NBER Working Paper*. No. 21766. National Bureau of Economic Research.

26 S. Berlinski and N. Schady. 2015. More Bang for the Buck: Investing in Early Childhood Development. In S. Berlinski and N. Schady, eds. *Early Years: Child Well-Being and the Role of Public Policy*. Palgrave Macmillan.

27 M. Ajwad et al. 2014. *The Skills Road: Skills for Employability in Uzbekistan*. World Bank.

Figure 5.13: Gross Enrollment Rates in Uzbekistan, 2003–2021
(%)

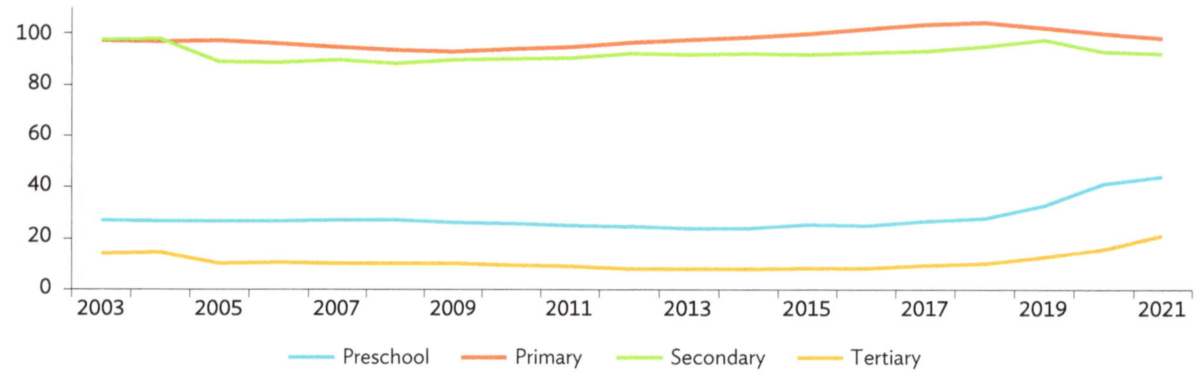

Source: UNESCO Institute of Statistics. Sustainable Development Goals (accessed July 2023).

The GER at the primary and secondary levels remained above or close to 100% from 2003 to 2019. Boys and girls are enrolling at high rates because of mandatory primary and secondary education. The GER declined in 2020 due probably to the pandemic. At the primary level, it decreased from 102.2% in 2019 to 100.1% in 2020, and from 97.4% to 93.0% at the secondary level. These declines align with UNESCO's projection that approximately 262,000 students in Central Asia alone were at risk of not returning to educational institutions in 2020 due to the pandemic.[28] It should be noted, however, that no decline was discernible in the GERs for preschool and higher education due to the pandemic. The reason may be that this was masked by a huge improvement in enrollment rates in these levels from boosted government spending.

The pandemic reversed a decline in out-of-school children at the primary level, according to UNESCO estimates (Figure 5.14). From 2007 to 2019, this had dropped from 167,000 to 15,000, but increased to 56,000 in 2020 and 100,000 in 2021, representing 3.9% of children of primary school age.

Figure 5.14: Number of Out-of-School Primary School Age Children in Uzbekistan, 2007–2021
('000)

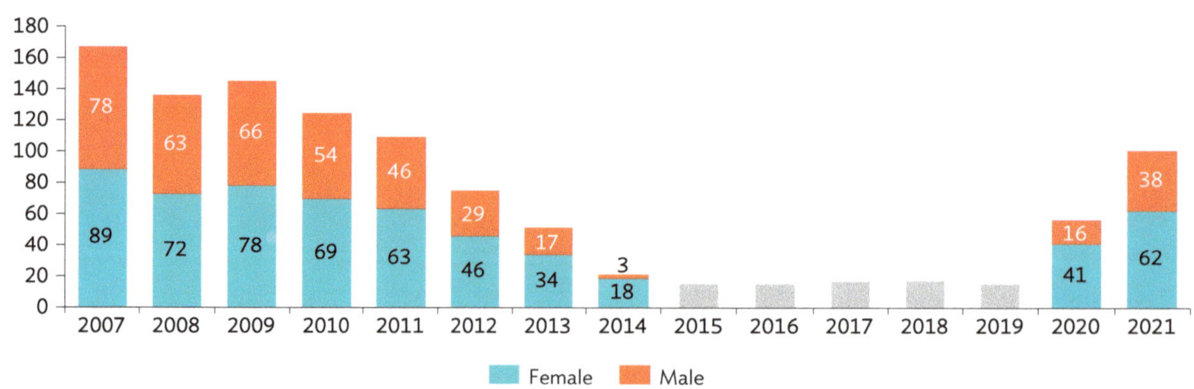

Note: Totals are provided only for 2015 to 2019 due to lack of gender breakdown.
Source: UNESCO Institute of Statistics. Sustainable Development Goals (accessed July 2023).

28 UNESCO. 2020. UNESCO COVID-19 Education Response: How Many Students Are at Risk of Not Returning to School? Advocacy Paper.

More girls than boys were out of school, at a ratio of 2:1 in 2021. Tackling this requires a comprehensive approach that includes setting up a monitoring and evaluation system to address data gaps, profiling out-of-school children, and developing context-appropriate policies and strategies.

Because access to higher education is limited in Uzbekistan, most school leavers opt for vocational training as an alternative. The GERs in tertiary education are relatively low, ranging from 8% to 14% over 2003–2019. Recent investments and reforms in higher education have, however, resulted in an increase in GERs at this level, which reached 16% in 2020 and 21% in 2021. The number of students enrolled in higher education doubled from 440,000 in 2019 to 1 million in 2022.[29] Despite this progress, Uzbekistan still lags behind most Central Asian countries on GERs at the tertiary level and is below the average of lower-middle-income countries (Figure 5.15).

Figure 5.15: Gross Enrollment Rates at the Tertiary Level in Central Asian Countries
(%)

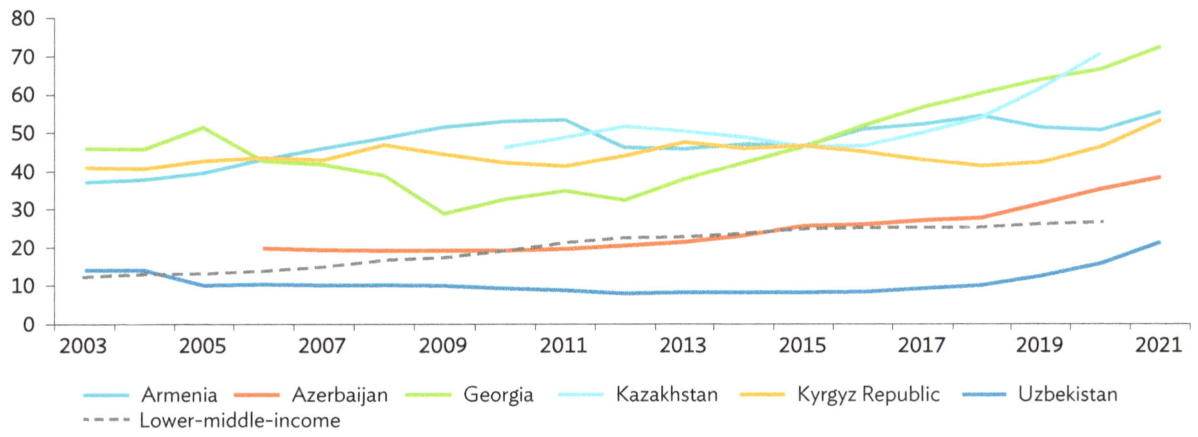

Source: UNESCO Institute of Statistics. Sustainable Development Goals (accessed July 2023).

The low participation in higher education is not due to lack of demand but rather to limited spaces, resulting in high selectivity. Although the number of applications to bachelor's degree courses increased fourfold from 2011 to 2022, only a small number of applicants were admitted. In 2011, for every 100 applications, 14 were admitted; this increased to 17 in 2021 (Figure 5.16). The rate of admissions has remained low despite a threefold increase in the number of higher education institutions, from 65 in 2011 to 191 in 2022.[30] The low admission rate, along with high costs and concerns about the quality of higher education, causes many students to study abroad, their numbers quadrupling from 23,100 in 2011 to 85,900 in 2020.[31] The Russian Federation is a popular destination given the similarities in language, the cheaper cost of education, and greater possibilities of combining studies with work.[32]

29 Statistics Agency under the President of the Republic of Uzbekistan. Education Outcomes (accessed July 2023).
30 Statistics Agency under the President of the Republic of Uzbekistan. Social Sphere, Minimum Indicators of Guarantees of Children's Rights (accessed 2 July 2023).
31 UNESCO Institute of Statistics. Sustainable Development Goals (accessed 2 July 2023).
32 M. Shagazatova et al. 2020. Unlocking the Potential for Labor Productivity Growth. In K. Anderson, E. Ginting, and K. Taniguchi, eds. *Uzbekistan: Quality Job Creation as a Cornerstone for Sustainable Economic Growth.* Asian Development Bank.

Figure 5.16: Application to and Acceptance in Bachelor's Degree Institutions in Uzbekistan, 2011–2022

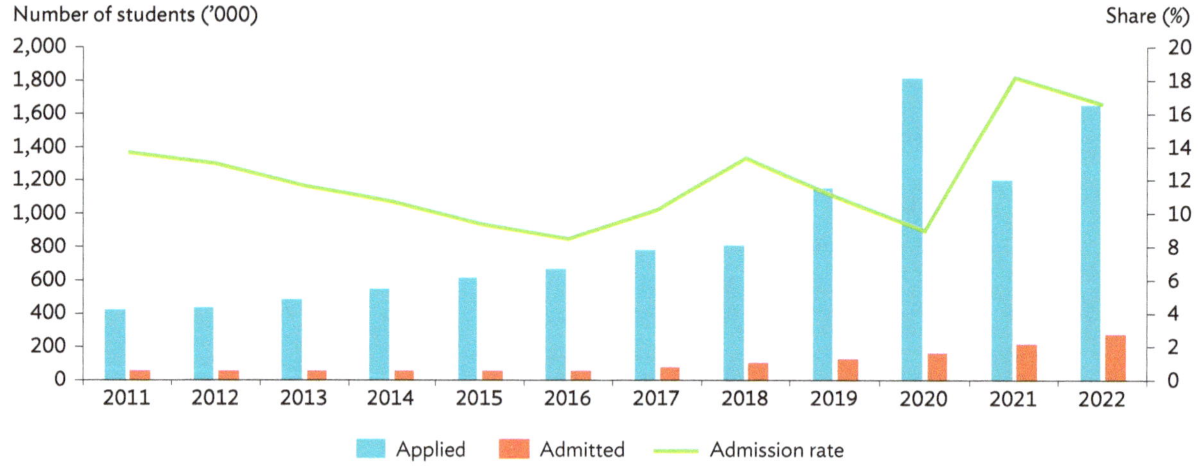

Source: Statistics Agency under the President of the Republic of Uzbekistan. Social Sphere, Minimum Indicators of Guarantees of Children's Rights (accessed July 2023).

The discrepancy in access to higher education across regions is huge. In 2021, students from Tashkent City, with less than 6% of the population aged 18–19, accounted for 35% of applicants for higher education and 30% of those admitted to bachelor's degree programs in universities. Kashkadarya, with 11% of the population aged 18–19, accounted for only 5.5% of applicants and 4.6% of admitted students (footnote 14).

A significant gender disparity exists among university students. The gender parity index (GPI) across all levels of education is close to 1.0, except at the tertiary level, where it is below 0.9.[33] Over 2003–2021, the GPI at the primary and secondary level remained stable at close to 1.0, while tertiary GPI showed a declining trend from 2003 to 2018, before increasing to 0.87 in 2021 (Figure 5.17). As of 2022, women accounted for 47.5% of the about 1 million students at public universities.[34]

Figure 5.17: Gender Parity Index in Education in Uzbekistan

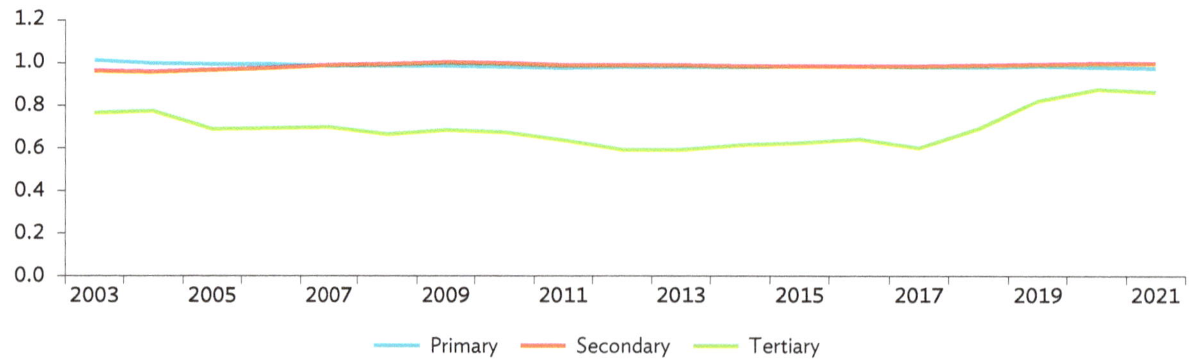

Note: A gender parity index from 0.97 to 1.03 signifies gender parity, indicating an equal representation of both genders. An index below 0.97 suggests a disparity that favors males, while an index above 1.03 indicates a disparity that favors females.
Source: UNESCO Institute of Statistics. Sustainable Development Goals (accessed July 2023).

33 The gender parity index compares the values of a particular indicator between males and females.
34 Statistics Agency under the President of the Republic of Uzbekistan. Education (accessed 2 July 2023).

The gender gap in higher education is particularly pronounced in the sciences, engineering, manufacturing, and construction—high-paying sectors predominantly pursued by male students. In 2017, the share of female graduates in these fields was 27.0%, although this increased to 36.1% in 2021.[35] Women are also underrepresented in research, where their share, hovering at 39%–43%, showed no significant improvement from 2008 to 2021. In 2021, women accounted for 41.4% of researchers in Uzbekistan, far lower than in other Central Asian countries, including Armenia (53.1%), Azerbaijan (55.4%), Georgia (53.3%), Kazakhstan (54.5%), and the Kyrgyz Republic (57.6%).[36]

Women, however, tend to have a higher representation in languages and teacher training in higher education courses. In 2020, women majoring in teaching accounted for 126,300 out of 260,000 enrollees. The preference for teaching and other stereotypically "female" courses rather than sciences, engineering, manufacturing, and construction can be attributed partly to societal expectations. Women in Uzbekistan are expected after marriage to prioritize the household and childcare, which hinders many from pursuing full-time careers. Teaching, however, is perceived as offering greater flexibility, which may explain the preference.[37]

Better access for women to higher education is an effective way to make the labor market more stable—and to this end the government is trying to bridge the gender gap. The Women's Education Support Program 2022–2026, adopted in March 2022,[38] aims to provide this support through the following measures:

(i) interest-free 7-year loans to cover the education expenses;
(ii) setting up universities and technical schools exclusively for women;
(iii) increasing the allocation of university slots by 500 to accommodate women with seniority and providing 300 doctoral positions in state research institutes and universities for women;[39] and
(iv) supporting 2,100 female students from socially vulnerable families by covering their education expenses.

Learning Outcomes and Quality of Learning

Lack of Adequate Assessment Methods

Literacy rates among men and women aged 16–24 in Uzbekistan is 100%, similar to most countries in Central Asia. Attaining this rate, however, cannot be solely attributed to the formal education system, as it requires a combination of both in-school and out-of-school learning. To gain a comprehensive understanding of the effectiveness of the educational system in delivering learning outcomes, it is necessary to test the level and quality of knowledge gained by students.

Gaining a better understanding of the quality of education in Uzbekistan is being impeded by the absence of adequate assessment methods specifically designed to capture quality. Comprehensive

35 Statistics Agency under the President of the Republic of Uzbekistan. Education (accessed 2 July 2023).
36 UNESCO Institute of Statistics. Sustainable Development Goals (accessed July 2023).
37 N. Saida. 2022. Closing the Gender Gap in Uzbekistan's Universities. *The Diplomat*. 9 August.
38 See International Labour Organization. Presidential Decree No. 87 (accessed 7 March 2022) for measures to further accelerate work on systematic support for families and women.
39 Seniority is defined as women who have at least 5 years of work experience in their specialty, but do not have a higher education.

assessment programs for primary and secondary levels that utilize internationally recognized standards and methodologies are lacking. Despite some effort by the government to test students in schools, this has not been successful for the following reasons (footnote 14):

(i) instruments and methods used were not standardized, making it difficult to compare the outcomes between years, tests, and grades;
(ii) data analysis focused only on calculating average scores by regions, omitting the underlying elements that affect students' learning levels; and
(iii) not enough initiatives were given to investigate the causes of the findings and use them to inform educational initiatives.

In a significant step toward getting a more comprehensive understanding of learning outcomes, Uzbekistan, in 2022, participated for the first time in the Programme for International Student Assessment (PISA). The PISA assesses the skills and knowledge of 15-year-old students in reading, math, and science, and provides rankings based on the country's average performance in each area. Eighty-five countries participated in the 2022 PISA, but the results were not yet out at the time of writing.

A study by UNICEF evaluated the "school readiness" of children aged 6–7 in Uzbekistan in pre-math and number concepts,[40] cognitive and conceptual areas, and preliteracy and language concepts. The study found that a significant majority of children showed proficiency in prenumber and space concepts, and their ability to understand and follow instructions (Figure 5.18). However, certain areas presented challenges, including making relative comparisons, understanding patterns, and constructing sentences. Students who received preschool education consistently outperformed nonattendees across various measures, with the most substantial difference observed in understanding patterns and constructing sentences (a 19 percentage-point gap). The research underscores the importance of preschool education in equipping students for secondary education.

Figure 5.18: School Readiness Among Children 6–7 Years Old in Uzbekistan

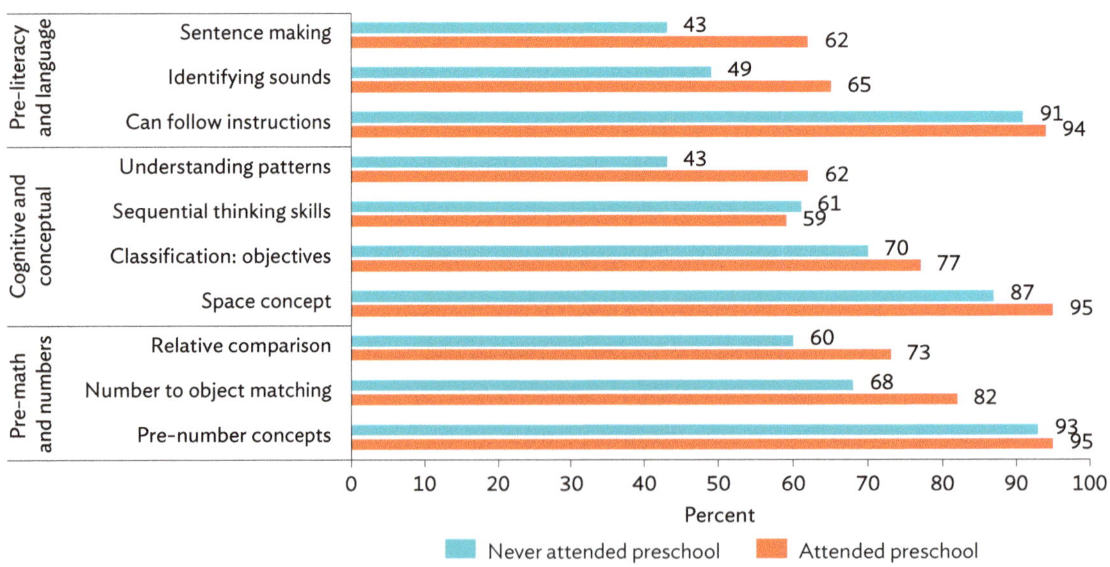

Source: UNICEF. 2021. Uzbekistan Education Sector Analysis 2021.

40 UNICEF. 2020. 2 in 5 Schools Around the World Lacked Basic Handwashing Facilities Prior to COVID-19 Pandemic—UNICEF, WHO. *Press Release*. 17 August.

In 2018, the Ministry of Public Education partnered with UNICEF to conduct the National Assessment Study among grade 4 students (end of the primary level) to assess learning outcomes for reading, math, and science. Some 7,000 students from 268 schools participated in the study that assessed two outcomes: the level of learning achieved by children at the end of primary grades, and the specific knowledge and skills attained by grade 4 students across different subjects and cognitive domains.[41]

The results showed the students could answer only 52% of the test questions correctly, and performed better in science and environmental studies (58.9% mean percentage score) than in reading comprehension (49.9%) and math (51.8%). Individual scores varied widely, highlighting significant disparities in learning outcomes. The gap between the best-performing students (top 25%) and the worst (bottom 25%) was substantial. Within individual schools, there was also a notable disparity between the top- and the bottom-performing students. Differences in school or teacher characteristics explain about half of the variation in the test scores.

Figure 5.19 benchmarks the results of the National Assessment Study with international tests. The share of Uzbek students scoring less-than-low and low benchmark was high in all subjects compared to the international median. It is important to note that the percentage of Uzbek students achieving advanced scores in all subjects is comparable to international standards. This finding underscores the presence of disparities in learning outcomes, with only a small portion of students performing well while the majority falls behind.

Figure 5.19: Benchmarking Uzbekistan's 2018 National Assessment Study with International Assessments

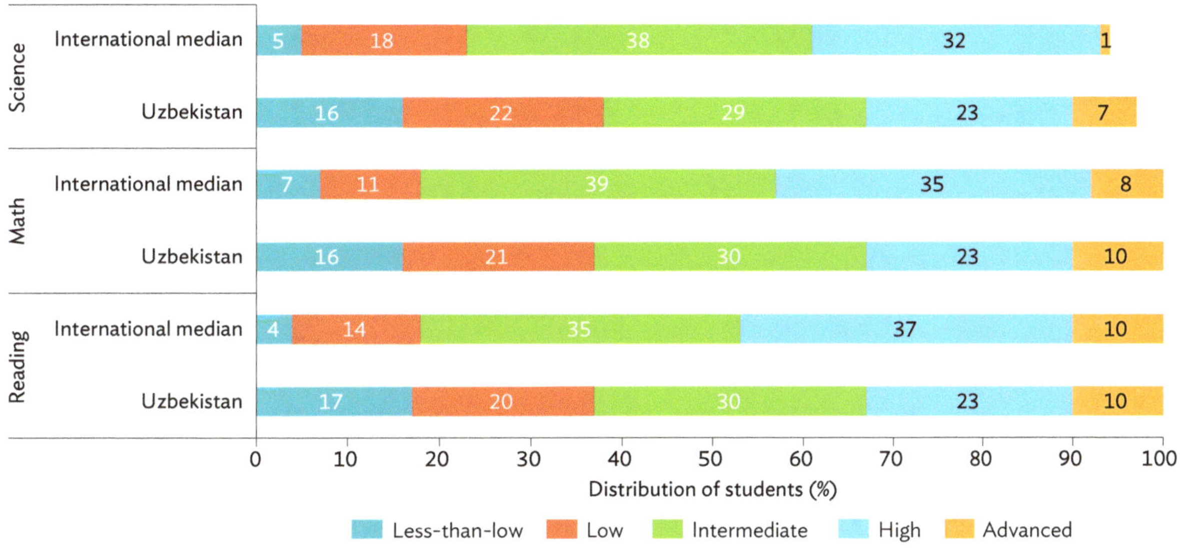

Note: Science and math were compared against the results of the Trends in International Mathematics and Science Study 2015; and reading against Progress in International Reading Literacy Study 2016.
Source: UNICEF. 2019. *Student Learning at Primary Grades in Uzbekistan: Outcomes, Challenges, and Opportunities—A Summary of Uzbekistan National Learning Achievement Study, Grade IV, 2018.*

41 This subsection draws heavily on UNICEF. 2019. *Student Learning at Primary Grades in Uzbekistan: Outcomes, Challenges, and Opportunities—A Summary of Uzbekistan National Learning Achievement Study, Grade IV, 2018.*

Skills Mismatch and Lack of Skills

A significant discrepancy exists between the number of graduates in various fields of study and the demand for jobs in those fields. From 2012 to 2019, humanities programs were the most popular choice among students in higher education, accounting for 48% of students. Social science courses, such as economics and law, were chosen by 10% of students and 7% chose health and medicine-related studies. Only about 25% of students in higher education chose courses relevant to industry and manufacturing (Figure 5.20). It is important to acknowledge that the overall rise in enrollment in recent years has primarily been driven by expanded opportunities in humanities-related fields (footnote 14). Given these trends, it is not surprising that the share of firms experiencing difficulties in hiring young workers is the biggest in industry (about 50%, according to a 2016 survey); followed by services (around 40%) and the construction, transport, and communication sectors (about 40%).[42] A survey of manufacturing firms in 2017 showed the lack of skilled engineers and workers was a primary concern for small firms (75% of respondents in this segment) and large firms (49%). The lack of access to skilled personnel due to the poor quality of education and training was ranked as the second most significant barrier (out of 13 barriers) by large firms, and the fourth by small firms in the same survey.[43]

Figure 5.20: Students in Higher Education Institutions by Course in Uzbekistan ('000)

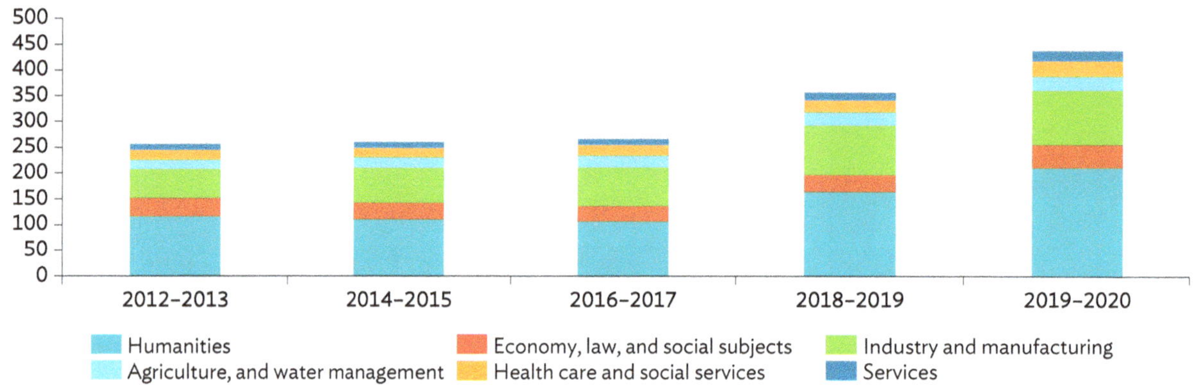

Source: UNICEF. 2021. Uzbekistan Education Sector Analysis: 2021.

In a 2020 skills needs assessment survey[44] among 150 micro and small enterprises employing a total of 9,415 workers in Uzbekistan, only two in three employers (68%) believed the training received from higher education institutions is aligned with market needs (Figure 5.21). The response for vocational graduates was 50% and 23% for graduates of academic lyceums. A 2021 survey shows that the lack of skills or work experience is the primary constraint faced by firms when hiring young workers.[45]

42 United States Agency for International Development (USAID). 2022. *Uzbekistan Youth Employment Skills (Yes) Activity: Labor Market Assessment and Skills Gap*.
43 World Bank. 2018a. Growth and Job Creation in Uzbekistan: An In-Depth Diagnostic.
44 Asian Development Bank. 2020. *Skills Needs Assessment for Micro and Small Enterprises in Uzbekistan: Enterprise Survey Report*.
45 World Bank. 2021. Firm Survey on Youth Employment Constraints.

Figure 5.21: Relevance of Education and Training to Labor Market Needs in Uzbekistan
(%)

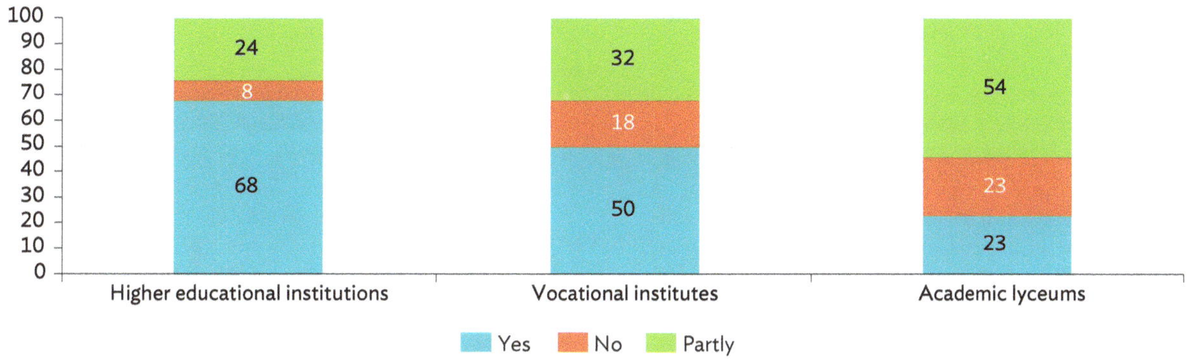

Source: Asian Development Bank. 2020. Skills Needs Assessment for Micro and Small Enterprises in Uzbekistan: Enterprise Survey Report.

Way Forward

Creating jobs and promoting employment, especially among the youth, is one of the government's top priorities in its development strategy. Effective investment in skills development will improve the employability of graduates, and these investments will make the economy more competitive and reduce socioeconomic inequality. The following offers recommendations to help achieve these goals:

(i) **Uzbekistan should continue investing in human capital as its working-age population steadily increases.** The country experienced a significant rise in the working-age population from 1990 to 2023 and has reached the early demographic dividend stage. A well-educated and trained workforce will help sustain long-term economic growth. Empowering women for work in the formal sector will be crucial to this end. The demographic dividend, however, is expected to close by 2040 as the working-age population declines and the proportion of older people grows at a faster pace. Thus, investments in human capital should be made now, not in the future.

(ii) **It is critically important to raise the quality of education and make the education system more aligned to developing labor market-relevant skills.** The government could consider introducing a merit-based system to link teacher promotion and career progression to teaching efficiency. The performance appraisal mechanism for teachers needs to be introduced and linked to teachers' career progression. Developing and adopting its own quality assessment framework, participating in international assessment processes, and learning from international best practices will be crucial to raise the quality of education. Collaboration between employers and training institutions needs to be improved to ensure that graduate skills are more aligned with the needs of the labor market. A functional labor market information system that produces reliable and accurate data will be crucial to achieve this.

(iii) **E-learning services need to be introduced to improve teaching quality and provide education in rural and remote areas.** Here, access to education and the availability of teachers are severely limited. To provide education services evenly across the country, e-learning and distance learning services should be introduced so that equal opportunities for learning will be given regardless of the geographic location. This will require improving internet access and improving digital literacy.

CHAPTER 6

Regional Cooperation and Integration

Turdakun Tashbolotov

Uzbekistan's efforts to boost regional cooperation and integration became an integral part of the country's deep socioeconomic and financial reforms to build an open economy. Trade liberalization and improving the investment climate have been key thrusts of the reform process. The newly adopted "Development Strategy of New Uzbekistan in 2022–2026" demonstrates the strong will to continue reforms taking into account lessons learned from the previous 5 years of reforms.[1]

International development agencies and expert communities recognize the early achievements of the reforms. *The Economist* named Uzbekistan the "Country of the Year" in 2019.[2] The economy's robust growth since 2017 is a fundamental indicator of that achievement. Even in 2020 amid the coronavirus disease (COVID-19) pandemic, Uzbekistan was among the few countries that demonstrated economic growth. The Asian Development Bank (ADB) reports that in 2022, the economy of Uzbekistan achieved 5.7% growth.[3]

The government is intensifying its regional and international integration and economic cooperation efforts. The National Strategy on Actions in Priority Directions 2017–2021 calls for a regional policy that builds a belt of security, stability, and good neighborship with countries in Central Asia.[4] Uzbekistan's improved bilateral relations with these countries have resulted in increased trade, which doubled between 2017 and 2019. Cross-border investments in the region have also risen, leading to more firms in Central Asian countries doing business in Uzbekistan, and vice-versa.

The reforms have also seen that Uzbekistan is actively engaging with international and regional organizations and initiatives, including the European Union (EU), Eurasian Economic Union (EAEU), and the World Trade Organization (WTO), and has resumed cooperation with the European Bank for Reconstruction and Development.

Uzbekistan is negotiating with various countries not only on trade agreements but also on essential aspects of strengthening regional connectivity. The country's efforts to reach more external markets have led to its participation in transport corridor development projects, and participation in other transport routes is being explored. Uzbekistan sees the Middle Corridor, the Trans-Afghan railway project, and a rail link with the People's Republic of China (PRC) as key regional initiatives that the country can boost its regional cooperation and development in the coming years.

1 President of the Republic of Uzbekistan. About the Development Strategy of New Uzbekistan for 2022–2026 (in Russian). President of the Republic of Uzbekistan. 2017. On the Strategy of Actions for the Further Development of the Republic of Uzbekistan (in Russian).

2 *The Economist*. 2019. Which Nation Improved the Most in 2019? 21 December.

3 ADB. 2023. ADB Forecasts 5% Growth for Uzbekistan in 2023 and 2024.

4 See the five priority areas of development in President of the Republic of Uzbekistan. 2017. On the Strategy of Actions for the Further Development of the Republic of Uzbekistan.

This chapter describes the recent trends in Uzbekistan's regional cooperation and integration efforts through analysis of the country's foreign trade, foreign direct investment (FDI), and connectivity development dynamics. The chapter also provides information on how Uzbekistan can benefit from active participation in key regional and global organizations. It also provides highlights of the bilateral cooperation of Uzbekistan with its neighbors and other regional economic partners.

Foreign Trade

Uzbekistan's foreign trade is markedly built on as a result of economic reforms since 2017 that focused on economic openness and liberalization. The National Development Strategy 2017–2021 set out sweeping structural changes in all sectors of the economy with the strategy significantly shaping the country's economic development path and trajectory.

The main impetus of reforms was to abandon, as much as possible, the policy based on self-reliance when the country's economic policy focused on substituting imports with locally produced goods. This policy, however, had its own logic, as the country was being impeded by growing inefficiency in production, resulting in deteriorating competitiveness of the economy. Early reforms saw the government removing restrictions on and constraints to trade and financial transfers, including restrictive tariffs and controlled foreign exchange operations. From 2017 to 2021, average custom tariffs fell from 18.5% to 6.45%.[5] These changes and the deregulation of foreign exchange operations led to a substantial increase in the number of domestic entities engaged in business activities internationally.

Figure 6.1 shows that trade liberalization drastically changed the volume and structure of the country's trade balance, with the total volume of foreign trade rising from $24 billion in 2016 to $50 billion in 2022.[6] Even though the coronavirus disease (COVID-19) disrupted and restricted Uzbekistan's foreign trade, it rose more than twofold in absolute numbers in 6 years. Exports increased by 37% from 2016 to 2022, and imports by almost 150%, creating a sizable trade deficit of $11 billion over this period, a first time for the economy.

Figure 6.1: Uzbekistan's Foreign Trade, 2000–2022
($ billion)

Source: UzStat (Statistics Agency under the President of the Republic of Uzbekistan). Foreign Economic Activity (accessed 2 August 2024).

5 G. Saidova. 2022. Trade Liberalization and Economic Integration. Statement in the Tashkent Investment Forum. 24 March, Tashkent.
6 UzStat (Statistics Agency under the President of the Republic of Uzbekistan). Foreign Economic Activity (accessed 2 August 2024).

As of 2022, Uzbekistan had signed trade agreements with 47 countries, according to the United States Department of Commerce (2022).[7] Since 2020, the country has been an observer in the EAEU and has expressed the possibility of becoming a full member of the Eurasian Development Bank.[8] Since 2017, the government has resumed negotiations to become a WTO member. Uzbekistan is a member of the Free Trade Zone of the Commonwealth of Independent States (CIS) and has signed free trade agreements with eight CIS countries that are immediate neighbors and large trading partners.[9] In 2005, Uzbekistan and the Russian Federation or Russia, currently Uzbekistan's largest trading partner, signed the Strategic Framework Agreement and Alliance Relations Treaty to boost economic ties, which was reaffirmed with a new Declaration on a Comprehensive Strategic Partnership between the two countries in 2022.[10] In 2021, the EU accepted Uzbekistan as a beneficiary of its generalized scheme of preferences, allowing Uzbekistan to export 6,200 tariff-free products to the EU.[11] A similar agreement was made with the United Kingdom (UK) to export 7,800 types of locally produced goods with zero tariffs.[12]

In 2022, the largest markets for Uzbekistan's goods were Russia (16% of total export volume) followed by the PRC (13%). Neighbors Kazakhstan (7.1%) and the Kyrgyz Republic (5%) remained important markets for exports of Uzbek goods and services. Exports to Türkiye are steadily increasing, accounting for 7.8% of total exports in 2022 (Figure 6.2). The export structure of Uzbekistan is shown in the Appendix as Figure A6.1.

Figure 6.2: Uzbekistan Exports to Major Markets, 2017–2022
($ billion)

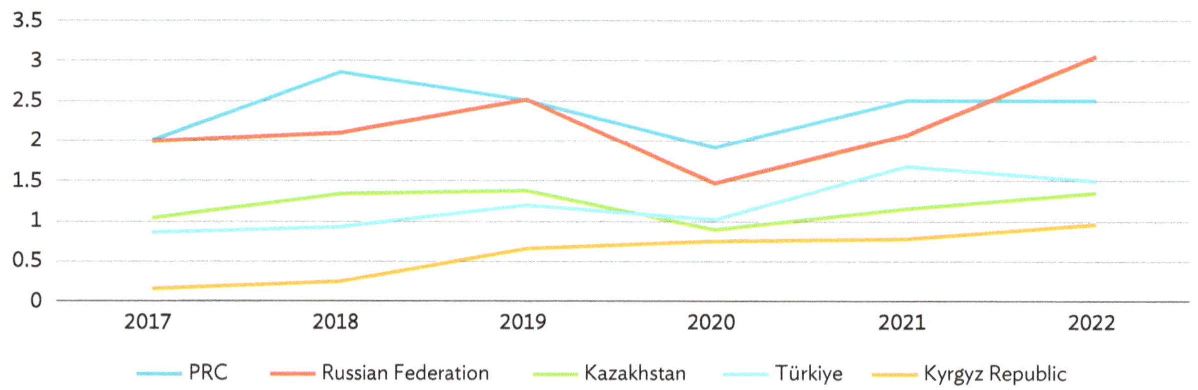

PRC = People's Republic of China.
Source: UzStat (Statistics Agency under the President of the Republic of Uzbekistan). Foreign Economic Activity (accessed 2 August 2024).

In 2022, Russia and the PRC were Uzbekistan's largest import markets, accounting for 21% of total import volume. Kazakhstan (10.5%), the Republic of Korea (7.5%), and Türkiye (5.5%) are other important import markets (Figure 6.3). The export structure of Uzbekistan is shown in the Appendix (Figure A6.2).

7 United States Department of Commerce. 2022. Uzbekistan—Country Commercial Guide: Trade Agreements.
8 *Tashkent Times*. 2021. Uzbekistan Eyeing Membership in Eurasian Development Bank. 19 November.
9 Ministry of Economic Development of the Russian Federation. Protocol of Using the Commonwealth of Independent States Free Trade Agreement of 2011 between Agreement Signatories and Uzbekistan (in Russian).
10 President of Russia. 2022. Declaration on Comprehensive Strategic Partnership between the Russian Federation and the Republic of Uzbekistan (in Russian).
11 A. Ten et al 2021. Uzbekistan to Get New Preferences from EU. Kursiv.
12 Gov.uk. 2021a. Uzbekistan is the First Beneficiary of the United Kingdom's EK Enhanced GSP Scheme.

Figure 6.3: Uzbekistan Imports from Major Markets, 2017–2022
($ billion)

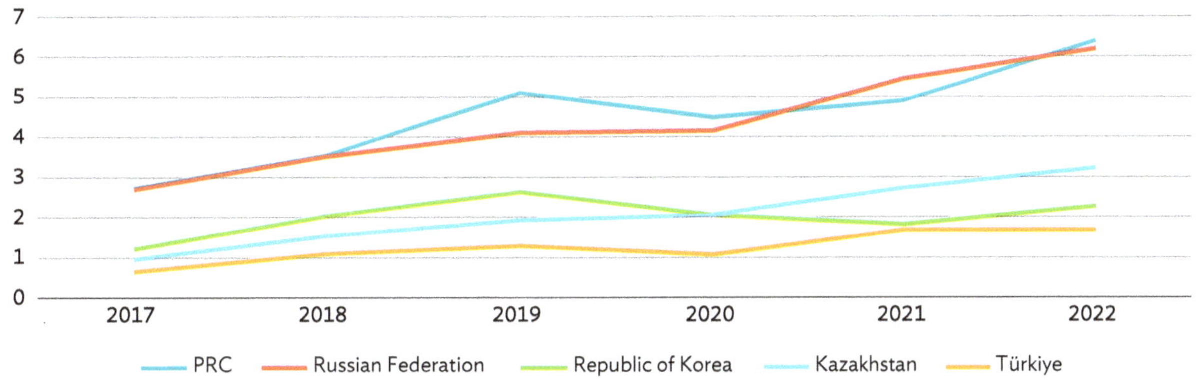

Source: UzStat (Statistics Agency under the President of the Republic of Uzbekistan). Foreign Economic Activity (accessed 2 August 2024).

The overall growth rate in exported value in 2020–2021 is smaller than the growth rate in 2017–2021 due to the global crisis caused by the COVID-19 pandemic that happened during this period. However, in 2020–2021 the growth rate with the main exporting countries (the PRC, Russia, Turkey, Kazakhstan) had increased, despite the overall (with the world) export growth rate remaining smaller (Table 6.1).

Table 6.1: Export Trends to Major Markets

Importers	Value of Exports 2021 ($ million)	Trade Balance 2021 ($ million)	Share in Uzbekistan's Exports (%)	Growth in Exports 2017–2021 (%)	Growth in Exports 2020–2021 (%)
World	14,035	(9,689)	100	9.0	7.0
PRC	1,744	(3,116)	12.4	1.0	36.0
Russian Federation	1,703	(3,628)	12.1	0	47.0
Türkiye	1,638	(17.0)	11.7	16.0	73.0
Kazakhstan	1,023	(1,677)	7.3	(4.0)	40.0
Kyrgyz Republic	770	613	5.5	51.0	8.0
Afghanistan	493	488	3.5	1.0	(3.0)
Tajikistan	329	231	2.3	44.0	16.0
Ukraine	225	(244)	1.6	21.0	89.0
Iran	167	(85.7)	1.2	(10.0)	24.0
Pakistan	126	75.9	0.9	99.0	30.0
Turkmenistan	95	(592)	0.7	21.0	28.0
Poland	86.8	(72.3)	0.6	25.0	53.0
Azerbaijan	73.2	31.1	0.5	31.0	43.0

() = negative, PRC = People's Republic of China.
Source: International Trade Centre. Trade Map.

The growth in imports has been steadily increasing, resulting in a negative trade balance with most of Uzbekistan's trading partners (Table 6.2).

Table 6.2: Import Trends with Major Markets

Exporters	Value of Import 2021 ($ million)	Trade Balance 2021 ($ million)	Share in Uzbekistan's Imports (%)	Growth in Imports 2017–2021 (%)	Growth in Imports 2020–2021 (%)
World	23,724	(9,689)	100	16.0	19.0
Russian Federation	5,332	(3,628)	22.5	18.0	31.0
PRC	4,861	(3,116)	20.5	15.0	10.0
Kazakhstan	2,701	(1.677)	11.4	27.0	29.0
Republic of Korea	1,742	(1,713)	7.3	9.0	(10.0)
Türkiye	1,656	(17)	7	22.0	54.0
Turkmenistan	688	(593)	2.9	53.0	74.0
Germany	646	(609)	2.7	2.0	(7.0)
Ukraine	470	(245)	2	20.0	50.0
India	458	(439)	1.9	16.0	9.0
Lithuania	437	(377)	1.8	17.0	(7.0)
Italy	386	(348)	1.6	24.0	19.0
Brazil	348	(346)	1.5	8.0	291.0

() = negative, PRC = People's Republic of China.
Source: International Trade Centre. Trade Map.

Foreign Direct Investment

Since 2017, the government has improved the country's investment climate by dismantling barriers and restrictions to doing business. The Law on Investment and Investment Activity adopted in 2019 and subsequent legislation changes made investment-related rules and norms more apprehensible for investors. The government's measures on reducing the overall tax burden, making access to commodities easier, and starting the privatization of state-owned enterprises together with improved investor relations mechanisms led to an increased FDI inflow to the country (Figure 6.4).

Ongoing investment reforms include liberalizing the foreign exchange rules and establishing special economic zones (SEZ) with a set of financial benefits for investors. As of early 2023, there were 22 SEZs: 12 industrial, 6 pharmaceutical, 2 agricultural, and 2 tourism (see Table A6.1 in the Appendix). The government used to provide generous benefits to firms registered in SEZs, which were exempted from customs duties on imports of raw materials and equipment; and income, land, and property taxes. Although some benefits were abolished in June 2020, this only applied to firms registered after that date. That notwithstanding, investment conditions in the SEZs are still quite attractive. Firms are still exempted from property and land tax, and land plots are provided free for the life of the SEZ. To enhance their attractiveness, SEZ infrastructure—roads, access to electricity and natural gas grids, and water supply—have been upgraded by the government. From 2008 to 2021, SEZs hosted 448 projects worth $2.4 billion of which $764.6 million was foreign direct investment. Special economic zones have created some 34,000 jobs.[13]

Figure 6.4: Foreign Direct Investment Inflows to Uzbekistan, 2000–2020
($ million)

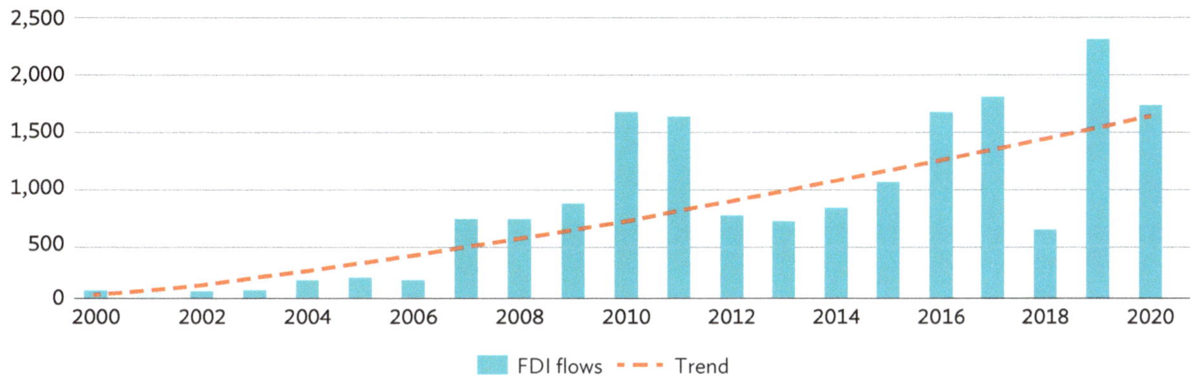

FDI = foreign direct investment.
Source: UNCTAD. Investment Policy Review 2021.

Reforms have undoubtedly increased Uzbekistan's appeal as a destination for international capital, and data clearly shows this. Even so, the pandemic's impact on the global economy weighed on FDI, with inflows declining by 25.5% to $1.7 billion in 2020 from $2.3 billion in pre-pandemic 2019. Landlocked Uzbekistan took a double hit from delayed investment projects caused by border closures and other restrictive measures taken by national and neighboring authorities. But as Table 6.3 shows, FDI inflows rebounded in 2021, when the FDI stock totaled $11.3 billion.

Table 6.3: Foreign Direct Investment Inflows to Uzbekistan, 2017–2021
($ million)

	FDI	2017	2018	2019	2020	2021	2020–2021 Growth Rate (%)
FDI flows	Inward	1,797	625	2,316	1,726	2,044	18.5
	Outward	9	2	3	2	3	51
FDI stock	Inward	10,045	8,993	9,582	10,288	11,278	9.6
	Outward	187	191	194	195	198	1.4

FDI = foreign direct investment.
Note: The World Bank defines FDI inflows as the value of inward direct investment made by nonresident investors in the reporting economy; FDI outflows are the value of outward direct investment made by the residents of the reporting economy to foreign economies.
Source: UNCTAD. *Country Fact Sheet: Uzbekistan*.

13 Ministry of Investment, Industry, and Trade of Uzbekistan. 2021. Free Economic Zones—Results for 2020 and Development Perspectives for 2021 (in Russian).

While new sectors such as electricity distribution, tourism, and banking are increasingly attracting FDI, the size of these sectors is smaller than traditional investment sectors, such as mining, manufacturing, construction, and agriculture, which dominate the FDI portfolio (Table 6.4).

Table 6.4: Foreign Direct Investment in Uzbekistan by Sector, 2021

Sector	Amount (SUM billion)	Share of Total Investment (%)
Manufacturing	63,225	25.8
Mining	23,199	9.5
Construction	20,274	8.3
Agriculture	18,934	7.7

Source: Halyk Research. 2021. *Republic of Uzbekistan: Results of 2021, Almaty* (in Russian).

A special short-term strategy to better facilitate FDI was adopted in 2020 by presidential decree.[14] The strategy includes a list of projects covering 24 sectors where the government will prioritize attracting foreign investment. The range of sectors shows a diversified approach that leans toward new industries. The geographic spread of the FDI portfolio includes not only traditional investors, such as the PRC, the Republic of Korea, European countries, and Russia but also newer investors from India, Iran, Japan, and the United Arab Emirates. Some 50 countries are investing in Uzbekistan. The top five in 2021 were the PRC ($2.2 billion), Russia ($2.1 billion), Türkiye ($1.18 billion), Germany ($800.7 million), and the Republic of Korea ($137.4 million).[15]

The Statistics Agency under the President of the Republic of Uzbekistan (UzStat) records only inward FDI flows. The government has no policies or mechanisms promoting outward FDI, thus; official statistics do not have available open data on this. Outward investment usually goes through three channels: (i) official bilateral external economic agreements; (ii) efforts by state-owned enterprises (SOEs) to boost exports by investing in joint ventures; and (iii) private investment for market expansion, access to resources in foreign countries, promotional marketing, and the expatriation of capital.

Figure 6.5 shows the FDI attractiveness of various sectors of the economy in Uzbekistan. The darker green area shows the sectors—electrical equipment, packaging materials, banks, and renewable energy—where it will be possible to promote FDI in the short to medium term. Sectors in the lighter green and other areas require additional policy reforms to unlock their potential to attract investment; these include food processing and construction materials. The challenge for these sectors is to identify the policy reforms that can ready them for investment promotion.[16]

14 President of the Republic of Uzbekistan. 2020. Presidential Decree PP 4563 on Measures to Implement the Investment Program of the Republic of Uzbekistan for 2020–2022 (in Russian).
15 A. Sim. 2022. Which Countries and How Much Invested in Uzbekistan in 2021 (in Russian).
16 World Bank. 2022. *Recommendations for a National Foreign Direct Investment Strategy and Roadmap for Uzbekistan: New Sources of Growth*.

Figure 6.5: Foreign Direct Investment Attractiveness by Sector

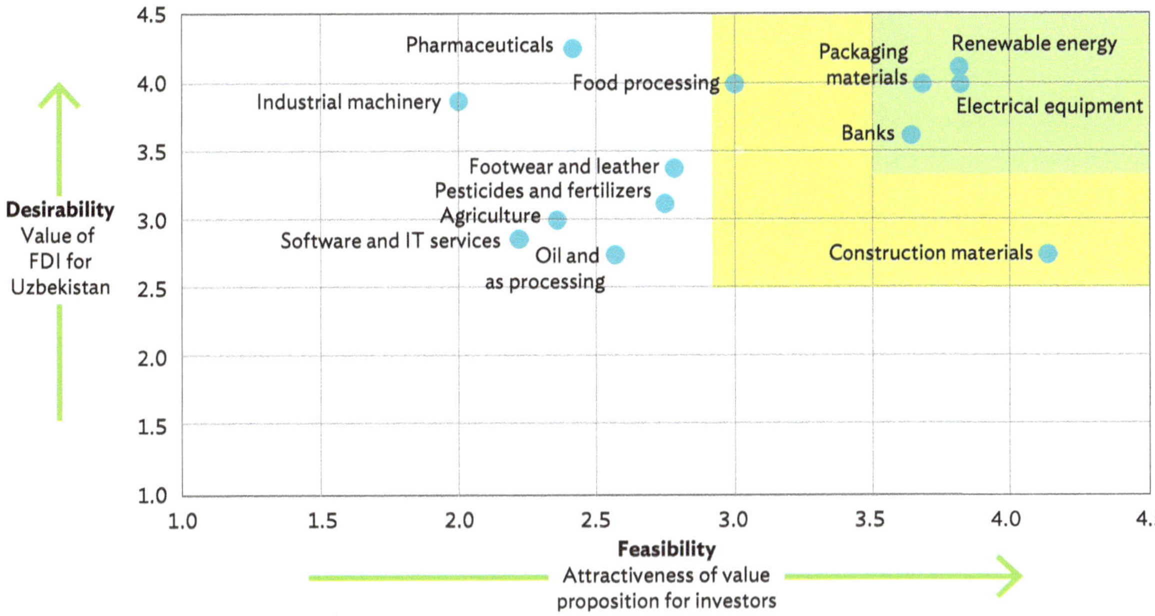

FDI = foreign direct investment, IT = information technology.
Source: World Bank. 2022. *Recommendations for a National Foreign Direct Investment Strategy and Roadmap for Uzbekistan: New Sources of Growth*.

Transport Connectivity

Transportation has been high on the agenda of the outward-looking, market-oriented growth policies that the government has been pursuing since 2017. To better coordinate the sector, a separate Ministry of Transport was created in 2019 by expanding the functions of the National Automobile Transportation Agency. The ministry oversees national development policies in all types of transportation and the development of logistics facilities and transport corridor networks. The vision for the sector is set out in the National Strategy on the Development of the Transport System until 2035.[17]

Regional connectivity is an important component of transportation development, as set out in the Program on Improving Transportation Infrastructure to Diversify Foreign Trade Routes, 2018–2022. Reforms have shown Uzbekistan's intention to actively participate in existing regional transport corridors and to join various regional intergovernmental activities to develop new routes. The country's international trade and volume of cargo transportation have increased since reforms started in 2017. The total volume of international cargo transportation in 2017 was 1,174 million tons, and in 2021 1,512 million tons of goods were transported.

Developing regional corridors is a key focus area of the country's foreign policy and domestic development strategy. Uzbekistan's geographic location in the middle of the Eurasian continent provides favorable conditions for the country to be connected from all sides—that is, eastward to the PRC, westward to the Middle East, northward to Russia and Europe, and southward to the Indian subcontinent. Uzbekistan could become an important transit hub by connecting these points.

17 President of the Republic of Uzbekistan. 2019. Presidential Resolution ID-3867 on Approval of the Strategy for the Development of the Transport System until 2035 (in Russian).

The closure of borders between Russia and the EU countries as a political reaction of Western countries to Russia's war in Ukraine increased the role of Central Asian countries, including Uzbekistan, as an alternative land route connecting the West and the East. This route, known as the Middle Corridor or TRACECA[18] corridor, came to prominence for its PRC–Central Asia–Caucasus–Türkiye–Europe connection. Uzbekistan has increased transport cooperation with Kazakhstan and Turkmenistan so that it can increase the volume and frequency of cargo through the Caspian Sea ports of Aktau and Turkmenbashi.

Uzbekistan's transport corridor development plans prioritize connecting with the PRC, a key trading partner, with alternative, faster, and economically cheaper routes. The current link to the PRC goes via Kazakhstan by rail. The alternative option reaching the PRC via the Kyrgyz Republic will be cheaper by 20%.[19] This option, however, requires midway transit by road. At the Samarkand Summit of the Shanghai Cooperation Organization in September 2022, the governments of Uzbekistan, the Kyrgyz Republic, and the PRC signed an agreement to do a feasibility study of the 523-kilometer (km) Uzbekistan–Kyrgyz Republic–PRC rail project, which was completed on 1 June 2023. A pilot multimodal transportation route was launched in 2022 to connect the PRC, the Kyrgyz Republic, Uzbekistan, and Afghanistan, where cargo from Kashgar in the PRC will be delivered by trucks to Osh in the Kyrgyz Republic, and the remaining legs to Osh–Andijan (Uzbekistan)–Hairatan (Afghanistan) will be by rail.

Connecting Uzbekistan to the Islamic Republic of Iran is another important transportation agenda. Talks between the two countries on developing trade and cooperation resulted in the signing of an agreement in 2022 giving Uzbekistan cargo access to Chabahar Port in Iran via Turkmenistan (and potentially via Afghanistan in the future). This agreement provides an opportunity for Uzbek goods to reach new markets in, for example, India and the Middle East. However, the international sanctions imposed on Iran and political tensions that regularly erupt in the Persian Gulf pose risks for relying on this route.

The Uzbek government considers Afghanistan an important country in the regional connectivity network. It is an active proponent of building a trans-Afghan rail link to connect Uzbekistan with Pakistan. Three countries have already negotiated a project to build the Termez–Mazar-i-Sharif–Peshawar rail link. Pakistan is not only a potentially large consumer market for Uzbek products but also provides agricultural products that have a niche in the Uzbekistan market. The ports of Karachi and Gwadar are attractive access points to sea lanes to Southeast Asian markets. While railroad projects are awaiting their own time of implementation in the future, the connection through automobile roads has already been activated. In May 2021, the first truck loaded with goods left Uzbekistan and reached Pakistan through Afghanistan, a 48-hour journey.

18 The Transport Corridor Europe-Caucasus-Asia (TRACECA) is an international transport program on cooperation between the European Union and partner countries in Eastern Europe, the Caucasus, and Central Asia on the organization of the Europe-Caucasus-Asia transport corridor.

19 *Podrobno.uz*. 2017. Opening of the Pilot Autorally China–Kyrgyzstan–Uzbekistan in Tashkent (in Russian).

National Priorities in Regional Cooperation

Relationship with Eurasian Economic Union

In December 2020, Uzbekistan received observer status in the EAEU. The rationale for deepening cooperation with the EAEU was Uzbekistan's increasing trade with the union's member countries, which, in 2022, reached 31.4% of total foreign trade (Figure 6.6). The EAEU countries imported 75% of Uzbekistan's agricultural production in 2020.20 Russia and Kazakhstan are Uzbekistan's second- and third-biggest trading partners, and the Kyrgyz Republic is the fifth. The trade with EAEU countries has clearly growing patterns. In **2022, it rose by 22.7% from the level in 2021, totaling $15.7 billion**.[21]

Figure 6.6: Uzbekistan's Exports and Imports with Eurasian Economic Union, 2022

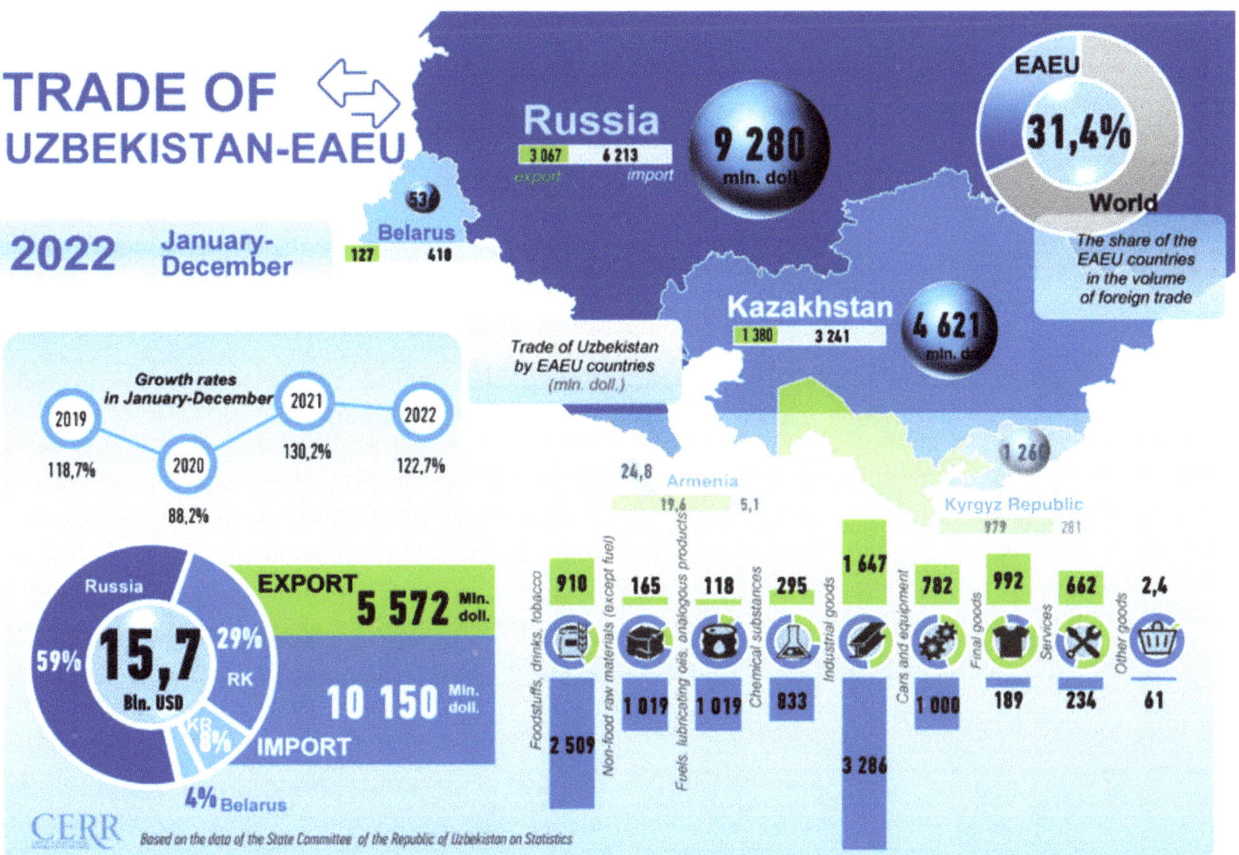

EAEU = Eurasian Economic Union, RK = Republic of Kazakhstan, KR = Kyrgyz Republic.
Source: Center for Economic Research and Reforms.

Russia remains one of the key trading partners for almost all countries of the former Soviet Union, including Uzbekistan (Figure 6.7). It is in Uzbekistan's best interest to maintain good trading relations with Russia and seek the economic benefits that can come from exporting goods and services to that country. Given the changes and transformations happening in the CIS, the Government of the Russian Federation may, in the future, seek to deepen economic cooperation with CIS countries through the

20 Grata International. 2020. Uzbekistan Received Observer Status in the Eurasian Economic Union (EAEU). 21 December.
21 Center for Economic Research and Reforms. 2023. Infographics: Development of Uzbekistan in 2022 (in Russian).

framework of the EAEU rather than CIS free trade agreements. For countries in the region, this may require their closer compliance with EAEU requirements if they want to maximize the benefits of closer economic cooperation with the Russian Federation.

Figure 6.7: Countries with the Highest Trade Share in Gross Domestic Product with the Russian Federation, 2020
(%)

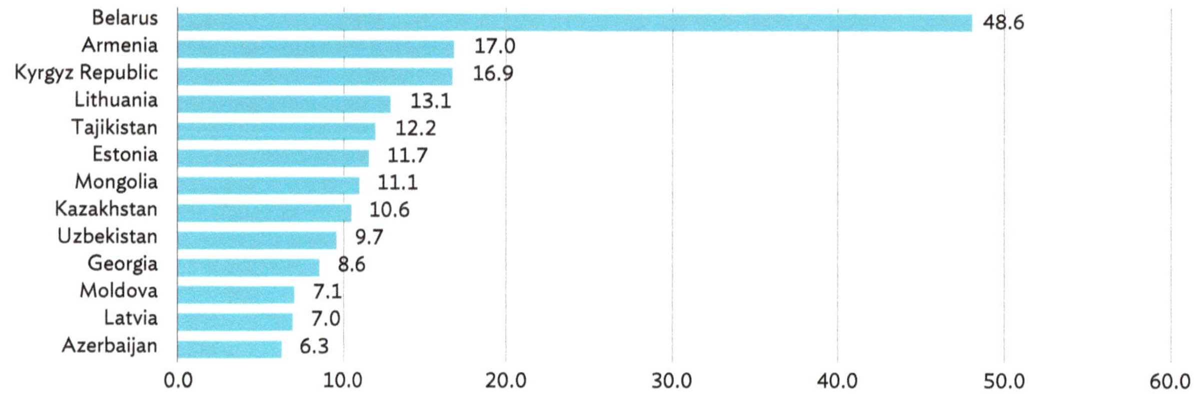

Note: Gross domestic product is the sum of merchandise imports and exports from and to Russia divided by total GDP in current United States dollars.
Source: Statista.com (accessed 15 August 2024).

The discussions on Uzbekistan's full EAEU membership have slowed as the country is still considering the cost and benefits of joining it. Doing so could bring the following benefits:

(i) Access to a large customs territory with common tariffs and regulations would allow exporters to not only benefit from nontariff agreements but also from better logistics with no or minimum barriers in crossing borders.

(ii) Membership in a large market zone with a population of 180 million could potentially attract more investment, boosting the scale of production, which already has a significant capacity for food and industrial goods.

(iii) Membership in an open market zone also would increase competition in certain sectors, including manufacturing and automaking. Given the similar level of technological development in other member countries, the competition would not be severe, but at a level that would encourage the manufacturing and automotive sectors in Uzbekistan to continuously improve product quality, while minimizing the operational cost.

(iv) Membership would benefit millions of migrants from Uzbekistan, mainly in Russia, by removing restrictions and simplifying procedures for employers. Education and skills diplomas and certificates from Uzbekistan would be recognized throughout the EAEU. Migrants from Uzbekistan could get access to the financial services of the banking system in EAEU countries, including loans, credits, and pension savings.

A potential downside is that the invasion of Ukraine and the Western sanctions against Russia could depress the Russian economy, which carries socioeconomic risks for trading partners, including Uzbekistan.

Membership in the Shanghai Cooperation Organization

Uzbekistan has had a long and dynamic partnership with the Shanghai Cooperation Organization (SCO), being one of the six founding countries. In November 2019, at a meeting of the heads of government of SCO countries in Tashkent, a new program of multilateral trade and economic cooperation up to 2035 was approved.[22]

Strengthening trade and economic relations with the SCO is of great importance for Uzbekistan, since SCO countries are already among its main foreign trade partners. Other SCO members India and Pakistan present new marketing opportunities for Uzbekistan in the near term. Trade between Uzbekistan and the SCO has accelerated in the last few years (Figure 6.8).

Figure 6.8: Uzbekistan's Trade with Shanghai Cooperation Organization Countries
($ billion)

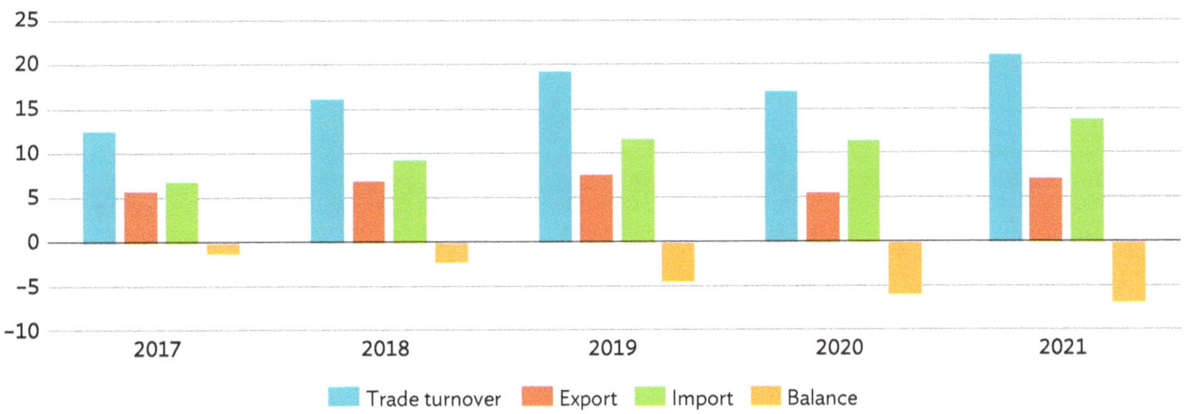

Source: *Rewiew.uz.* 2022. How Uzbekistan Trades with the SCO Countries. 13 September.

Given Uzbekistan's remoteness from the oceans, transport cooperation in the SCO could provide connectivity alternatives. An agreement on creating favorable conditions for international road transport was signed by SCO members in 2014 that could be useful for Uzbekistan's search for secure transport corridors to connect with external markets.[23] Under the agreement, SCO countries allow cargo from member countries to transit through each other's territory.

Membership in the World Trade Organization

In his Address to Parliament in December 2017, President Shavkat Mirziyoyev relaunched Uzbekistan's WTO membership process after a 15-year break. For Uzbekistan, joining the WTO will enable it to avail of the benefits of membership and help the country promote international trade using a rules-based approach. Almost all of Uzbekistan's trading partners are WTO members. Also, the market-oriented reforms that have been carried out in the country require exploring new foreign markets beyond its traditional partners and Uzbekistan's membership in WTO could create enabling conditions for such efforts.

22 U. Khasanov. 2019. The SCO and the Transformation of Modern Political Processes. 7 November.
23 Shanghai Cooperation Organization. Documents.

Joining the WTO is a complex process. The negotiations for Russia and Kazakhstan to join it lasted 19 years, almost 12 years for Tajikistan, and 14 years for Ukraine. The multistage negotiations affect all sectors of an economy to various extents and bring changes not only to a country's foreign trade regime (e.g., customs rates, technical regulation, sanitary and phytosanitary measures) but also to regulatory regimes, such as state support for agriculture and industrial production. Both are important sectors of the Uzbek economy and provide a sizable share of GDP and employment. As part of the negotiation process, Uzbekistan should improve intellectual property rights, regulations in the services sector, and public procurement, identify price regulation mechanisms by the state, and ensure transparency in the privatization activities of state-owned enterprises.

At the end of 2022, the negotiation process was at the multilateral stage that consists of three phases: fact-finding, negotiations, and a draft working party report on commitments (Figure 6.9).

Figure 6.9: World Trade Organization Membership Process for Uzbekistan

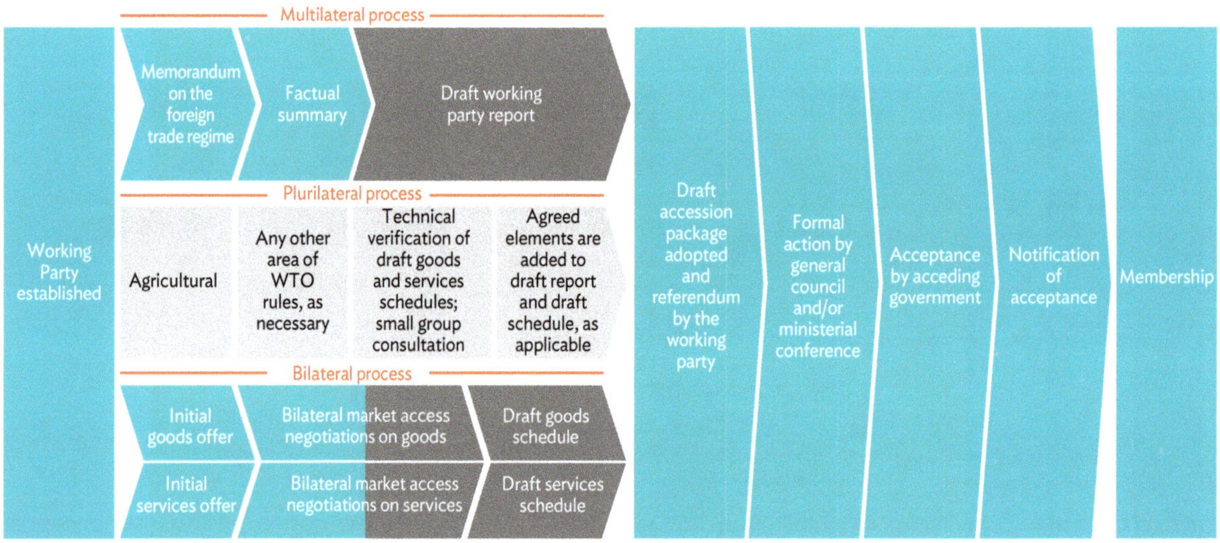

Source: World Trade Organization. Uzbekistan Accession Process (accessed 15 August 2024).

The government, at the time of writing, was providing no information on the state of the negotiations. All documents generated throughout the negotiation process are uploaded to the WTO's database, but access to these documents is restricted.[24]

Analyses of Uzbekistan joining the WTO are based on the general aspects of potential benefits and challenges. However, these are hypothetical because no information or data have been released on specific issues. The overarching argument for any country on the benefits of joining the WTO is based on studies showing the economic harm of protectionism is greater than its benefits, underlining protectionism as not being a viable policy for economic development in the long term.

24 WTO. Uzbekistan Accession Documents Database.

The benefits of Uzbekistan's membership can be summarized into four main reasons. The first is that Uzbekistan has signed bilateral free trade agreements with 47 countries. Becoming a WTO member would automatically expand that list to 164 countries and economies. And, as mentioned earlier, almost all of Uzbekistan's trading partners are WTO members. Joining would enable Uzbekistan to expand trade with new partners without negotiating separate trade agreements. Trade liberalization in the multilateral WTO system with lower tariffs and most favorable nation treatment will give Uzbekistan an opportunity to diversify its exports.[25] Second, under the most favorable nation regime, member countries cannot increase tariff rates beyond agreed bound levels. This will provide certainty and tariff security for domestic exporters in Uzbekistan as the tariff factor would eventually play a more significant role as the country steadily diversifies its exports toward processed and ready-made products (see Appendix and Figure 6.14). Third, the WTO's dispute resolution mechanisms would allow Uzbekistan to more effectively challenge other countries' trade policies and actions that it sees as unfavorable or posing a threat to its foreign trade. Fourth, as a rule, countries that pursue policies to liberalize their trade, finance sector, and monetary operations tend to attract more foreign investment than those with heavy regulations and limitations in these areas. Since Uzbekistan is actively pursuing a path of market liberalization, joining the WTO will demonstrate the irreversibility of these reforms, which should boost investors' confidence.

Still, there are economic challenges to joining the WTO. Despite ongoing efforts in increasing the export of processed goods, Uzbekistan's export structure is still dominated by raw materials (e.g., gold, copper, zinc, and natural gas), which have, as strategic commodities, easier access to foreign markets and are not affected by tariffs. WTO membership would bring minimal, if any, changes in these sectors. However, agriculture and industry, especially automaking and textiles, should be ready for increased competition from imports once protection mechanisms are reduced or abolished. Therefore, WTO's most favorable nation regime may not provide significant benefits to Uzbekistan if the country is unable to diversify exports by increasing processed and final products. Another challenge is that under WTO rules, it might be difficult for the government to easily enact sector or enterprise support measures providing grants, tax incentives, and subsidies without complying with those rules.

Participation in the Central Asia Regional Economic Cooperation Program

The CAREC Program facilitates projects and policy support programs that promote regional cooperation, economic integration, and connectivity to ensure sustainable economic growth and shared prosperity for 11 of its member countries in Central Asia. The program was established in 2001 and has been working with the Government of Uzbekistan to improve connectivity and logistics infrastructure to boost international trade by increasing the country's capacity to reach external markets. Uzbekistan received close to $8 billion (as of 2021) in the form of investment, loans, and technical assistance through the CAREC Program.

The program has identified three main transport corridors transiting through Uzbekistan: Europe–Mediterranean–East Asia, Russia–Middle East–South Asia, and Europe–Middle East–South Asia. Under CAREC corridor development initiatives, Uzbekistan receives support in areas related to CAREC's five operational clusters,[26] which include upgrading domestic transport infrastructure and expanding transportation systems to neighboring countries, namely, the rail link to Afghanistan,

25 R. Pomfret. 2020. Uzbekistan and the World Trade Organization. *Silk Road: A Journal of Eurasian Development*. 2 (1).

26 Information about CAREC operational clusters can be found in CAREC. *CAREC 2030: Connecting the Region for Shared and Sustainable Development*.

reconstructing the Bukhara–Nukus–Beyneu and the Tashkent–Osh international highways, and a 145-km railroad electrification project. The expanded transport infrastructure aims to foster regional cooperation and trade through better connectivity.

Highlights of Regional and Bilateral Relations

Economic Cooperation with Central Asian Republics

1. Kazakhstan

This is Uzbekistan's third-largest trading partner, and geographically, the largest of the countries with which Uzbekistan shares a common border. Kazakhstan and Uzbekistan account for 70% of regional trade in Central Asia.[27] In 2022, trade between the countries totaled $4.6 billion, up 18% from 2021. The two are implementing 38 joint projects worth $2.2 billion that could potentially create 11,000 jobs.[28] Foreign direct investment from Kazakhstan to Uzbekistan grew from $186.4 million in 2018 to $331.4 million in 2022, while Uzbekistan's investment in Kazakhstan increased from $8.6 million to $42.2 million for the same period.[29] The number of enterprises with Kazakh capital in Uzbekistan increased from 510 in 2019 to 1,056 in 2021, while 2,144 enterprises with Uzbek capital were registered in Kazakhstan. The volume of traffic between Uzbekistan and Kazakhstan in 2020, at 21 million tons, was up 19% from 2019.[30]

The two countries have begun building the Central Asia International Centre for Trade and Economic Cooperation on the Kazakhstan–Uzbekistan border near the Zhibek Zholy–Gisht Kuprik checkpoint. The aim is for the center to become a major industrial, trade, and logistics platform for joint investment projects, primarily in manufacturing, agro, and light industries. The center's workforce capacity is estimated at 35,000 people and it will be able to handle 5,000 trucks a day in both directions.[31] The center is being developed in stages: the preparatory stage was in 2019; the investment stage, over 2020–2023, includes building infrastructure; and long-term development is over 2023–2025. The center's primary tasks include building a new modern checkpoint, wholesale and retail trade facilities and adjacent infrastructure, and a transport and logistics center. The center is close to large agglomerations, Tashkent and Shymkent (Kazakhstan's third-largest city).

2. The Kyrgyz Republic

Trade with Uzbekistan surged from $167.4 million in 2016 to $1.3 billion in 2022, with exports rising from $121.5 million to $979.3 million,[32] making the Kyrgyz Republic the fifth-largest importer of products made in Uzbekistan.

In 2021, the two countries signed an agreement regulating water consumption and energy exchange for 2021–2023. That created an effective cooperative mechanism for water accumulation in the Toktogul reservoir in the Kyrgyz Republic so that Uzbekistan receives enough water for irrigation needs

27 Investment Promotion Agency under the Ministry of Investment and Foreign Trade of Uzbekistan.
28 *Astana Times*. 2022. Kazakhstan, Uzbekistan Sign 40 Agreements Worth $2.5 Billion at Tashkent Business Forum. 22 December.
29 A. Ten. 2023. Investments of Uzbekistan in Kazakhstan Collapsed by 62% (in Russian).
30 U. Nuriddinov. 2022. Bilateral Cooperation between Uzbekistan and Kazakhstan: Will the Dynamics Continue? Central Asian Bureau for Analytical Reporting. 14 January.
31 A. Satubaldina. 2021. Kazakh, Uzbek PMs Launch Construction of Central Asia International Centre for Trade and Economic Cooperation. *Astana Times*. 12 April.
32 UzStat (Statistics Agency under the President of the Republic of Uzbekistan). Foreign Economic Activity (accessed 2 August 2024).

during the growing season, while Uzbekistan supplies electricity to its neighbor in spring and autumn.[33] In early 2023, Uzbekistan, Kyrgyz Republic, and Kazakhstan signed a joint roadmap of building a large hydropower station Kambarata-1 with a capacity of 1,860 megawatts.[34] In transportation, both countries are promoting the PRC–Kyrgyz Republic–Uzbekistan rail project and multimodal transport links. In January 2023, the two countries signed an agreement on border demarcation, completing a long series of border negations.

3. Tajikistan

Its trade with Uzbekistan more than tripled from $196.8 million in 2016 to $674.4 million in 2022. A free trade regime between the two countries provides an enabling environment to intensify bilateral trade. In 2022, bilateral trade increased to 11.3% from the previous year with exports totaling $519.9 million and imports $154.5 million (footnote 33).

The volume of international rail cargo transportation between Uzbekistan and Tajikistan reached 6.7 million tons in 2021, up from 5.8 million tons in 2020, and international road cargo rose to 1.3 million tons from 408,200 tons for the same period. After 25 years, in 2017, the two countries resumed direct flights between capital cities. In 2021, Uzbekistan Airways had 440 regular flights transporting 46,600 passengers, 10.7% more than the previous year; and 113 tons of cargo, 3.3% more than the previous year.[35]

In 2022, Uzbekistan and Tajikistan started the construction of the new Yavan hydropower plant on the Zarafshan River in Tajikistan, which will have a capacity of 140 megawatts.[36] Once the plant becomes operational, it will be Central Asia's first example of intergovernmental cooperation in renewable energy.

4. Turkmenistan

Bilateral trade volume in 2022 reached $926.2 million. Exports from Uzbekistan to Turkmenistan have more than doubled since 2017, reaching $194.8 million in 2022, and imports from Turkmenistan rose more than fivefold, reaching $731.4 million. Over the same period, the number of enterprises with the participation of Turkmen capital in Uzbekistan rose from 11 to 160, and 61 companies operating in Turkmenistan with the participation of capital from Uzbekistan, including automotive firms.[37]

In 2021, international cargo transportation volume between Uzbekistan and Turkmenistan reached almost 2 million tons (1.7 million by rail, 1.3 million by road), an 18% increase from 2020.[38] The implementation of the large-scale regional rail project, Kerki–Akina–Andkhoy rail links, will not only contribute to better connectivity between the two countries but also create favorable conditions for increased international cargo transit through them. This will also be facilitated by the increased use of the Turkmenbash seaport and the full launch of a multimodal transport corridor along the Uzbekistan–Turkmenistan–Caspian Sea route.

33 K. Timofeeva. 2021 Kyrgyzstan and Uzbekistan Agree on Electricity Exchange (in Russian).
34 *Azattyk News*. 2023. Three Countries Decided to Jointly Build the Kambarata HPP-1 in Kyrgyz Republic (in Russian). 8 January.
35 *Eureporter*. 2022b. Uzbek-Tajik Relations: A New Period of Growth. 6 June.
36 National Electric Grid. 2022. Construction of Modern Hydroelectric Power Plant Starts. *News*. 2 June.
37 *Eureporter*. 2022a. Prospects of Trade and Economic Partnership between Uzbekistan and Turkmenistan. 21 July.
38 International Trade Centre. Trade Map.

Economic Cooperation with the People's Republic of China

In 2022, Uzbekistan signed a 5-year Program on Trade and Investment Cooperation with the PRC. Uzbekistan is deepening its cooperation with the PRC in various areas including those that promote Uzbekistan's capacity to effectively participate in regional cooperation and integration such as diversifying its transportation infrastructure network and reaching new export markets. The PRC is not only Uzbekistan's largest trading partner but also a key investor and lender to the Uzbek economy. In 2022, the PRC's share in Uzbekistan's foreign trade totaled 17.8%. In 2020, Uzbekistan's debt to the PRC reached $3 billion, 20% of total foreign debt. The PRC's investment in Uzbekistan totaled $9 billion at the end of 2021.[39] Investments of the PRC in Uzbekistan are diversified, varying from oil and gas to agriculture and logistics.

Exports from the PRC to Uzbekistan surged from $2.7 billion in 2017 to $6.4 billion in 2022, but imports from Uzbekistan to the PRC rose from only $2.0 billion to $2.5 billion (Figure 6.10). While the PRC's exports to Uzbekistan remain diversified across various industrial products, Uzbekistan mainly supplies mineral fuels, particularly natural gas, which comprises 38% of total exports, and cotton, which comprises 33% (footnote 40).

Figure 6.10: Uzbekistan's Trade with the People's Republic of China
($ billion)

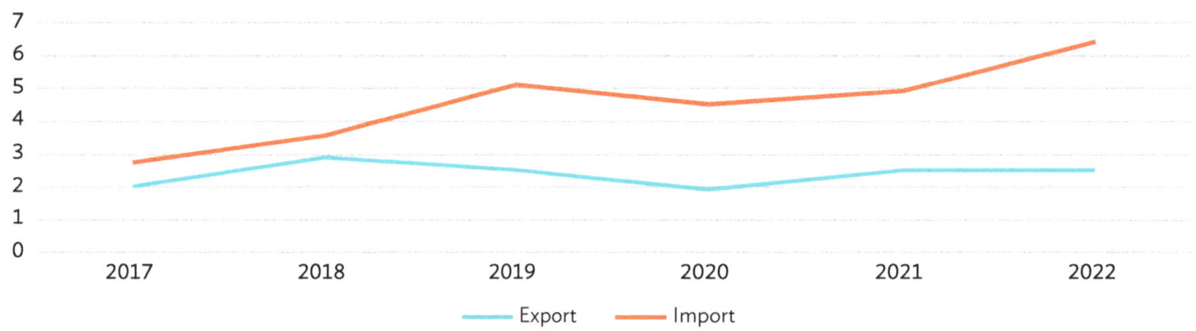

Source: UzStat (Statistics Agency under the President of the Republic of Uzbekistan). Foreign Economic Activity (accessed 5 August 2024).

A major goal for Uzbekistan is to strengthen connectivity with the PRC by diversifying transport connection options and further expansion of export capacity by finding a niche in the PRC. In the future, the PRC could become a key transit country for Uzbekistan and other Central Asian countries to connect with economic partners in South Asia via the China–Pakistan Economic Corridor and Southeast Asia.

The PRC also sees Uzbekistan as an important partner in its Belt and Road Initiative. Although the two countries do not share common borders, Uzbekistan's strategic location that borders all other Central Asian countries and Afghanistan means the country could become a vital transport hub between the PRC and Europe. Negotiations over the PRC–Kyrgyz Republic–Uzbekistan rail link have been revived after long and teetering talks. In September 2022, the three countries signed a

39 A. Khitakhunov. 2022b. *Economic Cooperation between Uzbekistan and China*. Almaty, Eurasian Research Institute.

cooperation agreement, and a project office was set up in Bishkek in January 2023 to coordinate the implementation stages. The 260-km rail line is estimated to cost about $4.1 billion[40] and will shorten by 900 km the travel distance between the PRC and Europe.[41] The two countries are also cooperating on improving domestic connectivity in Uzbekistan. In 2013, the PRC's Export-Import Bank provided a loan of $350 million to build the 14-km Kamchik tunnel on the new Angren–Pap rail line connecting regions in Fergana Valley with other parts of the country and bypassing Tajikistan, making cargo and passenger travel faster and cheaper. The line was completed in 2016.

Uzbekistan plays an important role in the Central Asia–PRC gas pipeline. The 1,833-km pipeline passes through 530 km of Uzbek territory, with the country supplying the PRC with 10 billion cubic meters (m^3) of natural gas per annum through the pipeline (out of the pipeline's total 55 billion/m^3).[42] Uzbekistan, however, is planning to stop exporting natural gas by 2025 to use it for domestic consumption; this means it will benefit only from transit fees from the regional pipeline.[43] The ongoing efforts of constructing a fourth pipeline (line D) in addition to the existing three parallel lines of Central Asia–PRC pipeline connecting Turkmenistan and the PRC via Uzbekistan, Tajikistan, and the Kyrgyz Republic could increase piping capacity from 55 billion/m^3 a year to 85 billion/m^3.[44] The project, if completed, could provide additional fees from transit services for Uzbekistan.

Economic Cooperation with Afghanistan and Pakistan

Strengthening transport connectivity and trade are the two main goals of Uzbekistan's bilateral cooperation with Afghanistan and Pakistan. Afghanistan, which shares common borders with Uzbekistan, is a potential gate point to South Asian markets and deep seaports.

In 2021, a potential Mazar-i-Sharif–Kabul–Peshawar railway was discussed. The project promises economic benefits not just for the countries involved but for all Central Asian countries. However, the political uncertainty in Afghanistan poses economic and financial risks to implementing the project.

Uzbekistan and Pakistan have signed two agreements that are expected to increase bilateral economic cooperation. A preferential trade agreement, signed in 2022, lowers duties and, where possible, removes them completely for 34 goods that represent the bulk of bilateral trade in commodities.[45] Both countries also agreed to recognize each other's quality standards to make customs procedures quicker and easier. The 2021 transit trade agreement allows Uzbek carriers to reach—via Afghanistan—Pakistan's Gwadar, Karachi, and Bin Qasim ports without reloading cargo onto Pakistan carriers at the Afghanistan–Pakistan border checkpoints.[46] In the first 6 months of 2022, 330,000 tons of cargo were transported on the Uzbekistan–Afghanistan–Pakistan route, up 2.6 times from the same period of the previous year.[47]

40 *Gazeta.uz*. 2022. The First Stages of the Implementation of the Railway Project Uzbekistan-Kyrgyzstan-China (in Russian). 16 December.
41 R. Preston. 2022. Work to Start Next Year on China–Kyrgyzstan–Uzbekistan Railway. *International Railway Journal*. 9 June.
42 F. Aminjonov and O. Dovgalyuk. 2023. Central Asia–China Gas Pipeline (Line A, Line B, and Line C). The People's Map of Global China. 7 February.
43 *Kun.uz*. 2020. Uzbekistan Plans to Cease Export of Natural Gas by 2025. 18 January.
44 D. Kroos et al. 2022. *Enhancing Energy Security in Central Asia* (in Russian). Vienna. Organization for Security and Cooperation in Europe.
45 S. Rana. 2022. Pakistan, Uzbekistan to Sign FTA. *The Express Tribune*.
46 *Agreement between the Government of the Isamic Republic of Pakistan and the Government of the Republic of Uzbekistan on Transit Trade*.
47 S. N. Burna-Asefi. 2022. Uzbekistan Looks South for New Trade Routes. *The Diplomat*. 1 April.

Economic Cooperation with the European Union, the United Kingdom, and the United States

In 2022, Uzbekistan and the EU signed the Expanded Partnership and Cooperation Agreement, which replaced the 1996 Partnership and Cooperation Agreement.[48] The new agreement covers a wide spectrum of bilateral cooperation priorities, including human rights; strengthening civil society; ensuring justice and the rule of law; and cooperation in trade, water, energy, transport, and other economic areas.

In 2021, the EU began applying special import tariffs for goods from Uzbekistan under the generalized scheme of preferences system that allowed 6,200 types of goods produced in Uzbekistan to enter the EU with either low or no customs duties.[49] Uzbekistan's trade with EU countries has increased from $2.6 billion in 2017 to $4.5 billion in 2022.[50] According to 2021 data, the EU countries accounted for 9.2% of Uzbekistan's total trade, 3.3% of exports, and 13.0% of imports. Uzbekistan's main trading partners in the EU are Germany (19.7% of total trade with the EU), Lithuania (13.0%), Italy (11.1%), the Netherlands (7.4%), France (7.2%), Poland (6.4%), Latvia (6.0%), Czech Republic (5.1%), Spain (4.1%), Hungary (3.0%) and Austria (2.7%).[51]

In 2017, 440 enterprises with the capital of European countries operated in Uzbekistan, which, in 2021, had risen to 1,052. Most of these firms have joint ventures with local firms, but 300 enterprises were fully owned by European investors (footnote 51).

In 2019, Uzbekistan and the UK signed a partnership and cooperation agreement that continued the reciprocal most-favored nation treatment in trade.[52] This document ensures the UK and Uzbekistan continue to grant each other most-favored nation treatment for trade. In 2021, an enhanced framework was signed under which the UK applied the generalized scheme of preferences to trade with Uzbekistan.[53] This allowed 91% of goods exported from Uzbekistan to the UK at a zero-tariff rate. Total trade between the UK and Uzbekistan has increased significantly since 2017, totaling £392 million in 2021 (Figure 6.11). According to the UK Department for Business & Trade, increased exports to the UK resulted in a £90 million surplus in Uzbekistan's balance of trade with the UK in 2021.[54]

48 Diplomatic Service of the European Union. 2022. Uzbekistan: The European Union and Uzbekistan Complete Negotiations for a New Enhanced Partnership and Cooperation Agreement.
49 Delegation of the European Union to Uzbekistan. 2021. Uzbekistan Joins the European Union Special Agreement GSP+. April 21.
50 *Eureporter*. 2023. Uzbekistan–EU: State of the Progress. 1 March.
51 O. Khakimov. 2022. Uzbekistan Expands Cooperation between Europe and Central Asia. EU Political Report.
52 Controller of Her Majesty's Stationery Office. 2019. *Partnership and Cooperation Agreement between the UK and Uzbekistan*.
53 Gov.uk. 2021b. UK Generalised Scheme of Preferences: Admission of Uzbekistan to the Enhanced Framework.
54 Department for Business & Trade, Government of the United Kingdom. 2023. Uzbekistan. *Trade and Investment Factsheets*. 18 May.

Figure 6.11: Trade Between the United Kingdom and Uzbekistan, 2012–2021
(£ million)

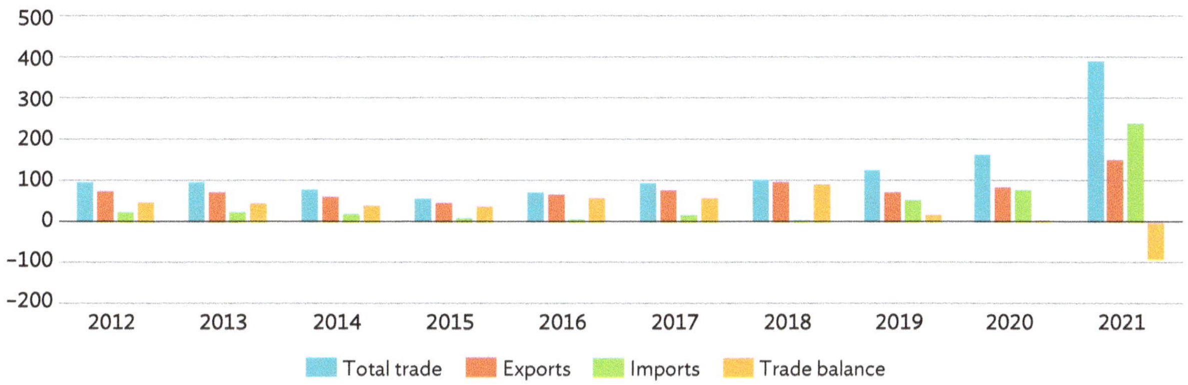

£ = British pound sterling.
Source: Department for Business & Trade, Government of the United Kingdom. 2023. Uzbekistan. *Trade and Investment Factsheets*. 18 May.

Uzbekistan is trying to strengthen bilateral relations with the United States, constantly striving to expand trade and economic cooperation. Trade between the two countries has been growing since 2020, but the volume remains small (Table 6.6).

Table 6.5: Trade Between the United States and Uzbekistan, 2020–2022
($ million)

Item	2020	2021	2022
Trade turnover	277.0	426.3	436.8
Export	28.5	60.8	68.5
Import	248.5	365.5	368.3

Note: Adapted from F. Ermanov. 2023 Uzbekistan–USA Partnership: A New Page in Their Relations (in Russian).
Sources: Institute of Strategic and Regional Studies under the President of Uzbekistan.

Conclusion

Policy Challenges

Uzbekistan's foreign trade policy should anticipate potential challenges that may intensify in 2023. Among these are WTO projections of slower global trade volume. In 2022, global trade is expected to have grown by 3.5%, but growth is forecast at only 1.0% in 2023 due to an easing in monetary tightening in the United States, and high energy prices caused by Russia's war in Ukraine. In the PRC, pandemic-related problems reemerged in 2022 that weakened external demand. For developing countries everywhere, rising energy and food prices may lead to socioeconomic instability. Given this backdrop, the government should create economic buffers against possible losses in external trade.

The export of commodities and raw materials still dominates Uzbekistan's external trade. In these uncertain times, the reliance on raw materials will increase the country's vulnerability to external price shocks.

The government should advance its membership in the WTO. Even before becoming a full member, accession measures adopted by Uzbekistan could help the country meet the stringent international requirements of developed countries that will eventually have a positive impact on the country's export potential. As part of the WTO's membership process, better compliance with international conventions on climate change mitigation, conservation of the environment, labor rights, and rule of law will enhance Uzbekistan's trade competitiveness.

Further trade liberalization while the WTO membership process is underway will enable the government to withstand pressure from domestic interest groups and monopolies such as SOEs. The country's accession to WTO will increase competition through which nonviable SOEs will disappear, bringing to economic prominence truly competitive enterprises.

External trade would benefit from small and medium-sized enterprises (SMEs) being more internationally oriented. The country has a good industrial base and is favorably located in terms of border access. But leveraging this will require linking SMEs to larger enterprises to facilitate their integration into regional and global trade and value chains, as they will need the technical competencies and skills upgrading to be able to enter these markets.

The winter energy crisis in 2022 showed that the energy system might not be able to cope with the growing demand. Systemic reforms and infrastructure investments are needed for the sector, and deepening energy cooperation in the region could be an effective solution to the country's energy security challenges.

Large FDI so far is attracted by the privatization of SOEs and channeled into already well-established enterprises and projects. New sectors and enterprises must receive support to attract FDI in the private sector or through public–private partnerships.

The government could further improve transparency in legal and regulatory processes in accessing various official information, including laws and regulations. Doing this will be needed to ensure there is transparency in the pursuit of new investments.

The further diversification of international routes and modalities is essential. Uzbekistan's dependency on just a few countries for transport connectivity could be a risk to its economic security. The government's initiatives to explore new connectivity options to the east, west, and south will provide access to new markets and help the country become a regional transit hub, ensuring regional interdependency. But because of the lucrative benefits of being a regional transit hub, Uzbekistan can expect serious competition from neighboring countries, especially Kazakhstan.

Way Forward

Uzbekistan has laid the foundations to become an economic powerhouse in Central Asia with growing industrial capacity and rich natural resources. The significant progress in pursuing reforms since 2017 together with a relatively good infrastructure and a large population in the region can offer attractive opportunities for investors. Efforts to improve bilateral relations after reforms were initiated in 2017 have also started to bear fruit.

Over the course of ongoing reforms, the government has tried to make the country more attractive to investors. The Law on Investments and Investment Activity, adopted in 2019, and other legislation streamlined interactions between investors and the state, reduced taxes, liberalized access to commodity markets, and started the privatization of major state-owned enterprises.

External factors, however, pose an increased risk to the country's economic outlook. Foreign direct investment inflows declined in 2020 because of the global economic impact of the pandemic. Russia's war in Ukraine has created economic and political uncertainty across the region, and while its long-term impact has yet to be understood, it has already caused a slowdown, albeit a mild one, in Uzbekistan's 2022 GDP growth.[55]

An important thrust of foreign policy is to transform Uzbekistan into a land-linked country within the wider Eurasian region connecting East and West to overcome some of the challenges of being a landlocked country. The destabilization of the Northern Corridor had created disruptions; however, at the same time, it brought opportunities for Uzbekistan to become an important transit hub in the region connecting large markets through the Middle Corridor (Trans-Caspian). The government's efforts to develop ramified transport connectivity in the region led to the launch of the PRC–Kyrgyz Republic–Uzbekistan–Afghanistan multimodal route, and the completion of the PRC–Kyrgyz Republic–Uzbekistan railway project is an important task for the coming years.

Uzbekistan set up ambitious goals underlined in its Development Strategy of New Uzbekistan, 2022–2026. The country is planning to increase the volume of exports to $30 billion by 2026 through measures that include growing the number of export-oriented enterprises from 6,500 to 15,000 and expanding the country's export destinations from the current 115 countries to 150. Uzbekistan also aims to attract $70 billion in FDI during this 5-year period. Therefore, regional cooperation and integration is becoming a very important instrument that can provide ample opportunities for the country in achieving its goals. Although Uzbekistan has been productively pursuing regional cooperation and integration activities with some positive results, the emerging geopolitical and economic challenges at the regional level and some sensitive aspects of reforms at the domestic level require cautious and well-planned policies.

55 International Monetary Fund. 2022. Uzbekistan: Staff Concluding Statement of the 2022 Article IV. Mission.

Appendix

Figure A6.1: Export Structure of Uzbekistan by Products, 2000–2021

($ billion)

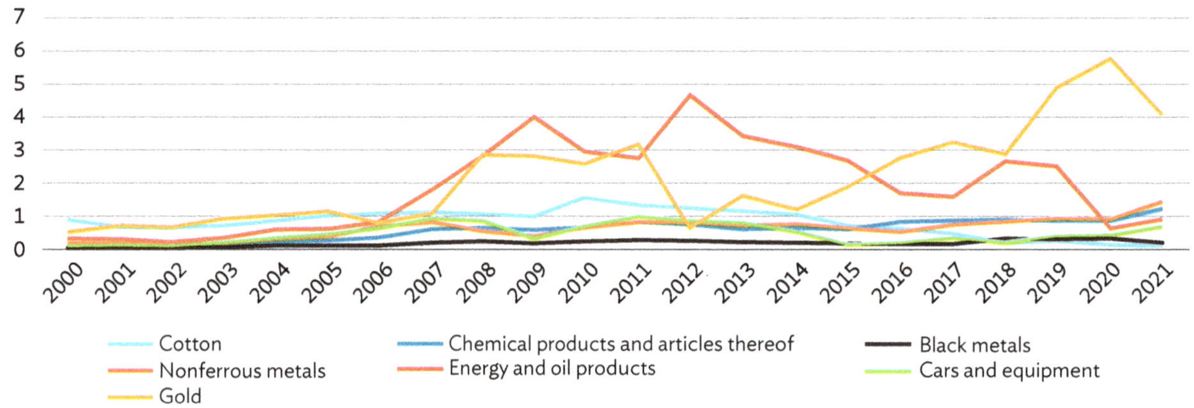

Source: UzStat (Statistics Agency under the President of the Republic of Uzbekistan). Foreign Economic Activity.

Figure A6.2: Import Structure of Uzbekistan by Products 2000–2021

($ billion)

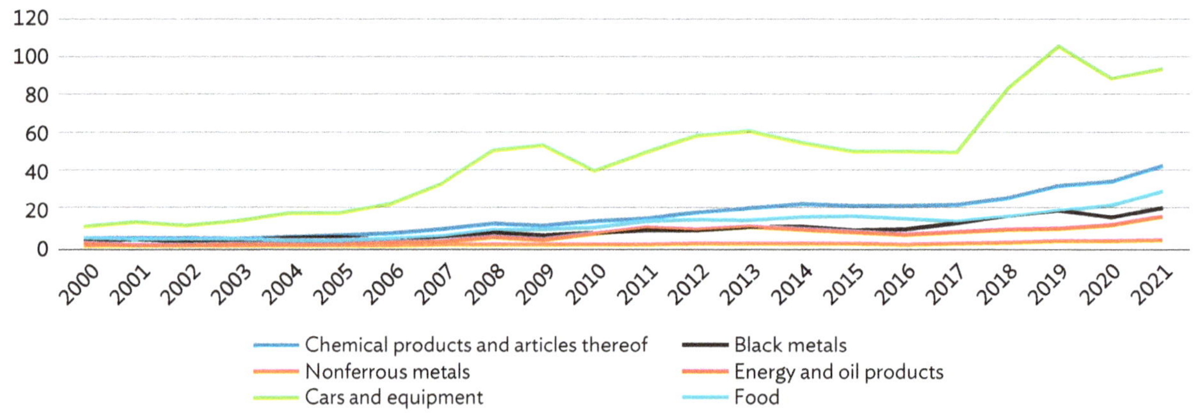

Source: UzStat (Statistics Agency under the President of the Republic of Uzbekistan). Foreign Economic Activity.

Figure A6.3: Export of Processed vs. Raw Products in Selected Sectors, 2000–2021
($ billion)

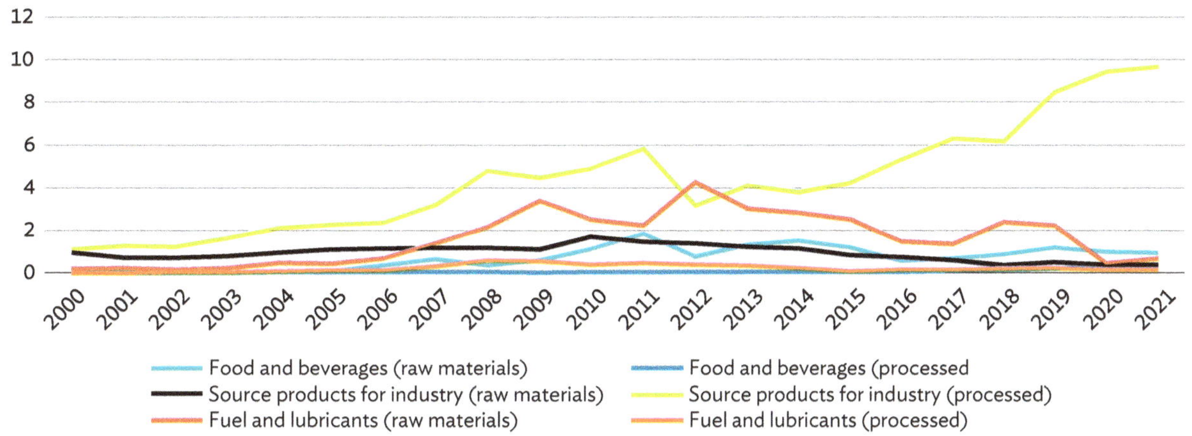

Note: Although the export structure of Uzbekistan is still dominated by commodities, there is an evident tendency for the steady expansion of the export of processed goods and end-products such as electronic equipment and devices. For instance, the export of computers and office machinery grew from $200,000 in 2016 to $63 million in 2021, and the export of electric equipment for vehicle engines increased from $400,000 to $12.2 million in the same period (source: J. Liuima. 2022. Uzbekistan to Benefit from EU GSP+ Trade Scheme. Euromonitor International. https://www.euromonitor.com/article/uzbekistan-to-benefit-from-eu-gsp-trade-scheme.).
Source: UzStat (Statistics Agency under the President of the Republic of Uzbekistan). Foreign Economic Activity.

Table A6.1: Special Economic Zones in Uzbekistan, 2019

Name	Type	Date of Establishment	Location	Description
Angren	Industrial	25 February 2018	Angren City, Tashkent Region	Projects: **75** Produced value: **$789.4 million** FDI: **$318.5 million** Created jobs: **913**
Andijan-Pharm	Pharmaceutical	14 January 2019	Andijan City	N/A
Bostonlik-Pharm	Pharmaceutical	3 September 2018	Bostanlik City, Tashkent Region	Project: **1** Produced value: **$0.6 million** FDI: **0** Created jobs: **10**
Bukhar-Agro	Agricultural	10 July 2010	Bukhara City	Projects: **114** Produced value: **$3270 million** FDI: **$105.4 million** Created jobs: **2,933**
Charvak Touristic Recreational Zone	Tourism	15 December 2017	Gazalkent City, Tashkent Region	Project: **1** Produced value: **$100 million** FDI: **$100 million** Created jobs: **350**
Chirokchi	Industrial	6 June 2021	Karshi City, Kashkadarya Region	N/A
Jizzakh	Industrial	18 March 2013	Jizzakh City	Projects: **23** Produced value: **$204,3 million** FDI: **$81,7 million** Created jobs: **3,673**
Gijvudan	Industrial	1 June 2021	Gijvudan District, Bukhara Region	Projects: **29** Produced value: **$106.2 million** FDI: **$7.7 million** Created jobs: **1,786**

continued on next page

Table A6.1 *continued*

Name	Type	Date of Establishment	Location	Description
Karakalpak-Agro	Agricultural	2 January 2020	Nukus City, Republic of Karakalpakstan	N/A
Kasansoy-Pharm	Pharmaceutical	3 May 2017	Kasansoy District, Namangan Region	Projects: **4** Produced value: **$6.9 million** FDI: **0** Created jobs: **221**
Khazorasp	Industrial	12 January 2017	Urgench City, Khorezm Region	Projects: **15** Produced value: **$49.6 million** FDI: **$15.6 million** Created jobs: **1,083**
Kokand	Industrial	12 January 2017	Uchkuprik District, Fergana Region	Projects: **49** Produced value: **$147.9 million** FDI: **$48.9 million** Created jobs: **4,222**
Namangan	Industrial	20 August 2018	Namangan City	Projects: **2** Produced value: **$25.0 million** FDI: **0** Created jobs: **973**
Navoyi	Industrial	2 December 2008	Karmana District, Navoyi Region	Projects: **65** Produced value: **$341.9 million** FDI: **$96.6 million** Created jobs: **4,225**
Nukus	Industrial	4 September 20019	Nukus City, Republic of Karakalpakstan	Projects: **3** Produced value: **$16.2 million** FDI: **$3.9 million** Created jobs: **436**
Parkent-Pharm	Pharmaceutical	3 May 2017	Parkent City, Tashkent Region	Projects: **2** Produced value: **$1.72 million** FDI: **0** Created jobs: **35**
Sirdarya	Industrial	12 April 2018	Gulistan City, Sirdarya Region	Projects: **25** Produced value: **$119.5 million** FDI: **$38.4 million** Created jobs: **3,230**
Sirdarya-Pharm	Pharmaceutical	12 April 2018	Gulistan City, Sirdarya Region	Projects: **6** Produced value: **$106.0 million** FDI: **0** Created jobs: **921**
Termez	Industrial	13 March 2020	Termez City, Surkhandarya Region	N/A
Urgut	Industrial	12 January 2017	Samarkand City	Projects: **56** Produced value: **$281.6 million** FDI: **$49.8 million** Created jobs: **3,884**
Zaamin-Pharm	Pharmaceutical	3 May 2017	Zaamin District, Jizzakh Region	Projects: **2** Produced value: **$6.0 million** FDI: **0** Created jobs: **37**
Zaamin Touristic Recreation Zone	Tourism	6 April 2021	Zaamin District, Jizzakh Region	N/A

FDI = foreign direct investment, N/A = not available.
Source: Single portal of Free Economic Zones and Small Industrial Zones in Uzbekistan. https://sez.gov.uz/.

www.ingramcontent.com/pod-product-compliance
Lightning Source LLC
Chambersburg PA
CBHW041755220926
51847CB00014B/212
9789292770716